Objects
of
Affection

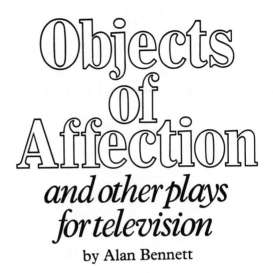

Objects of Affection

and other plays for television

by Alan Bennett

BRITISH BROADCASTING CORPORATION

Published by the
British Broadcasting Corporation
35 Marylebone High Street
London W1M 4AA
First published in 1982
Reprinted with revisions and corrections 1984, 1985

ISBN 0 563 20154 1

Filmset by August Filmsetting,
Haydock, Merseyside
Printed in Great Britain by
Spottiswoode Ballantyne Limited,
Colchester and London

Contents

Introduction

There are eight plays in this collection. Five of them were shown first on BBC2 in the autumn of 1982, and to these I have given the title *Objects of Affection*. The phrase seems to imply the existence of a theme, or at any rate a connection, but if so it never occurred to me while writing them. Even now, as I look at them in bulk, it's not what hits me in the eye. Repetitions, yes; preoccupations, certainly; but not a theme. And these repetitions and preoccupations are so particular and fiddling as never to get within spitting distance of the cosmic. Why am I obsessed with hang-gliding, for instance? It crops up three times. What is it compels the mind about indoor sports centres or life-saving, indoor rock climbing and sub-aqua? The number of ladies in little costumes in these plays must be well above the national average (though vicars in civvies come hard on their heels). If I have a favourite, imaginary landscape it seems to be an empty corridor. These are not comfortable facts for a writer in middle life to have to face. We are but the gloves great light is wearing. Gloves maybe, but not a seersucker slipover.

However, in this quest for the universal I'm cheered to find that three of these plays take place in hospital, another in a cemetery and one in both. In such unhelpful circumstances it's hardly surprising that several of the characters end up dead, which at least is some sort of universal. I seldom have the experience, supposedly common among writers of fiction, when characters take on a life of their own. On the rare occasions when *my* characters take on a life of their own, the first thing they do is make a bolt for the Exit door, two of them, it's disturbing to note, while other characters are indulging in sexual intercourse.

Most of these plays, and most of the television plays I have written, are set in the north of England. I don't have any illusions about the north being more 'real', or think that it is, like the muesli cake in *Intensive Care*, wholesome but gritty. I was brought up in the north, but, like the hero of the same play, in such humdrum circumstances that I was deprived only in that I suffered no deprivation. The language and the rhythms of northern speech come naturally to me. Its characteristic habit of saving the subject until the very end of a sentence gives northern dialogue a tension lacking in standard English. It also helps the jokes. This collection includes the first television play I wrote, *A Day Out* (1972), and I see from the script that as a beginner I thought it necessary to write the dialogue in dialect, or an approximation to it. This practice I later abandoned as being no help to anybody, but I've left the dialogue in *A Day Out* as I originally wrote it, though it sometimes makes irritating reading.

Whenever I can, I attend all the rehearsals of my plays and go on location with the films. I wouldn't do it if I didn't enjoy it, and it's only possible if one is on terms of trust with the director and the cast (though if one isn't, then there's not much point in doing the play at all). Even so, the position of the playwright is a delicate one, though not as delicate, it seems to me, as when rehearsing a play for the stage. For a stage play an actor's performance is built up gradually over at least four weeks of rehearsal. The playwright has to learn to bide his time, watch and wait, while an actor achieves a performance often by a tortuous process of trial and error. To the playwright the errors may seem grotesque and the trial all his but to speak too soon (and that always through the director) may mean one ends up with no performance at all. Love and encouragement is the order of the day. I was once told off by the director Ronald Eyre because in watching a rehearsal of a stage play I had been rocking gently in my seat, this slight and involuntary motion being taken by him to indicate some deep, unspoken unease with the performance. It was actually piles.

The rehearsal of a television play, and certainly the filming of one, is much less fraught, for everyone except the director. The fact that all filming and much television is done in relatively short takes and without an audience removes the main source of an actor's nerves, namely that at some particular point in the near future the curtain is going to rise and the audience will eat him/her alive. Moreover the director has his hands full with so many of the technicalities of the production besides the acting that in a relaxed atmosphere the author can be of some help, though again only provided he and the director see eye to eye. Sometimes the script does not sit easily with the location and has to be adjusted and one needs to be on hand for this. There is a small instance in *Rolling Home*. Harold, singing the praises of the old people's home, remarks: 'It's a tip-top place. It's not often you see a lawn like that. And I looked at the menu: they have a choice of puddings.' The location we were using had one scrubby patch of grass that didn't achieve the status of a lawn, let alone a choice example of the genre. There was, however, a cherry tree on hand, so as filmed the dialogue goes: 'It's a tip top place. This is a cherry tree. And I looked at the menu . . . etc.' It's a better line, because madder and more thoughtless.

In one department, though, I've learned to keep quiet. It's possible to give an actor the pronunciation of a word; it's unwise to tamper with its emphasis. In *A Day Out* Baldring (played by Paul Shane) gets off his bike after a long ride and remarks: 'My bum's numb', the emphasis rightly falling on 'numb'. Paul, however, put it on 'bum', with the implication that while his bum might be numb, the rest of him remained vibrantly alive. I queried this emphasis and he made valiant but unsuccessful attempts to correct it. Subsequent experience has shown me that the more a phrase is repeated, the less meaning it has, and the harder it is to get right. At such times the writer's function is not all that different from, say, the props man or the make up girl, who dash onto the set just before a take to tweak a doyley into position or powder a nose. And it is at moments like this, getting an actor to repeat 'My bum's numb' for the seventeenth time, that one wonders if this is a proper profession for an adult person.

For all that, I've found filming an enjoyable process. It gets one out of the house and away from the typewriter. To be filming in a strange place with a group of congenial people seems to me the best sort of holiday, and at such times one feels blessed in one's profession. Inevitably the more one does, the more an element of the chore enters in. But so it is with most things. Sooner or later in life everything turns into work, including work.

Some of these plays seemed to demand a foreword, others not. *A Day Out*, for instance is prefaced with extracts from a diary I kept during the filming, which I hope gives some flavour of what being on location with a television film is like. *A Woman of No Importance* also carries a note, explaining how the form of the piece was dictated in the first instance by my intention to direct it. I've also added an introduction to *An Englishman Abroad*. It's in many ways the odd one out among these plays and the circumstances in which it came to be written seemed to me to be of interest and worth recording.

These are not camera scripts. When writing it's seldom that I think in terms of shots or camera angles, simply writing out the dialogue in scenes with any stage directions that seem necessary for a master shot. Within the text I've included notes where the material as filmed and edited differs from the written text.

I'd like to thank all those who worked on these plays, in particular my directors Stephen Frears, Giles Foster, Piers Haggard, Gavin Millar and Malcolm Mowbray. They were all produced by Innes Lloyd, the epitome of what a producer should be, tactful, good humoured and, above all, an ally.

Our Winnie

WINNIE   Sheila Kelley
CORA   Elizabeth Spriggs
IDA   Constance Chapman
ERIC   Peter Lorenzelli
INTERVIEWER   Veronica Roberts
LIZ   Lesley Manville
FIRST ATTENDANT   Max Hafler
SECOND ATTENDANT   Jim Broadbent
IVY   Avril Elgar
CHARLES   Jimmy Yuill
UNDERTAKER   Jackie Shinn

Produced by Innes Lloyd
Directed by Malcolm Mowbray
Designed by Stuart Walker
Music by George Fenton

1. Interior suburban living room. Day

A middle-aged girl in ankle socks, long coat and woollen gloves stands expressionless in a room. Her shoes are too young for her. There is no movement in her face. Her name is Winnie. She stands immobile long enough for it to seem odd, then a woman in her sixties comes in: her name is Cora. She is dressed, like Winnie, ready to go out. She opens Winnie's coat and hitches the girl's skirt up.

CORA. Fasten your buttons. Come on. This button. (*Winnie fastens it with great concentration.*) This button. (*Winnie fastens it.*) This button. (*Winnie fastens it.*) And this button. (*Winnie fastens it.*) There. You can look really nice if you want to. It's done well has this coat. (*Cora pulls the flaps out from the pockets.*) Your hair'll want cutting in a bit. (*She turns to go out of the room and Winnie sits down.*) Don't sit down, Winnie. We're all ready. You don't sit down when we're all ready. (*Cora puts on her hat and makes up her face.*) We don't want to keep your Aunty Ida stood waiting. She likes us there on the dot.

Cora goes out. Winnie remains standing until Cora returns with a bunch of carnations.

If you're good you can carry the flowers. (*They go out and we hear the outside door closed and locked.*) Now – wait at the gate – Winnie.

The empty room. The sideboard. A wedding photograph of Cora and Frank, her husband. A later photograph of them with a baby.

2. Exterior. Street. Day

Cora and Winnie walk down various suburban avenues of nice semi-detached houses.

CORA. Mind where you're treading. (*Cora has to keep stopping for Winnie, who tends to stare in at gates.*) Winnie! Keep up. (*Winnie keeps up, and then draws ahead.*) And don't take such big strides. Either racing on in front, else lagging behind. You never get it right. I don't think you concentrate. (*Winnie stops and stares at people and Cora, catching her up, smiles apologetically as she takes her hand and bustles her on.*) Watch where you're walking. This is where Doctor Handley used to live. He delivered you. Flats now. His wife died. Right refined woman. Always used to speak. Kept that garden lovely. Somebody's chucked a mattress out. It's a right tip now. (*Winnie has started to pick some flowers, which she puts with the carnations.*) See, Winnie! (*Cora takes the flowers Winnie has picked and throws them away.*) Dogs go in there, and all sorts. Look at your nice gloves. It's really disheartening. Keep in. They go mad round this corner. Now then. You run on and see if you can see your Aunty. Only think on, don't cross over. (*Winnie runs on, as Cora calls after her:*) And mind them carnations.

3. Exterior. Eric's street. Day

(*Winnie runs heavily down the street, and we see a woman waiting at the corner, the same age as Cora but more spinsterly. This is Ida. Winnie throws her arms round her with extravagant affection as Cora catches them up.*)

IDA. I think she's losing her knickers.

CORA. Oh. (*Cora undoes Winnie's coat and hoists them up.*) You wouldn't lose your knickers if you were sensible and walked properly. Stand up straight.

They walk down another street. More semi-detached houses.

IDA. I thought you said your Eric was going to his Sub-Aqua. He's in their garden.

CORA. No.

IDA. He is. He's just bobbed down.

We see Winnie bent over the gate of a house, looking behind a hedge. Cut to the garden of the house where a young man is crouched behind the hedge, being watched by Winnie.

ERIC. Go away. Go on. Sod off.

CORA'S VOICE. Eric. Eric?

Eric stands up shamefacedly. He has been cutting the hedge.

ERIC. Hello, aunty.

CORA. Have you not gone to your Sub-Aqua?

ERIC. Christine just thought I could dispose of the hedge first. (*He looks apprehensively back at the house.*) I'm sorry I can't run you up there.

A car stands in the drive.

CORA. Never heed. It's only a bus ride. We don't mind, do we Ida?

IDA. Where'd you do it?

ERIC. What?

IDA. Your Sub-Aqua.

ERIC. Down at the Sports Centre.

CORA. One of them torpedo things on your back?

ERIC. We haven't actually got into the water yet. To date it's all been theory.

IDA. Oh. I thought you'd have been a fully qualified frogman by now.

ERIC. These things take time.

IDA. Put paid to our little jaunts anyway. It was nice, the Capri. Breath of fresh air.

Cora ignores this.

CORA. What will you do with it when you've got it, the Sub-Aqua?

ERIC. Well . . . (*He is at a loss.*)

IDA. Another string to his bow.

CORA. There's all sorts gets chucked in the canal. Prams and what not. You could use it for that. You know, the environment.

IDA. (*Drily.*) And folks are always drowning.

CORA. Come away from that bell, Winnie.

Winnie has gone up to the front door and is twizzling the bell. The three of them go off down the street as Christine opens the door and looks crossly after them. Eric catches her eye and attacks the hedge again.

4. Another street. Day

IDA. It wasn't as if we didn't chip in for the petrol. We were very scupulous about that. We even put in a bit for wear and tear on the car. Well, we were no wear and tear, I'm sure. Then suddenly it's Sub-Aqua.

CORA. It's Christine. She'll have put her spoke in.

IDA. Sub-Aqua!

CORA. He's young.

IDA. Last year it was all Hang-Gliding. He went off that. It was just an excuse. He never liked taking us, that was the trouble. There was always some excuse. What was it the time he was supposed to be taking us out to Bolton Abbey? I know. That ox-roasting affair.

CORA. It's her. She rules him.

IDA. That's his fault.

CORA. You don't know, Ida. You've never experienced it.

IDA. What?

CORA. Marriage. (*Cora suddenly trips over Winnie, who has bent down to look at the pavement.*) I'll give you such a clatter in a minute, young lady.

IDA. Never mind, love. Come hold your aunty's hand.

> *Cora looks aggravated. The three of them walk on, Winnie happily holding Ida's hand.*

CORA. Young. Able to drive Heavy Goods Vehicles. You had the ball at your feet, Ida, if you'd only known.

IDA. What's that supposed to mean?

CORA. The war. You could have got a man then. It was all in the melting pot then.

IDA. I didn't want a man.

CORA. Well, you have to say that.

IDA. I *didn't*. It's something you've never understood, you.

CORA. Frank used to say: she'd have made a grand wife for somebody, would Ida. Frank liked you, Ida.

IDA. I liked Frank.

CORA. We had some grand times, the three of us. Real pals. Even after Winnie came along.

> *We see them approach a bus-stop, where a young woman with a clip board in hand steps out to meet them.*

INTERVIEWER. I wonder if you'd object to answering one or two questions. It's a survey.

IDA. What sort of survey?

CORA. A girl in Lewis's last week gave me a bit of experimental cheese. Got up as a Dutch girl.

INTERVIEWER. It's a survey of public transport for the corporation.

CORA. Well, it wants surveying. You can be stood half an hour some times. (*To Ida*) Bonny little face. Mind you, we wouldn't ordinarily be using this bus. My nephew used to run us up.

IDA. He's gone overboard for this Sub-Aqua.

CORA. Shut up about Sub-Aqua. We live in the modern world. It's only a phase.

INTERVIEWER. This is a random sample anyway. You don't have to be regular users.

CORA. The eleven's better than the fourteen. The fourteen's very spasmodic.

Winnie is looking at a boy and girl, also waiting for the bus, who are leaning up against the wall, necking. Ida notices this, takes Winnie's hand and pulls her away.

INTERVIEWER. Now, you're three?

CORA. Two really. You'd better not put Winnie down. We never do. She's not right.

INTERVIEWER. She's a passenger unit. She counts from a statistical point of view.

CORA. She doesn't have a vote.

INTERVIEWER. Now, you say you have access to a car.

CORA. Yes.

IDA. No, we don't. Not since he started doing this . . . silly diving thing.

CORA. It'll pass. The Sub-Aqua will pass. The Hang-Gliding passed. He's like that is our Eric. Very volatile. Put down 'occasionally'.

IDA. Very occasionally.

CORA. I wouldn't care, but Ida used to drive. She was a lorry driver. During the war. ATS. Heavy lorries. You wouldn't think so to look at her now.

IDA. I couldn't do it now.

CORA. You should have kept it up. A skill like that.

IDA. I'd look a bit silly driving lorries now.

CORA. She could dismantle an engine in thirty minutes flat.

IDA. Well the Queen was the same. She was in the ATS. I bet she hasn't kept it up.

CORA. Yes, but you've more reason.

INTERVIEWER. What's your starting point?

CORA. How do you mean?

INTERVIEWER. Where did your journey commence?

CORA. Here. Amberley Road.

INTERVIEWER. And what's your destination?

CORA. Heywood. The cemetery.

5. Exterior. Cemetery gates. Day

We see the three of them getting off a bus. The bus goes, and they walk towards some large gates. It is a cemetery-cum-crematorium on the outskirts of the city.

CORA. All that's come in, these last few years, surveys, asking folk what they think. Consultation's the keynote.

IDA. I reckon nothing to it. It's these computers, wanting feeding. They install them, so they have got to give them something to do.

CORA. No. I think they realise now. It's like these phone-in things. People matter. Now Winnie, we don't want you running off. This is not a playground. See. (*She takes back the carnations from Winnie.*) Would you credit it? Twenty-five pence a bloom!

IDA. Shocking.

6. Interior. A room in the Crematorium offices. Day.

A public room, with seats round and in the centre a glass case in which is kept the Book of Remembrance. It is open and we see a list of names of those who had died on this particular day. A girl, a student named Liz, is looking at the book. She has a camera. Outside the room an Attendant waits, dressed in dark blue uniform. Another attendant sits at the side of the room, watching. The door opens and the Attendant comes in. Steps up to the case, unlocks it, lifts the lid, turns over a page of the book, closes the case and goes to the door again, where he stops and waits.

LIZ. Is that what you usually do?

FIRST ATTENDANT. Yes. I come in. I open the case. I turn the page over. I shut the case.

SECOND ATTENDANT. Better turn it back. You turned it forward. It's been turned once to-day.

FIRST ATTENDANT. All right, all right.

He does this, rather crossly.

SECOND ATTENDANT. He does it reverently. You do it reverently.

FIRST ATTENDANT. Course I do it reverently. I'm not doing it reverently now because there's nobody here. If it's just me I come in and do it. I don't make a big performance of it. Only if there are any bereaved about I make it a bit more ceremonial. A bit more . . . military.

LIZ. Try that then. (*As he goes back to the door, Liz takes out her camera.*) More . . . formally.

First Attendant comes in as before, but more smartly; gets to the case and stops.

FIRST ATTENDANT. Do you want me to pause?

LIZ. Would you pause?

FIRST ATTENDANT. No, I mean besides that. Won't it blur?

SECOND ATTENDANT. Blur? How do you mean blur? It won't *blur*. If you come in like Sebastian Coe it won't blur. It's one of these Japanese jobs. They don't blur. (*To Liz*) You should have asked me. I understand what you're on about.

FIRST ATTENDANT. It's my day on.

SECOND ATTENDANT. Yes and any other day you'd be belly-aching.

FIRST ATTENDANT. I'll start again.

SECOND ATTENDANT. Blur!

The First Attendant comes in through the door and goes through the routine again. Liz snaps him at various points.

LIZ. Would you do it again?

FIRST ATTENDANT. Again? What am I doing wrong?

SECOND ATTENDANT. Well I don't mind doing it if you don't want to.

FIRST ATTENDANT. No. I'm quite happy.

The First Attendant repeats the process, and is almost at the case when he is interrupted.

SECOND ATTENDANT. And you'll have to turn the page *back* this time, remember.

The First Attendant stops, very cross.

FIRST ATTENDANT. You've put me off. He's put me off. (*He is furious with the Second Attendant, and Liz snaps him at this point.*) Don't. That's not what I do. I thought you wanted an accurate picture. (*He goes out again, comes in, goes through the whole routine, gets to the Book of Remembrance and can't remember whether to turn the page forwards or back.*) Oh sod it.

LIZ. Never mind. In any case the background's a bit dead. I really want somebody else in the picture.

SECOND ATTENDANT. Your own fault, love, for coming on a Monday. Sundays you can't move. I'll go and get Ivy. She'll welcome the excitement.

He goes out. The First Attendant looks at the Book of Remembrance.

FIRST ATTENDANT. This is what they call an illuminated manuscript. The monks invented it. This . . . it's a work of art.

Liz looks sceptical. It's plainly not what she'd call a work of art.

7. Exterior. Cemetery. Day.

Cora, Winnie and Ida are walking up a drive lined with laurels and rhododendrons.

IDA. Keep in, Winnie. We don't want running over.

CORA. Well if we were they wouldn't have far to take us.

They laugh, just as a hearse passes.

IDA. We shouldn't be laughing.

CORA. It's all done with split-second timing, this. Fast as one comes out there's another ready to go in. No slump here. They're not on short time, undertakers. This is where we cut through.

IDA. No, it is further up.

CORA. Ida, he was my husband: we cut through here.

Ida shrugs, and they cut through into the cemetery.

8. Interior. Office. Crematorium. Day.

Liz is looking out of the window and she sees Cora, Ida and Winnie go by en route for Frank's grave. Liz is watching them when the Second Attendant returns with Ivy, who is resentful and morose. Bereavement is her bread and butter, and some of it has obviously rubbed off.

FIRST ATTENDANT. (*From outside.*) Ready?

IVY. Mondays is when I like to break the back of my correspondence. Sad?

LIZ. No. Just look.

IVY. I would look sad, though wouldn't I? Under the circumstances.

SECOND ATTENDANT. You might not have liked them.

IVY. Who?

SECOND ATTENDANT. The deceased.

IVY. Why did I bother to come up, then?

FIRST ATTENDANT. (*From outside.*) Can we get on with it?

LIZ. O.K.

As the First Attendant marches in to turn the page, Ivy clutches her bosom in a parody of grief. Liz is not happy and takes no picture.

LIZ. I don't want you to . . . feel anything.

IVY. You're too young, you. You've never lost a loved one, probably.

LIZ. Try talking.

IVY. What about?

LIZ. Chat.

IVY. I wouldn't chat, would I, if I were bereaved. The bereaved don't chat.

SECOND ATTENDANT. Some do. Some gab their heads off.

There is a strained pause.

IVY. I got the thumbs down this morning. (*First Attendant says nothing.*) I said I got the thumbs down.

FIRST ATTENDANT. Sorry, I thought you were just . . . chatting . . . you know, for her. For the camera.

IVY. Well if I were I wouldn't say that, would I? 'I got the thumbs down this morning.' If someone tells you to chat you don't suddenly say 'I got the thumbs down this morning' out of the blue. You say something like 'Haven't we been having some weather?' I'm carrying on a real conversation. I got the thumbs down. Over the trouser suit.

SECOND ATTENDANT. She's been trying to persuade them to let her come in a trouser suit.

IVY. Let me tell her. I'm supposed to be the one who's supposed to be chatting.

SECOND ATTENDANT. What'd he say?

IVY. He said it smacked too much of leisure wear. Said, what was the matter with a plainish frock? I said I was fed up with plainish frocks. I said, if it's genuine grief it doesn't matter a toss what I wear.

FIRST ATTENDANT. You didn't say that?

IVY. I did. More or less.

SECOND ATTENDANT. What did he say?

IVY. Gave it the thumbs down. Said we were treading a thin line. How much longer is this going to go on? It's eroding my morning is this.

She looks at her watch. Liz snaps her.

LIZ. That was good.

FIRST ATTENDANT. What did you do?

IVY. Nothing.

SECOND ATTENDANT. I'm getting it. I see what it is you're after. It's life, isn't it. The genuine article. The camera cannot lie.

First Attendant glances through the open door.

FIRST ATTENDANT. Ivy. You've got somebody waiting.

IVY. Oh blood and sand! (*She hurries out.*) They've come for some ashes and I haven't done the documentation.

LIZ. Sorry. Look, is there anywhere else we could go?

9. Exterior. Cemetery. Day.

Cora and Ida are walking along a path. We see Winnie, who is behind them, run off among the graves.

CORA. I don't remember there being this path.

IDA. We cut through too early.

CORA. This is where I've always cut through.

IDA. No. We cut through further up.

CORA. You always have to be right, don't you?

IDA. These are old graves.

CORA. Some are and some aren't. They're that fast for room, they put new ones amongst the old ones. They have to budge up. Land, it's at a premium. He's next to somebody called Eastlake. It's near a seat. (*She looks round.*) Where's Winnie? Oh, hell and damnation! Winnie! Winnie! Winnie! (*They set off looking, and pass a student, Charles sat on a gravestone, drawing.*) Have you seen a big girl go past in a fawn coat?

CHARLES. I'm sorry. I haven't been looking. I've been drawing.

CORA. (*To Ida.*) You go that way.

She goes off, calling 'Winnie'.

IDA. (*To the boy.*) She's not right, you see. Winnie!

Cora searches the cemetery. We see other students dotted about, sketching. Cora sees Winnie stood among the graves.

CORA. Winnie! (*calls*) Ida! I've found her. She's here. (*She runs through the graves to Winnie.*) You've no business wandering off. Your Mam's going to smack you. (*Cora hits the back of Winnie's legs, as we see behind Winnie the name Eastlake. Winnie starts crying.*) It's for your own good, love. You don't understand. There's all sorts of fellers about.

The student Charles is sitting not far away, and sees all this. Ida comes up as Winnie is still crying.

IDA. Is she all right?

CORA. Yes.

She wipes Winnie's face.

IDA. It's all right, love. Your Mam and me are here. You're not lost.

CORA. No. I gave her a smack.

Ida looks round.

IDA. Well she's found it. The grave. (*Cora sees her husband's grave.*) She knew where it was. And there's the seat.

Cora is mortified.

CORA. Oh, Winnie. I'm sorry, love. Your Mam's sorry. Give your Mam a kiss. It was your Mam's mistake. They've cut down that tree, that's what confused me. You can smack me if you want. Go on. Give your Mam a smack.

She bends over, inviting Winnie to smack her bum. Winnie giggles, but doesn't.

IDA. You're a clever girl, Winnie.

CORA. (*Pointing to the next grave.*) Yes, you see: Eastlake.

IDA. It was your Mam's fault.

CORA. All right, Ida. It was a genuine mistake.

She starts snipping at the grass on the grave with some household scissors she has brought.

10. Exterior. A colonnade outside the chapel. Day.

The colonnade is lined with plaques, recording the names of the dead. There is the sound of singing from the nearby chapel as the Second Attendant lays out some wreaths. Liz hovers with her camera.

LIZ. Talk, if you want.

SECOND ATTENDANT. There's a service going on. (*Pause.*) They'll let you study aught now, students. Projects. We never went on projects. It's a hobby in my book, photography. It's pleasure.

The First Attendant arrives with more flowers. He is about to put his cigarette out but Liz, anxious to get a shot of him laying out the wreaths with a fag in his mouth, stops him.

LIZ. No, don't put your cig out.

FIRST ATTENDANT. No smoking in the chapel precincts. You'll have me sacked.

LIZ. Nobody gets sacked these days. Do they?

She is talking for the sake of talking, to distract attention while she is photographing them.

FIRST ATTENDANT. It's not nice for the relatives.

LIZ. Try leaning against the wall. No, keep the wreath.

SECOND ATTENDANT. You'll have to be sharp. They'll be coming out in a minute or two.

LIZ. They've only just gone in.

SECOND ATTENDANT. It doesn't take long. It's only a formality after all.

Pause.

LIZ. Talk – chat –

FIRST ATTENDANT. Chat. Chat. We wouldn't chat here anyway, would we? The procedure is, we disembark the flowers, lay them out, then hop it. The bereaved don't like to see the staff.

LIZ. Why's that?

Again, keeping them talking.

FIRST ATTENDANT. Why is it? Well why is it, Harry?

SECOND ATTENDANT. I don't know why. But I'm off.

FIRST ATTENDANT. You were wanting to be in on it when she was taking me.

SECOND ATTENDANT. Aye, but once you've had one or two goes it gets boring.

FIRST ATTENDANT. Like everything else.

Liz, pissed off, waits as the doors of the chapel open and the mourners come out to look at the wreaths. Some bend over, looking at the names on the wreaths.

11. Exterior. The grave.

Cora talks to Charles, who is sketching a statue on a grave.

CORA. You've got her nose wrong. My husband could draw a bit. He was very good at horses. Horses are quite hard to draw, but they just happened to be his strong point. Can you draw horses?

CHARLES. I haven't tried.

CORA. Is that next term? (*They both laugh, and he goes on drawing.*) Will you get marked on it?

CHARLES. Yes. And not so well either.

CORA. Is that my fault? I'm not disturbing you?

CHARLES. No.

12. Exterior. Colonnade. Day.

Mourners. Liz quite discreetly snaps them. The undertaker notes this. He edges over to her without looking at her and says:)

UNDERTAKER. Are you official?

LIZ. Yes.

UNDERTAKER. In pink trousers? You never are. Out, lady, sharp. It's not a wedding. These are grief-stricken people.

LIZ. I'm a student. We have got permission.

UNDERTAKER. Not from me. Get lost.

Liz walks disconsolately away from the chapel, with her gear. She has a folded-up tripod as well as her camera.

13. Exterior. Cemetery. Tap. Day.

Ida and Winnie are walking through the graves, Winnie with some dead flowers, Ida with a vase. Liz, Ida and Winnie are plainly on a collision course.

IDA. Here's the bin. Throw them in. There's a clever girl.

Winnie holds the vase while Ida mans the tap. Together they fill the vase.

Liz has spotted them and is desperately focusing her camera. Then she finds she is out of film.

LIZ. Shit.

By the time she has got another roll in Ida and Winnie are slowly going back towards the grave.

14. Exterior. Cemetery. Day.

Charles sketches while Cora chats.

CORA. Your hair's nice and short. That's all come in again, short hair. I'd just got used to it being long, and now they've started with it short again. My forte was composition.

CHARLES. Composition? Music?

CORA. No! English. 'My holidays.' Composition was what it was called. I used to have to stand up and read mine out many a time. It's whether you have imagination or not. Course it's all altered now. I was asking this little kiddy next door what she liked best and she said environmental studies. I was staggered, she's only nine. Then she talks about it – turns out she means nature study. Here comes my party. (*Ida and Winnie are approaching, trailed at a distance by Liz, camera at the ready. Winnie has been allowed to carry the vase, which she is doing with exaggerated care. Cora takes it from her.*) That was a risk. It's her best coat.

IDA. (*indulgently.*) Well.

CORA. Winnie, look at your new shoes. All plastered up. Oh, you are a mucklump. Go and sit on that seat. Go on.

Winnie goes and sits on the seat. Cora arranges the carnations in the vase.

IDA. You expect too much of her.

CORA. She knows more than you think.

IDA. You ought to give her responsibility, not take it away. They all say that nowadays.

CORA. Who?

IDA. Television.

CORA. You don't know what it's like, day in, day out.

IDA. She's company.

CORA. She is and she isn't.

IDA. It's a person. Someone there, choose what you say. You've two plates to put out. Two cups. Someone to follow.

CORA. You've no right to complain. It's what I say. You should have got wed.

Ida says nothing, just stands looking at the grave. Liz stands by Charles, watching.

CHARLES. You can't. She's retarded. It's not fair.

LIZ. It doesn't matter. Does it?

Charles goes on drawing, looks furtively now and again as we see Liz go up to Cora and Ida and start talking. Cut to the graveside.

LIZ. Can I take your photograph?

CORA. What do you think?

IDA. I take a terrible picture.

CORA. We've been interviewed once today. Now we're going to have our picture taken. You students, I don't know.

IDA. They get it all done for them now.

CORA. We were born too soon, you and me, Ida. We should have been students.

LIZ. I could be taking some now while you're talking.

CORA. Oh no. I want to look nice. (*Winnie has come over.*) Winnie, what did I say? Go sit on that seat. Your shoes are all daubed up as it is. Your Aunty Ida and me are having our pictures taken.

LIZ. Can't I take you all together?

CORA. No. Winnie doesn't want her picture taking. She never has her picture taken. Her Dad wouldn't have liked it.

IDA. Nay, Cora, go on. Frank wouldn't have minded.

CORA. Ida. She's my daughter. (*Liz nearly snaps this exchange, but doesn't. Meanwhile Cora has taken out her powder compact and is just putting on a bit of make-up.*) Just doll myself up a bit. (*Ida waits as Cora puts on her make-up and Winnie stares straight at the camera. Liz takes a photograph.*) You little monkey! I'm not ready. And I told you, I didn't want our Winnie's picture taking.

LIZ. It wasn't a picture. I'm just focusing. You have to get the exposure right.

Charles hears most of this and looks fed up.

CORA. We're not up in the mechanics of it. Anyway, Winnie, you've been told. Go and sit down. (*Liz poses them, Ida on one side, Cora on the other. She takes out her tripod.*) Oh, legs! Look, Ida, legs!

LIZ. Talk.

They don't, but she takes one or two snaps. In the background Winnie sits on the seat, looking miserable.

CORA. Easier for you than your friend.

LIZ. What?

CORA. Just clicking. Easier than your friend. Drawing. She's using a lot of pictures. Our Eric'll make a film last months.

IDA. What's matter with Winnie? What is it, love? (*Winnie is crying.*) She wants her picture taking.

CORA. No. I'm thinking of Frank.

IDA. Go on, let her. Pretend. Don't click it.

Cora is uncertain.

CORA. If she promises.

LIZ. All right.

IDA. Put it on the legs. She'll want it on the legs, like ours. (*Ida does Winnie's hair and tidies her up.*) Sit up, love. That's it. Big smile for your Aunty Ida!

Winnie smiles. Liz takes her photograph.

15. Exterior. Grave. Day.

Cora, Ida and Winnie have gone. Liz has her tripod set up. She has just taken a still photograph of the grave with its vase of carnations. Charles walks over as Liz packs her gear.

LIZ. You'd draw her. Wouldn't you?

CHARLES. It's not the same.

LIZ. Why?

CHARLES. I don't know.

LIZ. You attend to people, that's all it is. You photograph people, you attend to them. (*It's not enough of an explanation for Charles, who senses also that Liz's photograph will be better than his drawing. He screws up the drawing and chucks it in a waste basket.*) Attention, these days, it's what people want.

16. Interior. Cora's home.

Tea is set out. Ida is looking at a photograph album as Cora comes in with the tea tray. There is a plate of cream cakes and Ida gives Winnie one, which she eats messily throughout this scene.

CORA. That was taken in Leeds. We were just walking down Boar Lane and Frank says, 'Look out, this feller's taking our photograph.'

IDA. You can just see him saying it. I can see him in Winnie so clear sometimes.

Cora pours out some tea.

CORA. We haven't done so bad to-day. We've been interviewed vis-a-vis the bus service. We've come into contact with the younger generation and we've had our photographs taken. They're quite nice some young people now, whatever you read in the papers. Those two were all right.

IDA. Eric's two are demons. They look straight through you. You get the feeling you don't exist.

CORA. (*Looks at Winnie.*) They don't know they're born some of them. (*Cora goes back to the album.*) Redcar. Just after we were married. Cleethorpes. I won that doll. That's Winnie when she was little. That's you when you were little, Win. I don't think we can quite have known then. I think I realised first, only I didn't let on. Then I found he hadn't been letting on either. It turned out we both knew.

IDA. I knew. He told me.

CORA. He blamed himself. Putting it off till we got a house. We left it too late.

IDA. You're not to know these things.

CORA. We put her in for the Evening Post Bonny Babies competition. Sent her pictures in. I can't bear to think of it still. And people used to stop me with the pram and say what a grand baby. (*Winnie's face is smeared with cream. Cora spits on her hanky and cleans her up.*) Oh Win, you are a mucky trollop.

IDA. Never mind. She's my friend, aren't you, love?

CORA. Once we knew for certain, I didn't go out. Didn't go anywhere. I wouldn't take her out. Dad had it all to do. Dad and you. The housework. The shopping. Everything. It was long enough before I came round. Still, life has to go on, I suppose. Folks stare. They look at her and they don't realise. Then when they do realise, they look away. You don't want them to stare, and yet you don't want them to look away either. I don't know.

IDA. It's a good job there's love.

17. Interior. Art college. Exhibition room. Day.

The camera tracks along a gallery, past various paintings and drawings of the cemetery done by the students, ending up on the photograph taken at the grave: Cora is putting on some lipstick, Ida stands looking into the distance, and Winnie stares directly into the camera. It is a heartless photograph, but a striking one. It is also the one Liz said she had not taken, and it has won a prize. The final shot is of another photograph, the one Liz promised was only a pretend picture, of Winnie, sat on a seat, smiling vacantly.

A Woman of No Importance

PEGGY   Patricia Routledge

Produced by Innes Lloyd
Directed by Giles Foster
Designed by Vic Meredith
Music by George Fenton

I wrote *A Woman of No Importance* thinking I might direct it myself. I have never directed either for the stage or television and the possibility of having to do so accounts for the simplicity (not to say crudity) of the form: the piece is for one actress, who speaks directly to camera.

Thinking I would be able to manage at the most two cameras, I planned the play as a series of midshots with the camera tracking in very slowly to a close-up, holding the close-up for a while then, just as slowly, coming out again. I didn't figure on there being any cuts within scenes, though this would place a heavy burden on the performer, some sections being pretty lengthy: the first speech, for instance lasts twelve minutes. To shoot in such a way makes cutting virtually impossible: one fluff, and it's back to the top of the scene again. Autocue is one answer, but Patricia Routledge, for whom the piece was written, was anxious to avoid this, and quite rightly. Even when a performer is in full command of the text, the sight of it slowly reeling down over the camera lens exercises an hypnotic effect, and an element of the rabbit fascinated by the snake enters in. I therefore planned on using a second camera, shooting Miss Schofield in profile. This would provide a shot to which one could cut if it proved necessary to do so.

In the event, because I was working on one of the other plays I didn't direct the piece, which was done by Giles Foster. He adhered faithfully to the form I'd given the play, though to begin with finding the restrictions it imposed irksome and unnerving. He began by moving the play around, with Miss Schofield traversing the studio to match the movements described in the text. Rehearsal was a process of simplification whereby these movements were taken back inside the character, who ended up static in front of the camera as I had originally imagined. There are in fact some cuts within sections, when a gesture or slight turn of the head make it possible to switch to a slightly different shot without being false to the fairly relentless nature of the piece. Of course such directness and simplicity may not be thought to work. 'Talking heads' is a synonym in television for boredom, and here is just one head, not two. And Miss Schofield is a bore. But to have her in full close-up, retailing in unremitting detail how she borrowed the salt in the canteen takes one, I hope, beyond tedium.

The first few lines of the play are poached. In the Festival of Britain, which I visited as a boy, there was a pavilion (I suspect I might be irritated by it now) called The Lion and the Unicorn, devoted to Englishness. It included a console where, by pressing a button, one heard snatches of typical English conversation. These had been written by (I think) Stephen Potter and were performed by Joyce Grenfell. One in particular concerned a disaster that befell a middle-class lady, and began: 'I was perfectly all right on the Monday. I was perfectly all right on the Tuesday. I was perfectly all right on the Wednesday. I was perfectly all right on the Thursday until lunchtime, when I just ate a little poached salmon: five minutes later I was *rolling about the floor.*'

Peggy is a middle-aged woman. She talks directly to camera against a neutral background.

PEGGY. I was all right on the Monday. I was all right on the Tuesday. And I was all right on the Wednesday until lunchtime, at which point all my nice little routine went out of the window.

Normally, i.e. provided Miss Hayman isn't paying us one of her state visits, come half past twelve and I'm ready to down tools and call it a morning. I put on a lick of paint, slip over and spend a penny in Costing . . . I should technically use the one in Records but I've told them, that lavatory seat is a death trap. And I'm not ringing up again. 'Try a bit of sellotape.' What are they paid for? I'll then rout out Miss Brunskill from 402 and we'll meander gently over for our midday meal. But you just have to hit it right because, give it another five minutes, and believe me that canteen is dog eat dog.

However if you can manage to nip in before the avalanche you have the pick of the tables and there's still some semblance of hygiene. Our particular stamping ground is just the other side of the bamboo framework thing they tried to grow ivy up. It's what Miss Brunskill calls 'our little backwater'. We're more or less fixtures there and have been for yonks. In fact Mr Skidmore came by with his tray last week just as we were concluding our coffee and he said, 'Well, girls. Fancy seeing you!' We laughed. Girls! Mr Skidmore generally gravitates to the table in the far corner under that silly productivity thermometer-type thing. 'Export or Die'. It's actually broken – stuck anyway – but it's where management tend to foregather since we've had this absurd 'All Barriers Down' policy. Once upon a time management had tables roped off. That's gone, only they still congregate there. 'Huddling together for warmth,' Mr Rudyard calls it. I said to Mr Cresswell, 'You can tell who's an activist.' We laughed, because anybody more conformist than Mr Rudyard you couldn't want, and he has beautiful fingernails. Of course once the management started frequenting that particular table sure enough Miss Hayman and the Personnel brigade pitch camp next door. And she'll turn around and chat to Mr Skidmore over the back of her chair. She never used to have all that hair.

Our table though we're very much the happy family. There's me, Miss Brunskill, Mr Cresswell and Mr Rudyard, Pauline Lucas, who's ex-Projects . . . to tell the truth she's still Projects, only she's in Presentation wearing her Projects hat. Then there's Trish Trotter (when she's not in one of her 'bit of cheese and an apple' phases); Joy Pedley pays us the occasional visit, but by and large that's the hard core. Trish Trotter is the only one with a right weight problem but we're all salad fanatics and keep one another in line. I have to watch my stomach anyway and salad suits Miss Brunskill because she's a big Christian Scientist. But to add that bit of excitement I bring along some of my home-made French dressing. Mr Cresswell keeps pestering me to give Mr Rudyard what he calls 'the secret formula'. He's a keen cook, Mr Rudyard. Little moustache, back like a ramrod, you'd never guess it. I pretend there's a mystery ingredient and won't let on. We laugh.

People are a bit envious of us, I know. I ran into Mr McCorquodale the other day when we were both queueing in (guess!) Accounts and he said, 'You do seem to have a good time at your table, Peggy. What do you talk about?' And I didn't know. I mean, what do we talk about? Pauline's mother keeps getting a nasty rash that affects her elbows. We'd been discussing that. Mr Cresswell and Mr Rudyard were going in for some new curtains for their lounge and were debating about whether to have Thames Green. And I was saying if Thames Green was the green I thought it was I liked it in a front door but wasn't keen on it in curtains. So that made for some quite lively discussion. And Trish Trotter had got hold of some new gen on runner beans as part of a calorie-controlled diet, and we kicked that around for a bit. But honestly, that was all it was. I don't know what we do talk about half the time! My secret is, I don't talk about myself. When Joy Pedley went to Thirsk on a 'Know Your Client' course that was apparently the whole gist of it: concentrate on the other person. I said, 'Well, I've no need to go to Thirsk to learn that. It's something I've been born with.' We laughed.

Once we've lined up our eats and got the table organised Miss B. gets her nose into her crossword while I scan the horizon for the rest of the gang. I have to be on my toes because there's always some bright spark wanting to commandeer them and drag them off elsewhere. I don't think people like to see other people enjoying themselves, basically. Take Pauline Lucas. The other day, she came in with young Stuart Selby. He's ginger, and when Mr Oyston went up into Accounts and Mrs Ramaroop moved to Keighley, Stuart did a bit of a dog's hind leg and got into Costing. Him and Pauline were making a bee-line for the window, which is in the Smoking area. Now Pauline doesn't smoke, in fact rather the reverse. So I sang out, 'You're not deserting us, are you

Pauline? Fetch Stuart over here. See how the other half lives!' So she did. Only halfway he ran into Wendy Walsh and it ended up just being me and Pauline. I said to her 'That was a narrow escape.' She said, 'Yes.' We laughed. Her acne's heaps better.

And then look at Mr Cresswell and Mr Rudyard. It's the biggest wonder last week they didn't get sat with the truck drivers. They were dawdling past with their trays and there was room but luckily I just happened to be going by en route for some coffee and saw which way the wind was blowing and rescued them in the nick of time. They were so grateful. I said 'You two! You don't know you're born!' They laughed.

However, as I say, on this particular Wednesday I'm in the office, it's half past twelve and I'm just thinking, 'Time you were getting your skates on, Peggy,' when suddenly the door opens and nobody comes in. I didn't even look up. I just said, 'Yes, Mr Slattery?' He was on his hands and knees with a pro forma in his mouth. Anybody else would have got up. Not him. He crawls up to me, pretending to be a dog and starts begging, this bit of paper in his mouth! I thought, 'You're a grown man. You've got a son at catering college; your wife's in and out of mental hospital and you're begging like a dog.' I enjoy a joke, but I didn't laugh.

Surprise, surprise he's after a favour. The bit of paper is the Squash Ladder. Would I run him off two dozen copies? I said, 'Yes. By all means. At two o'clock.' He said, 'No. Now'. Wants to put them round in the lunch hour. I said, 'Sorry. No can do.' I haven't forgotten the works outing. Running round with that thing on his head. He was like a crazed animal. I said, 'Anybody with an atom of consideration would have come down earlier. Squash Ladder! It's half past twelve.' He said, 'It's not for me.' I said 'Who's it for?' He said, 'Mr Skidmore.'

Pause.

Well, as luck would have it I hadn't actually switched the machine off. And, knowing Trevor Slattery, Mr Skidmore had probably asked him to do it first thing and he'd only just got round to it. I know Mr Skidmore: courtesy is his middle name. But it did mean I didn't get out of the office until twenty to, by which time of course there's no Miss Brunskill. Any delay and La Brunskill's off like a shot from a gun, plastic hip or no plastic hip.

By this time of course the canteen is chock-a-block. I was five minutes just getting inside the door, and if I'd waited for a please or thank you I'd be stood there yet. They looked to be about to introduce martial law round the salad bowl so I thought, 'Little adventure, I'll opt for the hot dish of the day, steak bits or chicken pieces.' I knew the woman doling it out because she gets on the fifty-six. She's black but I take people as they come, and seeing it was me she scrapes me up the last of the steak bits. I topped it off with some mushrooms, and trust me if I didn't get the last of the yogurts as well. I heard somebody behind me say 'Damn'. I laughed.

I beetled over to our table but no Pauline, no Mr Cresswell and no Mr Rudyard. It's a cast of unknowns and only Miss Brunskill that I recognise. I said, 'Didn't you save me a place?' She said, 'I thought you'd been and gone.' Been and gone? How could I have been and gone, she knows I'm meticulous. But I just said, 'Oh' rather pointedly, and started touring round.

Eventually I pinpoint Pauline sat with little Stuart Selby, only there's no room there either. 'Scattered to the four winds to-day, Pauline,' I said. 'Yes,' she said, and he laughed. I see she's starting another spot.

I trek over to the far side and blow me if Mr Cresswell and Mr Rudyard aren't sat with all the maintenance men, some of them still in their overalls. Mr Cresswell is smoking between courses, something he never does with us, a treacle sponge just stuck there, waiting. Mr Rudyard is having a salad and I wave my jar of French dressing in case he wants some but he doesn't see me because for some reason he's not wearing his glasses.

Just then I spot somebody vacating a place up at the top end. I say, 'Room for a little one?' only nobody takes on. They're young, mostly from Design, moustaches and those little T-shirty things, having some silly conversation about a topless Tandoori restaurant. I start on my steak bits, only to find that what she's given me is mainly gristle. I don't suppose they distinguish in Jamaica. I thought, 'Well, I'll have a little salt, perk it up a bit,' but as luck would have it there's none on the table, so I get up again and go in quest of some. The first salt I spot is on the table opposite, which happens to be the table patronised by the management; and who should be sat there but Mr Skidmore. So I asked him if I could borrow their salt. 'Excuse me, Mr Skidmore,' was what I said, 'but could I relieve you temporarily of your salt?' I saw Miss Hayman's head come round. She'd naturally think I was crawling. I wasn't. I just wanted some salt. Anyway, Mr Skidmore was very obliging. 'By all means,' he said. 'Would you like the pepper too?' I said, 'That's most civil of you, but I'm not a big pepper fan.' So I just took the salt, put a bit on the side of my plate and took it back. 'Much obliged,' I said. 'Don't mention it,' Mr Skidmore said. 'Any time.' He has impeccable manners, they have a big detached house at Alwoodley, his wife has had a nervous breakdown, wears one of those sheepskin coats.

I suddenly bethought me of the Squash Ladder, so just after I'd
replaced the salt I said, 'Oh, by the way, I ran you off those copies of the
Squash Ladder,' not in a loud voice, just person to person. He said,
'What?' I said, 'I ran you off those copies of the Squash Ladder.' He
said, 'Squash Ladder?' I said, 'Yes.' He said, 'Not my pigeon.' I said,
'Why?' He said, 'Didn't you know? There's been a flare-up with my
hernia.' Well I didn't know. I can't see how I would be expected to
know. Somebody laughed. I said, 'Oh, I am sorry.' He said, 'I'm not.
Blessing in disguise. Squash is Slattery's pigeon now.'

I went back to my table and sat down. I felt really sickened. He'd
done it on me had Mr Slattery.

After a bit Trish Trotter rolls up and parks herself next to me. She
says, 'Are you not eating your steak bits?' I said, 'No.' She said, 'Don't
mind if I do,' and helps herself. She shouldn't wear trousers.

Anyway it was that afternoon that I first began to feel really off it. I
went home at half past four.

*Fade quickly to black. Still shot of her desk: very neat. A single flower in
a glass. Typewriter with its cover on.*

I want the tableaux between scenes to look like still life paintings.

*Peggy is now sat against another neutral background, wallpaper
possibly – something to indicate she is at home.*

PEGGY. I don't run to the doctor every five minutes. On the last occasion
Dr Copeland sat me down and said, 'Miss Schofield. If I saw my other
patients as seldom as I see you I should be out of business.' We laughed.

He's always pleased to see me: gets up when I come into the room,
sits me down, then we converse about general topics for a minute or two
before getting down to the nub of the matter. He has a picture of his
children on the desk, taken years ago because the son's gone to Canada
now and his daughter's an expert in man-made fibres. He never
mentions his wife, I think she left him, he has a sensitive face. Cactuses
seem to be his sideline. There's always one on his desk and he has a
Cactus Calendar hung up. This month's was somewhere in Arizona,
huge, a man stood beside it, tiny. I looked at it while he was diddling his
hands after the previous patient.

There was a young man in the room and Dr Copeland introduced me.
He said, 'This is Miss . . .' (he was looking at my notes) '. . . Miss
Schofield. Mr Metcalf is a medical student; he's mistaken enough to
want to become a doctor.' We laughed, but the boy kept a straight face.
He had on one of those zip-up cardigans I think are a bit common so
that didn't inspire confidence. Dr Copeland said would I object to Mr
Metcalf conducting the examination provided he was standing by to see

I came to no actual physical harm? We both laughed but Mr Metcalf was scratching a mark he'd found on the knee of his trousers.

Dr Copeland put him in the picture about me first: 'Miss Schofield has been coming to me over a period of twelve years. Her health is generally good, wouldn't you say Miss Schofield? –' and he was going on, but I interjected. I said, 'Well, it is good,' I said, 'but it's quite likely to seem better than it is because I don't come running down to the surgery with every slightest thing.' 'Yes,' he said. 'If I saw my other patients as seldom as I see Miss Schofield I should be out of business.' He laughed. The student then asked me what the trouble was and I went through the saga of the steak bits and my subsequent tummy upset.

He said 'Is there anything else beside that?' I said 'No.' He said. 'Any problems at work?' I said, 'No.' He said, 'Any problems at home.' I said, 'No.' He said, 'You're single.' I said, 'Yes.' He said, 'Where are your parents?' I said, 'Mother's in her grave and father is in a Sunshine Home at Moortown.' He said, 'Do you feel bad about that?' (He didn't look more than seventeen.) I said, 'No. Not after the life he's lived.'

I saw him look at Dr Copeland, only he was toying with the calendar, sneaking a look at what next month's cactus was going to be. So this youth said, 'What life did he lead?' I said, 'A life that involved spending every other weekend at Carnforth with a blondified piece from the cosmetics counter at Timothy Whites and Taylors.' He said, 'Is that a shoe shop?' I said, 'You're thinking of Freeman, Hardy and Willis. It's a chemist. Or was. It's been taken over by Boots. And anyway she now has a little gown shop at Bispham. His previous was a Meltonian shoe cream demonstrator at Manfields, and what has this to do with my stomach?'

Dr Copeland said, 'Quite. I think it's about time you took an actual look at the patient, Metcalf.' So the young man examined me, the way they do pressing his hands into me and whatnot, and then calls over Dr Copeland to have a look. 'That's right,' I said. 'Make way for the expert.' Only neither of them laughed.

Dr Copeland kneaded me about a bit, but more professionally and while he was washing his hands he said, 'Miss Schofield. I'm not in the least bit worried by your stomach. But, you being you, it wants looking at. There aren't many of us left!' We laughed. 'So just to be on the safe side I want to make an appointment for you to see a specialist, Mr Penry-Jones. I said, 'Isn't his wife to do with the Music Festival?' He said, 'I don't know, is she?' I said, 'She is. I've seen a picture of her talking to Lord Harewood.' He took me to the door of the consulting room, which he doesn't do with everybody, and he took my hand (I'm not a private patient). 'Thank you,' he said. 'Thank you for being a guinea pig.' We laughed. Only it's funny, just as I was coming out I saw the student's face and he was looking really pleased with himself.

She very slightly presses her hand into her stomach.

Fade to black and up again to still shot of bedside table. Clock. Bedside lamp. A bottle of white medicine.

Fade to black and up again: Peggy is in a hospital bed.

PEGGY. I've just had a shampoo and set. She's not done it too badly, bearing in mind she doesn't know my hair. Lois, her name is. She has a little salon. You go past Gyney, and it's smack opposite Maternity. It's a bit rudimentary, they just have it to perk up the morale of the pregnant mums basically, but, as Lois says, it's an open door policy just so long as you can find your way because this place is a rabbit warren. Lois said my hair was among the best she'd come across. It's the sort Italians make into wigs apparently, they have people scouring Europe for hair of this type. I should have had a perm last Tuesday only when Mr Penry-Jones whipped me in here it just went by the board.

Caused chaos at work. Miss Brunskill said after I'd rung up Mr McCorquodale and Mr Skidmore went into a huddle for fully half an hour and at the end of it they still couldn't figure out a way to work round me. In the finish Miss Hayman had to come down from the fifth floor – though not wearing her Personnel hat, thank God – and Pauline did her usual sideways jump from Records, but it's all a bit pass the parcel. Miss Brunskill says everybody is on their knees praying I come back soon.

I'd actually been feeling a lot better when I went along to see Mr Penry-Jones. He's got one of those big double-fronted houses in Park Square: vast rooms, wicked to heat. There was just one other woman in the waiting room, smartish, looked to have arthritis. I said, 'I wouldn't like this electricity bill,' but she just smiled. Then the housekeeper came and conducted me upstairs. I made some remark about it being spring but she didn't comment, a lot of them are Spanish these days. Mr Penry-Jones though was very courtly oldish man, blue pin striped suit, spotted bow-tie. I said, 'What a lovely fireplace.' He said, 'Yes. These are old houses.' I said, 'Georgian, I imagine.' 'Oh,' he said. 'I can see I'm in the presence of a connoisseur.' We laughed.

He examined me and I went through the story again, though I didn't actually mention the steak bits, and it was a beautiful carpet. Then he looked out of the window and asked me one or two questions about my bowels. I said, 'I believe your wife has a lot to do with the Music

Festival.' He said, 'Yes.' I said, 'That must be very satisfying.' He says, 'Yes. It is. Last week she shook hands with the Queen.' I said, 'Well that's funny, because I stood as near to her as I am to you, at York in 1956. What an immaculate complexion!'

When I'd got dressed he said, 'Miss Schofield, you are a puzzle. I'm very intrigued.' I said, 'Oh?' He said, 'Have you got anything special on in the next couple of weeks?' he said. 'Because ideally what I would like to do is take you in, run a few tests and then go on from there. I'm absolutely certain there's nothing to get worked up about but we ought to have a little look. Is that all right?' I said 'You're the doctor.' We laughed.

He made a point of coming downstairs with me. It was just as some other doctor was helping the better-class-looking woman with arthritis into a car – it looked to be chauffeur driven. I went and sat on a seat in the square for a bit before I got the bus. The trees did look nice.

Go to black and up again. Miss Schofield is now sat by her hospital bed in a candlewick dressing gown.

PEGGY. I've appointed myself newspaper lady. I go round first thing taking the orders for the papers, then I nip down and intercept the trolley on its way over. I said to Sister Tudor, 'Well, with a candlewick dressing gown I might as well.' Most of the others have these silly shorty things. Mine's more of a housecoat. The shade was called Careless Pink, only that's fifteen years ago. It's mostly the Sun or the Mirror, there's only two of us get the Mail and she's another Miss. I could tell straight away she was a bit more refined. Hysterectomy.

Of course I shan't be able to do the papers tomorrow because of my op.

When Princess Alexandra came round, this was the bed she stopped at, apparently.

I get on like a house on fire with the nurses. We do laugh. Nurse Trickett says I'm their star patient. She's little and a bit funny-looking but so goodhearted. 'How's out star patient?' she says. 'I hope you've been behaving yourself.' We laugh. She hasn't got a boy friend. I've promised to teach her shorthand typing. Her mother has gallstones, apparently. Nurse Gillis is the pretty one. I think she's just marking time till she finds the right man. And then there's Nurse Conkie, always smiling. I said to her, 'You're always smiling, you're a lesson to any shop steward, you.' She laughed and laughed the way they do when they're black.

Sister came in while she was laughing and said wasn't it time Mrs Boothman was turned over. She's all right is Sister, but she's like me:

she has a lot on her plate. I said to her, 'I'm a professional woman myself.' She smiled.

Pause. Miss Schofield turns the name tag she has on her wrist.

Name on my wrist now: 'Schofield, Margaret, Miss.'

Pause.

Mr Penry-Jones comes round on a morning, and he fetches his students and they have to guess what's wrong. I said to Miss Brunskill, 'It's a bit of a game. If he doesn't know what the matter is, they won't.' He said, 'Gentlemen, a big question mark hangs over Miss Schofield's stomach.' They all laughed.

So tomorrow's the big day. He was telling the students what he's going to do. 'I'm just going to go in,' he said, 'and have a look round. We're not going to do anything, just a tour of inspection.' I chipped in, 'More of a guided tour, if all these are there.' They did *laugh*. Not Sister though. She can't afford to, I suppose. He's like a God to them, Mr Penry-Jones.

I do my bit here in different ways. I'm always going round the beds, having a word, particularly when someone isn't mobile. I run them little errands and tell the nurse if there's anything anybody's wanting. Mrs Maudsley opposite's on a drip and she was going on about getting her toenails cut, they catch on the sheet. I located Nurse Gillis and told her, only it must have slipped her mind because when I went across later on Mrs Maudsley was still on about it. I mentioned it again to Nurse Gillis just in case she'd forgotten and she said 'I don't know how we managed before you came, Miss Schofield, I honestly don't.' Actually I found out later her toenails *had* been cut. Apparently Nurse Conkie must have cut them the same day as she cut mine, the day before yesterday, only Mrs Maudsley wouldn't know because she's no feeling in her feet.

Mrs Boothman's another of my regulars. Can't move. Can't speak. Doesn't bother me. I sit and chat away to her as if it was the most normal thing in the world. She'll sometimes manage a little movement of her hand, but the look in her eyes is enough.

Miss Brunskill's been down to see me. Nobody else much. Plenty of cards. I've got more cards than anybody else on this side.

She reads them.

'Feel kinda sick without you. Trish.' Trish Trotter. Picture of an elephant. 'Wishing you a speedy recovery. All in 406.' 'It's not the same without you. You're missed more than words can tell. So I'm sending this card to say, Please hurry and get well.' It says 'from all on the fifth floor' but I bet it's Mr Skidmore, it's such a classy card. A thatched cottage. I should imagine it can be damp, though, thatch. Silly one from Mr Cresswell and Mr Rudyard. 'Sorry you're sick. Hope you'll soon be back to normal. Whatever that is!'

I thought they might have been popping down, but Mr Cresswell hates hospitals, apparently, and they're going in for a new dog. A Dandy Dinmont. They think it'll be company for Tina, their Jack Russell. Well, they're out all day.

> *Pause.*

Miss Brunskill's knitting me a bedjacket. I said, 'You'll have to be sharp, I shall be home next week.'

> *Pause.*

I've got one nice neighbour, one not so nice. She's been quite ill. Just lies on her side all day. Karen, her name is. I offered her one of my women's books but she just closed her eyes. She's young. But however poorly I was I think I'd still try to be pleasant. The woman this side is as different again. Very outgoing. Talks the whole time. She's in with her chest. She's a lifelong smoker, so I don't wonder. Her daughter's marrying a computer programmer whose father was a prisoner of the Japanese, and she's inundated with visitors. She's a big TV fan so she's often down the other end. I reckon to be asleep sometimes when she's going on. You can't always be on your toes.

> *Pause.*

Could just drink a cup of tea. Can't when you're having an op. They get you up at six, apparently. Give you a jab. Nurse Trickett says I won't even know I've gone and I'll be back up here by twelve. I've warned sister I shan't be able to get the papers, she thinks they'll manage.

> *Pause.*

Solve the mystery anyway.

> *Go to black.*

> *Still of the bedhead. Bed empty, as if she has gone for her operation.*

> *Go to black and up again.*

> *Miss Schofield is sitting by a radiator near a window in her dressing gown.*

PEGGY. Hair in my dinner again today. Second time this week. Someone

must be moulting. I mentioned it to Sister and she said she'd take it up
with the kitchen staff and get back to me. She hasn't though. It isn't that
she's nasty. Just crisp. I don't complain. Nurse Gillis can be sharp as
well, but I try and meet her half way. I said, 'Don't apologise. I deal
with people myself. They don't realise, do they?'

Pause.

I'd such a shock yesterday. Nurse Conkie and Nurse Trickett had just
given me my bath, and the little trainee nurse with the bonny face and
cold hands was combing my hair, when I bethought me of the bedjacket
Miss Brunskill had knitted me. I'd put it away in my locker because
she'd made it too tight round the sleeves, but I tried it on again and it
was just right. She says she hates knitting. I'm the only person she'll
knit for, apparently. Of course, I paid for the wool. She's never ailed a
thing, Miss Brunskill. Still, I hadn't until this do. Anyway I'd just got
the bedjacket on and she'd fetched Nurse Conkie to see how nice I
looked and they got me out my lipstick and I put a bit of that on. I was
just sitting there and Nurse Conkie said, 'All dressed up and nowhere to
go,' and a voice said, 'Hello. Long time no see!' And it's Mr Skidmore!

And I said it, loud, like that 'Mr Skidmore!' I said to him, I said,
'Five minutes earlier and you'd have seen me being bathed. He said
'That's the story of my life.' We laughed.

He chatted about work. Said they were still only limping along. Said
my job is open whenever I feel up to it and what's more it'll stay that
way. They've got a special dispensation from Mr Strudwick. He says it's
open-ended. They've never done that before. When Wendy Walsh had
her infected sinus they ended up giving her a deadline. Still she wasn't
the lynch-pin I am.

He did say there were other factors quite unconnected pushing them
towards some degree of revamping. 'But,' he said, and patted my hand,
'in that event we shall find you a niche.' I said, 'Well I'm honoured.
Fancy making a special journey for me'. Only it transpires that Mrs
Skidmore's mother is in the psychiatric wing with another of her
depression do's, and he'd left Mrs Skidmore sitting with her while he
popped along to see me. 'Killing two birds with one stone,' he said.
Then realised. 'I didn't mean that,' he said. 'Don't be silly,' I said. We
laughed. He does look young when he laughs.

He'd just gone when Nurse Conkie came down to turn Mrs
Boothman over. Great big smile. 'Who was your gentleman friend?' she
said. She's got a nice sense of humour. I said 'That was my boss. He
says they can't wait till I'm back.' 'I'm not sure we can spare you,' she
said. We laughed.

I've been here the longest now, apart from Mrs Boothman and she's been resuscitated once. I potter around doing this and that.

Mr Penry-Jones is very proud of my scar. He fetches his students round to see it nearly every week. He says he's never seen a scar heal as quickly as mine. It's to do with the right mental attitude apparently. They stop longer at my bed than with anybody. What he does is take the students a bit away, talks to them quietly, then they come up, one by one and ask me questions. I whisper to them 'He doesn't know what it is, so don't worry if you don't.' Mrs Durrant on this side, she won't have them. She goes on about 'patients' rights'. She's a schoolteacher, though you'd never guess it to look at her. Long hair, masses of it. And I've heard her swear when they've given her a jab.

Pause.

I have a laugh with the porters that take me down for treatment. There's one in particular, Gerald. He's always pleased when it turns out to be me. 'My sweetheart,' he calls me. 'It's my sweetheart.' He's black too. I get on with everybody.

Pause.

I've started coming and looking out of this window. I just find it's far enough. There's naught much to see. There's the place where they put the bins out and a cook comes out now and again and has a smoke. And there's just the corner of the nurses annexe. A young lad comes there with a nurse. He kisses her then goes away. Always the same lad. Nice. Though I don't like a lot of kissing, generally.

Pause.

I keep wondering about my Dad.

Go to black.

Up on a jug and tumbler on the bedside table.

Black.

Up again on Miss Schofield in bed. Her hair should be straight, as if it has been washed but not set. The speeches are more disjointed, and feebler.

PEGGY. I'm lucky. I'm standard size. I've got stuff off the peg and people have thought I'd had it run up specially. I've got a little fawn coat hanging up at home that I got fifteen years ago at Richard Shops. I ring the changes with scarves and gloves and whatnot, but it's been a grand little coat.

Pause.

I fetched up ever such a lot of phlegm this morning. Nurse Gillis was on. She was pleased. She said I'd fetched up more phlegm than anyone else on the ward. I said 'Was there a prize?' She laughed. I've never had that trouble before, but that's the bugbear when you're lying in bed, congestion.

Pause.

She said it's a good job all the patients aren't as little trouble as me or else half the nurses would be out of work. Funny, I didn't use to like her, but she's got a lot nicer lately. Her boy friend's a trainee something-or-other. I forget what. She did tell me. They're planning on moving to Australia.

Pause.

I've never been to Australia. She said if I wanted I could come out and visit them. I said, 'Yes.' Only I couldn't go. I couldn't be doing with all that sun.

Pause.

When Princess Alexandra came round this was the bed she stopped at, apparently.

Pause.

Sister's been better lately, too. The one I can't stand is Nurse Conkie. Never stops smiling. Great big smile. When they took old Mrs Boothman away just the same. Great big smile.

Pause.

Vicar round today. Think it was today. Beard. Sports jacket. Student, I thought, at first.

Pause.

Chatted. Bit before he got round to God. Says God singles you out for suffering. If you suffer shows you're somebody special in the eyes of God. He said he knew this from personal experience. His wife suffers from migraine.

Pause.

Do without being somebody special, this lot.

Pause.

There's a vicar goes round at Farnley, where my Dad is. Sits.

Pause.

Miss Brunskill came. Revolution at work. 406 and 405 knocked into one. Do your own photocopying now. Do it yourself, cut out the middleman. I said, 'Where did I fit in?' and she was telling me, only I must have dropped off and when I woke up she'd gone. Niche somewhere.

Pause.

I've been lucky with buses when I think back. I don't know what it is but just as I get to the bus stop up comes the bus. It must be a knack. I don't think I've ever had to wait more than two minutes for a bus, even when it's been a really spasmodic service.

Pause.

I wish they wouldn't laugh.

Pause.

There shouldn't be laughing.

Pause.

If they just left me alone I should be all right. 'Schofield, Margaret, Miss.' I've got a fly: keeps coming down. Must like me. There's a woman comes over and talks to me sometimes. Telling some tale. I close my eyes.

Pause.

Somebody was telling me about Rhyl. Still very select, apparently. No crowds.

Pause.

Here's my friend. This fly.

She smiles.

I said to Nurse Gillis, 'It's singled me out.' She laughed.

Go to black then up. The final shot is of an empty bed with the mattress folded back. The light is hard and white.

Fade out.

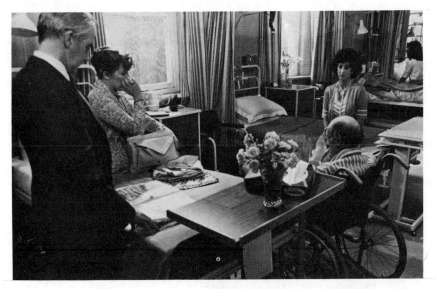

Rolling Home

MR WYMAN   John Barrett
VAL   Maureen Lipman
MOLLY   Pat Heywood
HAROLD   Bernard Gallagher
DONALD   David Threlfall
VIC   David Foxxe
MATRON   Isabelle Lucas
PAM   Anna Quayle
MR RISCOE   Jack Le White
MR METCALF   Leslie Pitt
ALBERT   Ernest Jennings
ERNEST   Charles Simon
KEVIN   Geoffrey Staines
MISS MUSCHAMP   Gladys Spencer
ALICE   Jeanne Doree
CONNIE   Beatrice Shaw
HANNAH   Molly Veness
NURSE   Michael Worsley

Produced by Innes Lloyd
Directed by Piers Haggard
Designed by Ray Cusick
Music by Geoffrey Burgon

1. Exterior. Hospital. Day.

Various shots: buildings, car park, etc. The odd patient or medical orderly passing. Some visitors arriving.

2. Interior. Corridor. Day.

A long, institutional corridor in a nineteenth-century building, a workhouse, probably, that has been converted into a hospital. It has been painted cream and some attempt has been made to modernise it in small ways. The lamps are modern and there are pictures on the walls. At the end are double doors.

For some moments nothing should happen, and the corridor remain empty, over it the sounds of an oldfashioned hospital. Somewhere someone is washing up, and there is the faint clatter of pans. The double doors open slowly, and an old man comes through in pyjamas. He comes along the corridor towards the camera. He is in his bare feet. He gets quite close to the camera before the doors open again, more quickly, and Vic, a male nurse in a short white coat comes through.

VIC. Mr Riscoe. Mr Riscoe.

From the tone of voice one should be able to tell this flight and pursuit has happened many times before. The old man takes no notice and carries purposefully on, until the male nurse catches him up, steers him round and they go back down the corridor.

Where was it this time?

RISCOE. Scarborough.

VIC. Scarborough! You gone off Whitby then?

RISCOE. There's no shagging in Whitby.

3. Interior. Corridor. Day.

Vic and Riscoe go through the doors and there is a further corridor beyond with more radiators along it, and more pictures. Old men sit on some of the chairs by the radiators. Vic takes Riscoe through to the ward at the end of this corridor, and we stay with another old man, Mr Wyman, who sits with his hands on the radiator looking out of the window. We see through the vast window to the grounds of the hospital. There is a lawn, neat flower beds and a high wall. Donald, another male nurse is sitting with one of the old men. Vic passes with Mr Riscoe.

VIC. On another Awayday, this one. Scarborough!

Donald smiles, then comes and sits with Mr Wyman, adjusting the sheet of paper in his clipboard as he does so. Donald is about thirty.

DONALD. Now then, Joey. What day is it?

WYMAN. (*Pause.*) Is it Wednesday? Wednesday.

DONALD. Try. Try Saturday.

WYMAN. It's more like Wednesday to me.

DONALD. What date?

WYMAN. *Saturday.* I'm not so daft.

DONALD. *Date.*

WYMAN. (*Shakes his head.*) It's raining. I can see that.

DONALD. What's four from seven?

WYMAN. You can't take four from seven. Oh no. I'm thinking you mean seven from four. Three. (*Donald smiles.*) Not so daft. Don't ask me money. I never bothered to learn all that when they had the alteration. (*Donald writes something down.*) Have I passed?

DONALD. What day is it?

WYMAN. Wednesday. Well, it's Wednesday to me.

DONALD. Do you know where you are?

WYMAN. I'm on the ward. There's them rhododendrons. (*Pause.*) I sit here every day and still don't know what's the other side of that wall.

Donald groans. Clearly Mr Wyman has said this umpteen times before. But then on this ward most things have been said umpteen times before.

DONALD. You do. (*He gets up.*) I'll tell you one thing, Joey. I wish they were all like you.

He helps Mr Wyman to his feet and they start towards the door.

WYMAN. By! My leg does hurt.

Donald looks briefly anxious.

DONALD. We'll get you a tablet.

4. Exterior. Grounds. Day.

A car draws up. Molly and Harold get out. They are a comfortable couple in their forties.

5. Interior. Ward. Day.

Vic looks through a window, checks his watch, and moves off down the ward.

VIC. Toilet anybody? Speak now. All got clean bums, have we, ready to face our loved ones? What about Jackie? No. You wouldn't dream of it, would you? Mr Metcalf? You haven't got a little parcel saved up for your niece, have you? Right. Where are they this eager, laughing throng laden with Lucozade?

On cue Molly, Mr Wyman's daughter comes through the double doors with her husband, Harold.

MOLLY. Now then, precious. Have you been waiting?

She gives him a kiss and sits down.

WYMAN. What've you come today for?

MOLLY. Why? It's Saturday.

WYMAN. I thought it was Wednesday.

Molly looks at Harold.

HAROLD. (*Shrugs.*) Well, I'm getting like that now.

He goes and gets a chair from another radiator. They sit in silence looking out of the window.

MOLLY. It's next week Stephen's going in for his bronze medal.

WYMAN. Which is Stephen?

MOLLY. The youngest, Dad. Paul, Melanie, then Stephen. You know Stephen. You were big pals, you and Stephen. I brought you those snaps.

WYMAN. What snaps?

MOLLY. In a little leather case. We bought it for your birthday. To keep on your locker. You said it was the one thing you'd been wanting. (*Aside:*) I bet it's been pinched.

HAROLD. No. (*Pause. She mouths, 'He can't remember Stephen.' She blows her nose.*) It's hot, is this radiator. The heating side of it's tip top.

MOLLY. We thought Val'd be here. We were expecting to see her.

HAROLD. She has to fit it in with her appointments.

MOLLY. Well, so do we.

WYMAN. I keep looking at yon wall.

HAROLD. What wall? (*He looks.*) Why? It's only a wall.

MOLLY. Melanie's no different. She's got a little spot on her chin. Taking up all her time. You know what they're like at that age. How's your foot? About the same, is it, your foot?

WYMAN. It's about the same.

MOLLY. (*Aside to Harold.*) How long has he had it?

HAROLD. What?

MOLLY. His foot.

HAROLD. I don't know.

Mr Riscoe appears in his pyjamas and makes for the corridor exit. Harold sees him go.

MOLLY. Your hands have gone nice, Dad. Haven't his hands gone nice, Harold? Real lady's hands. Never think you were a bricklayer.

HAROLD. No. Man of leisure now. Everything done for you.

6. Interior. Corridor. Day.

Cut to corridor outside. Val, Molly's sister, slightly younger and an altogether smarter woman, is walking along the corridor. Mr Riscoe pads past her. Val looks perplexed. Harold comes through the doors.

HAROLD. Hold on, old lad. You're not supposed to go on your travels. Hold on. Hallo, Val.

Donald comes out in pursuit of Mr Riscoe.

DONALD. Thanks.

HAROLD. He fair shifts, doesn't he?

DONALD. Oh ay. Could play for the under twenty-ones, this one.

He takes the old man back in, and Harold and Val follow into the ward.

7. Interior. Ward. Day.

HAROLD. Here's Val.

Val gives a brave smile.

VAL. Dad. (*Kissing him.*) Mol. Have I had a journey! Easterly Road packed solid. Football fanatics. I've been in Bradford all morning.

MOLLY. We were just saying how his hands have gone nice. Haven't his hands gone nice, Val?

VAL. He looks thinner. You look thinner to me, love. (*She turns away and mouths to Molly*) I wonder if they get enough to eat. (*Molly and Harold exchange looks.*) They talk about cutbacks, yet they keep the heating on at this pitch. I always have a sinus do when I've been here. The air's that dry. (*Pause.*) Off to Harrogate next week, Dad. My annual jaunt. Northern Fashion Show.

MOLLY. Val's a buyer for a gown shop, Dad.

VAL. He knows that. You know that, love, don't you?

MOLLY. He forgets.

HAROLD. It's to be expected. Look at me. I can never remember our postcode.

MOLLY. DS7 2NU.

HAROLD. (*Weakly.*) Yes.

VAL. I'm RB6 4A. (*Pause.*) Mr Stillman says that if things go on the way they're going on, there's no reason why next year I shouldn't eventually have a stab at Paris. Fancy Dad, your little Val in Paris.

MOLLY. Stephen's going in for his bronze medal.

HAROLD. You told him that.

MOLLY. I'm telling Val.

HAROLD. Are you being affected by the recession? We've been having a bit of a downturn.

VAL. Well, Harold, I think I'm entitled to say 'What recession?' With our class of customer it really makes no odds. Woman came in the other day. In the shop ten minutes. Spent six hundred pounds. I wondered whether I'd be seeing little Stephen today. Or Melanie. What's happening to all my nephews and nieces?

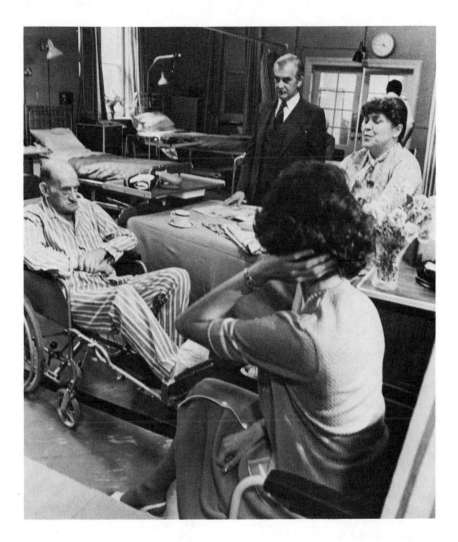

MOLLY. It's what I was saying: Stephen's doing his bronze medal and Saturdays is when Paul does his Indoor Rock-Climbing. Have you come across that Dad? Indoor Rock-Climbing? They do it down the Sports Centre. They have this make-do rock face, so's when they graduate to the real thing they don't have to jump in at the deep end. They climb up on these crampons.

HAROLD. Pitons.

MOLLY. You haven't been. Rock climbing, Dad, little Paul. Not so little now. It was a toss-up between that and hang-gliding. You've got to let them go their own way.

HAROLD. I was just thankful it wasn't pot-holing.

Val is powdering her nose, very bored by Molly's talk of the children.

MOLLY. But he's a beautifully proportioned is Paul, isn't he Harold?

HAROLD. Well, he's big.

MOLLY. Up here now. Bigger than his Dad. He said the other day, 'You're getting a bald patch, Dad.' Can look right down on him now.

HAROLD. I'll just have a wander out. I'm a bit worried about the car.

VAL. What did you have for your dinner, Dad?

WYMAN. Oh, one thing and another, you know.

VAL. And how's your foot? (*To Molly.*) How is his foot?

MOLLY. Same, I thought we'd have a word with the nurse before we go. You're not in pain, are you, Dad?

WYMAN. No. Only it hurts.

MOLLY. Our Melanie, she's got a nasty little spot on her chin. Otherwise we're all champion.

Pause.

8. Exterior. Hospital grounds by wall.

Harold is walking round the back of the hospital, inspecting a pile of coke or smokeless fuel. An orderly comes out and puts some rubbish in a large mansize bin.

HAROLD. Grand bins.

ORDERLY. What?

HAROLD. Grand bins. Capacious.

ORDERLY. Ay. They have to be.

The orderly goes back inside. Harold wanders on round the hospital.

9. Interior. Ward. Day.

Donald comes up with a tablet and a glass of water.

DONALD. Here we are, Joey.

The old man takes the tablet and swallows it.

MOLLY. You see, he takes that like a lamb. At home it would have been a shouting do.

VAL. Why do you call him Joey? His name's Wilfred.

DONALD. We call them what they like to be called.

VAL. Joey makes him sound like a budgie.

MOLLY. How is his foot? We wondered if we could have a word.

They follow Donald up the ward to the orderly's room. We pick up Harold as he's walking down the ward, looking for them. He comes into the orderly's room in the middle of the conversation.

10. Interior. Orderly room and corridor. Day.

VAL. Gangrene? How's he managed to get that?

HAROLD. Is this his foot?

DONALD. They do at his age. The circulation's poor.

HAROLD. That's right.

VAL. But he must have got the infection from somewhere. I saw somebody as I was coming in in their bare feet. That's like an open invitation to germs.

MOLLY. (*Tearful.*) Gangrene.

DONALD. Sometimes it clears up.

HAROLD. Well if it's not one thing it's another. My mother fell down the cellar steps. It was a two minute job. I've never been sorry.

DONALD. Oh hell. Vic!

Mr Riscoe has gone by again, headed for the door. Donald runs after him.

VAL. He doesn't look very sensitive to me. It's a job for most of them, like any other. Funny job for a man anyway, I think nursing.

MOLLY. Why?

VAL. Oh . . . odd.

Donald comes back and Mr Riscoe is led away by Vic.

VIC. You can't go without your bucket and spade.

MOLLY. Why don't you lock the door?

DONALD. We can't. Unless they're violent.

HAROLD. I think you deserve a medal.

Harold and Val go, Molly turns back.

MOLLY. He had a little leather folder. For snaps. We bought it him when he came in, to stand on his locker. He gets confused over his grandchildren.

DONALD. It'll be in his drawer. I'll look for it next time.

MOLLY. If you would. I know you're busy.

Donald and Molly have been talking outside the office, and we have seen Val kiss Dad and go up the corridor, where she is now waiting to go, Harold with her.

11. Interior. Ward. Day.

Molly goes back to the ward.

MOLLY. We're off now, Dad. Harold's a bit worried about the car so we won't linger. Goodbye chick. There. I've given you a right good kiss. Ta ta pet.

She goes.

12. Interior. Corridor. Day.

Molly and Harold and Val go through the door and walk down the corridor.

HAROLD. It's coke, the central heating. Some sort of smokeless stuff. Beats oil any day.

13. Exterior. Grounds and car park. Day.

Molly, Harold and Val leave the hospital and go and stand by Val's car in the car park.

VAL. I don't know. You read these stories.

HAROLD. What stories?

VAL. Old people. Nurses.

MOLLY. It's under the corporation.

VAL. We know *that*. I could weep.

MOLLY. We couldn't have managed. Up night after night. Paul's got his O levels to do. I think he's happy.

VAL. Gangrene!

HAROLD. Is a tip-top place. I mean, this is a cherry tree. And I looked at the menu: they have a choice of puddings.

VAL. Mr Stillman asked where my father was. I just said Moortown, but he knew it was a corporation place, I could tell.

MOLLY. We'd no choice. We've been over it again and again. Anyway, I'm not sure he knows where he is.

VAL. Well I do. They have Mr Stillman's mother at home with them. Eighty-odd, and bright as a button. Incidentally, if you want a nice little frock, now's the time. We've got some lovely costumes in, discontinued lines at giveaway prices. They'd suit you.

She kisses Harold and Molly and gets into her car.

HAROLD. Belt up.

VAL. (*Startled.*) What?

HAROLD. Clunk-click.

VAL. Oh.

She goes as Molly and Harold walk over to their car.

HAROLD. Don't say it.

MOLLY. (*Mimicking Val.*) Fancy, Dad, your little Val in Paris. Your little Val. She was never his little Val. If she were his little Val why didn't she take him in? She's the single one. Discontinued lines!

He starts the engine and listens.

HAROLD. Can you hear a little ticking noise?

MOLLY. No.

HAROLD. I can. I wouldn't care but it's just been serviced. I reckon they just dust it.

14. Interior. The ward. Night.

Vic is going off duty. He and Donald are sat at the night table going through a list of patients, both doing clerical tasks and talking quietly as they do.

DONALD. You haven't heard anything?

Vic shakes his head.

VIC. She's a real wind-up merchant, that matron.

DONALD. It's got to be either you or me.

VIC. Neck and neck in the race to get our pips up. I just don't see myself wiping bums ad nauseam.

DONALD. It's not that. I need the money.

VIC. How is all that?

DONALD. Fine.

VIC. Named the day? (*Donald shakes his head.*) It looks like I'm going to be an old maid.

DONALD. What happened to the racing driver?

VIC. Roared off into the sunset. Usual story. Men just think nurses are a pushover. (*He gets up.*) Anyway, don't do anything I wouldn't do. You do though, don't you?

DONALD. It's practically the only time we get.

VIC. (*Mimicking Matron.*) I'm thinking of the patients, nurse.

He goes. Donald is left alone. After a while he walks down the sleeping ward.

15. Interior. Corridor. Night.

A girl is walking down the corridor. She looks through the window into the ward and then goes into the orderly's office.

16. Interior. Ward. Night.

In the ward Donald is checking the beds. He stops and goes to Mr Wyman's locker.

WYMAN. Donald.

DONALD. You're supposed to be asleep.

He looks in the locker for the folder of photographs, takes it out and puts it on top of the locker.

WYMAN. What's that?

DONALD. Your family.

WYMAN. Buggers.

DONALD. Language.

WYMAN. You know that wall?

DONALD. Why?

WYMAN. What's the other side?

Donald is fed up of telling Mr Wyman.

DONALD. Oh Joey it's . . .(*He stops.*) I'll tell you what. I'll go and have a look tomorrow. Then you'll be satisfied. Right? We'll ascertain once and for all. Now go to sleep. Wall!

WYMAN. Is it a field?

DONALD. Go to sleep.

Donald walks up the ward.

WYMAN. It's quiet whatever it is.

Jenny, who is Donald's girlfriend, now comes into the ward. We see them begin to walk slowly up and down the ward between the beds without hearing what they say, until we cut in one the whispered conversation.

JENNY. I mentioned savings. He said how much? I said about two thousand pounds.

DONALD. Well nearly. Did he sound pleased?

JENNY. Oh yes.

DONALD. I think two thousand's good. Did he think it was good?

JENNY. Oh yes. He said they were being squeezed by the government. He said that was happening all down the line.

DONALD. All what line?

JENNY. Just all down the line. Squeezed by the government all down the line.

DONALD. But he sounded hopeful?

JENNY. Oh yes. Only it's all to do with interest rates.

DONALD. Did you tell him I might be going up a grade soon?

JENNY. No.

DONALD. You should have told him that. It affects our income.

JENNY. I said we'd tried the Halifax, and the Bradford and Morley.

DONALD. Should you have said that?

JENNY. I wondered after. But he laughed. The more the merrier that's what he said.

DONALD. He sounds nice.

JENNY. He was nice.

DONALD. Did you tell him we'd be willing to become depositors?

JENNY. Oh, he said we'd have to become depositors. There wouldn't be any question. (*This conversation should be punctuated by the noises of old men sleeping, and with Donald stopping and checking on patients. Pause.*) He lives at Lawnswood.

DONALD. What's that got to do with it?

JENNY. He just happened to say.

DONALD. But he sounded hopeful?

JENNY. He said they weren't the villains.

DONALD. Who?

JENNY. The Building Societies. He said the government was the villain.

The economic situation was the villain. He said personally he'd give mortgages on a first come first serve basis and none of this to-ing and fro-ing.

DONALD. He sounds nice.

JENNY. He was nice.

DONALD. You should have told him my grading was going up though. Status, that's what they're interested in.

JENNY. Have you heard?

DONALD. Well, it's between me and Vic.

JENNY. He'd have given me some coffee if I'd wanted some.

Donald checks that Mr Wyman is asleep. Donald and Jenny walk back towards the orderly room.

DONALD. Did he say when they'd let us know?

JENNY. He didn't say.

She breaks down.

DONALD. Don't cry.

He kisses her, and they go into the orderly room, out of view. The camera stays in the ward, possibly focuses in on the family pictures in the leather folder, with the sleeping noises and grunting of the old men. Then it slowly goes up the ward past the open door of the orderly room where Donald is embracing Jenny, his white coat still on, trousers round his ankles, bare bum to the camera; but the sound is not the sounds of sex but still of old men sleeping.

17. Interior. Corridor. Day.

A slow procession of old men. Some have got walking frames, another is being wheeled. Mr Wyman is in a wheelchair, but one foot is now in a slipper. Donald is pushing him. They are all going in the same direction. As the procession moves along Vic gives a Peter O'Sullivan-type commentary, as he also pushes one of the patients along in a wheelchair.

VIC. Come on, lads. Only another four furlongs to go and it's Mr Dyson in the lead. Mr Dyson in the lead with Mr Riscoe coming up on the far side. Mr Riscoe's coming up on the far side but Mr Wyman's making a last minute bid . . .

Donald is pushing Mr Wyman.

. . . a surprise spurt here by Donald on Mr Wyman, and at the post it's Mr Wyman with Mr Riscoe second and Mr Dyson third.

Donald is laughing, as are some of the old men. It should be a cheerful scene.

18. Interior. Another corridor. Day.

Old women also on the move, also encumbered by walking frames etc. and surveyed magisterially by Matron who is black, assisted by three female nurses.

MISS MUSCHAMP. I was a big hiker. All during the war. My friend and me. We were in the Bradford Ladies. Went all over. Distance no object.

MATRON. Help each other. Keep up, Muriel. Help her, Nora. Imagine we're striding over the moors. Deep breaths. You don't want to keep your boyfriends waiting, do you?

19. Interior. Various corridors etc. Day.

The race. Montage of old people walking, music over. Close shots of feet, walking frames, wheelchairs etc. The two streams finally mingle.

20. Interior. Hospital. Assembly hall. Day.

The old men and women have assembled in a hall which also functions as a theatre. There is a piano. Posters on the walls, notices. My Wyman is at the back. Pam, a jolly therapist in her thirties, is taking the class.

PAM. Now, is everybody ready? No. We are not ready. Are we, Alice? Are we, Ernest? What did I say last week? (*Miss Muschamp puts her hand up.*) Don't tell me, Miss Muschamp, do it. *Mix.* We don't just stay in our own little group. Alice, you come over here. Hannah, you here. Ernest. We aren't frightened of them, are we, girls? They're only men. Some ladies would fall over themselves to get a boyfriend like this. That's right, Iris. That's better. No, not you, Mr Riscoe. You keep here.

Donald half-sits in the window sill, watching. Mr Wyman looks out of the window. It is another view of the wall.

We'll kick off with a song: 'I've Got Sixpence'.

She sits down at the piano and they begin to play. Pam half turns round while she's playing so she can mouth the words at them. Mr Wyman isn't singing, but staring out at the wall.

PAM and OLD PEOPLE. (*Singing.*) I've got sixpence,
Jolly, jolly sixpence.
I've got sixpence, to last me all my life.
I've got twopence to spend,
And twopence to lend
And twopence to send home to my wife.
No cares have I to grieve me,
No pretty little girls to deceive me,
I'm happy as a king, believe me,
As I go rolling home.
Rolling home. Rolling home.
By the light of the silvery moon etc.

21. Exterior. Park. Day.

Shot of the outside of the hospital wing, taken from the wall that Mr Wyman is looking at. Faintly, the sound of singing. Singing stops and we go back inside again.

22. Interior. Hall. As before.

PAM. So it's Gentlemen versus The Ladies, and we're starting off with the names of birds. Names of birds everybody, please, and Donald's going to keep the score. Off we go.

At intervals throughout the following dialogue an old lady in a wheelchair says, 'I'm not here. I'm not here.' As if to confirm this, no one takes any notice of her.

VARIOUS VOICES. Sparrow.

PAM. Sparrow.

VOICE. Thrush.

PAM. Thrush.

VOICE. Blackbird.

ANOTHER VOICE. Wren.

RISCOE. Shitehawk.

VOICE. Crow.

PAM. Crow, good, yes.

RISCOE. Shitehawk.

Vic signals to Pam that Mr Riscoe has a contribution to make.

VIC. Pam.

Pam, who has been trying to ignore Mr Riscoe, gives Vic a dirty look.

RISCOE. Shitehawk.

PAM. I didn't hear that, Mr Riscoe.

VIC. Shitehawk.

PAM. I'll kill you, Vic.

RISCOE. Shitehawk's a bird. They had them in India.

PAM. Well that wouldn't be their real name. Hawk perhaps but not the other bit.

RISCOE. When you came out of the cookhouse with your plate they'd swoop down and pinch your dinner.

PAM. I don't believe that but anyway shall we give it him, ladies? Just this once, seeing he's a man. Come on then, more birds.

Miss Muschamp, who is sitting near Donald and is rather refined, suddenly comes to life.

MISS MUSCHAMP. Osprey. Osprey.

DONALD. What?

MISS MUSCHAMP. Osprey.

DONALD. (*Calling out.*) Osprey here.

PAM. Osprey? That's good. Who's that? Miss Muschamp. I might have known.

MISS MUSCHAMP. Kingfisher.

PAM. Kingfisher! What colour's that, Connie? (*Connie shakes her head.*) Blue.

MISS MUSCHAMP. Heron. Jackdaw. Magpie.

PAM. Heron, yes. Jackdaw, Magpie. Give the others a chance Miss Muschamp. They haven't had your education.

VOICE. Hen. Hen.

PAM. Hen. That's good.

RISCOE. Cock.

PAM. (*Wearily.*) Yes, all right, Mr Riscoe.

RISCOE. Cock.

PAM. I said all right.

Miss Muschamp covers her face.

RISCOE. Tits. Tits.

Pam makes a face at Donald.

PAM. You spoil it for everybody else, Mr Riscoe. I think we'd better play Rivers and Seas.

Mr Wyman is still looking out of the window. Donald follows his look. It is just the wall.

23. Interior. Treatment room. Day.

Donald is bandaging Mr Wyman's foot, which is plainly getting worse. We see the wall outside. An occasional orderly passes.

DONALD. I've said. I'll go. When I've done this. So shut up about it. You get on my nerves. It's wall, wall, wall.

WYMAN. Don't you tell me. I was a bricklayer. You didn't know that, did you?

DONALD. Yes.

WYMAN. I built . . . now then. I built somewhere famous in Leeds. I built the Queen's Hotel.

DONALD. Not single-handed?

WYMAN. That hurts.

DONALD. Sorry.

WYMAN. The Princess Royal opened that. She shook hands with me. Right performance. Hands clean first. Fingernails inspected. Told what to say if she asked me this that and the other. All over in a minute or two. Tap tap. Silver trowel. Did it properly after she'd gone. She'd have never made a bricklayer. Launch ships. Plant trees. Lay bricks. It's a right job.

DONALD. What?

WYMAN. Royalty.

DONALD. Never do this job, though, do they?

WYMAN. It hurts like Billy-o does that.

DONALD. Right, I'll go look on the other side of the wall for you?

WYMAN. That's right.

DONALD. There's other patients on this ward you know besides you.

WYMAN. You're my pal.

Donald goes out. Mr Wyman stares out of the window and in a moment Donald passes. He pretends to shake his fist at Mr Wyman. Mr Wyman laughs.

24. Exterior. Grounds by wall. Day.

When he is safely out of sight of Mr Wyman, Donald waits until it will seem he has had time to go and look beyond the wall. He takes out a cigarette. To the casual onlooker he seems to be skiving. Cut to exterior of the ward block, looking in on the corridor. Matron is passing through and glances out of the window and sees Donald. She stops. She taps on the window. Donald turns. She beckons sternly.

25. Interior. Corridor with seating area. Day.

Donald comes through looking pissed off. He strides down the ward, going past Mr Wyman without looking at him.

DONALD. Now have you all been to the toilet? (*He goes down the corridor, stopping in front of each one.*) Toilet? Toilet? Toilet? (*An old man nods.*) Come on, then.

OLD MAN. No, I've been.

DONALD. When?

OLD MAN. Just this minute.

Donald feels his trousers.

DONALD. Oh bloody hell.

WYMAN. Well, I don't do that. I never do that. I know when I want to go. I always sing out.

Donald takes no notice and helps the other old man out.

VIC. Oh dear. What's got into your friend, then? She's cross.

26. Interior. Ward. Night.

Donald is sat at the night table.

WYMAN. Donald.

Donald takes no notice, at first, then he gets up and goes down the ward. He stands at the foot of Mr Wyman's bed, but we don't hear the conversation. He goes and gets a cradle, which, he puts under the bedclothes to lift the clothes off Mr Wyman's feet.

DONALD. Better?

WYMAN. Yes.

DONALD. I got into bother with you, you know. I was told off. Flaming wall.

WYMAN. I'm sorry.

DONALD. Never mind. Night night.

WYMAN. Donald. You never told me. What's there?

At this point Jenny, Donald's girl comes and stands waiting for him just inside the doors of the ward. Donald sees her, so this following speech is partly done watching her. He sits down by the bed.

DONALD. It's a house. A really nice little house. Two up, two down. Porch, path up to the door. Honeysuckle. There's a little garden. Flowers. Apple tree. And a vegetable patch. It's ideal.

WYMAN. Who's it belong to?

DONALD. A young couple. I think they've just got married.

WYMAN. Yes? What's he got in the garden?

Donald hesitates.

DONALD. Beans?

WYMAN. It could be beans. Beans'd do well. Runner beans.

DONALD. Runner beans. Go to sleep. Is that better with your foot?

WYMAN. Runner beans.

He smiles and closes his eyes as Donald goes back up the ward where Jenny has opened the door and is waiting for him. He puts his arm round her and they go out.

27. Interior. Ward. Day.

The ward. Mr Wyman sits by his bed in a dressing gown, walking frame by the bed, foot bandaged. Molly and Harold are sitting by the bed, Val also. Pause.

MOLLY. Stephen got his bronze medal. (*Val gets up, and goes and stares out of the window.*) Life-saving. Nice to have something like that up your sleeve. In an emergency. (*The leather folder is laid flat on the locker. Molly stands it up.*) Our Melanie's got going on this indoor rock climbing now. Her and Paul. You know little Paul that's big now? And she's doing another course besides in this Jappy wrestling. They do it at the new centre. I said to her, 'You might as well: there's all sorts of fellers about.' She can throw her Dad. You can do anything you want, at the centre in the way of sports. Harold's even been talking about squash.

HAROLD. I'm too old for squash.

MOLLY. Nobody's too old for anything these days, are they Dad? Look at President and Mrs Reagan. We think they've got a look of Mr and Mrs Brewster.

VAL. (*Returning.*) Who?

MOLLY. President and Mrs Reagan.

VAL. (*Sniffs her sleeves.*) It gets into your clothes. I go home and I need a complete change of outfit.

Donald passes with an old man.

HAROLD. You deserve a medal.

VAL. They're nicely off now, nurses. I've no sympathy for anybody that works for the local authority, choose what they do. They aren't living in the real world. (*Donald passes with the same old man, walking him back.*) They don't lie awake worrying about profit margins, being undercut. I see it in Mr Stillman's face. He went over to Blackpool the other week. A round table on man-made fibres. He was practically the only Englishman there. All Japanese.

MOLLY. We're thinking of going in for one of these new fridge-freezers, Dad, did we tell you?

VAL. He had some Japanese food. Said it was all right, only more what we'd call hors d'oeuvres really. He had to let three people go last week. All men.

MOLLY. Oh dear.

VAL. I'm all right. Mr Stillman said to me, he said, 'Don't you worry, Val. The right man for the job is often a woman.'

Donald comes back and Molly gets up.

MOLLY. How is his foot?

DONALD. About the same.

Mr Wyman raises his hand.

WYMAN. Now then, Donald.

VAL. He speaks to you. Doesn't speak to us, do you Dad? We're your family. We love you, chick.

DONALD. He's tired.

MOLLY. We'll go.

She and Val kiss him. Harold to Donald:

HAROLD. You're doing a great job. (*They pass Vic, who has just recaptured Mr Riscoe for the seventeenth time that day.*) Keep up the good work.

28. Exterior. Car park and grounds. Day.

VAL. I'm not wasting any sympathy on him. I remember the way he made mother suffer. He killed mother.

MOLLY. No. . . . It was Gilbert dying that killed mother.

VAL. I went in one morning and she was crying and you could see there was a right blotch on her cheek. I said, 'What's that mark, Mam?' She said 'Oh, nothing I must have been bitten.' He'd hit her.

HAROLD. Nobody's perfect.

VAL. If something does happen to him we shall have to think what to do about Rothwell Street.

HAROLD. Put it on the market.

VAL. What market? It's due for demolition all round there. I'm surprised it hasn't been squat. It's all students.

HAROLD. They have to live somewhere.

MOLLY. Our Melanie fetched a lad in the other night. Mascara.

VAL. A lad?

MOLLY. He was quite nicely spoken but it was definitely mascara.

HAROLD. She'd met him at rock-climbing.

MOLLY. Rock-climbing, mascara; you can't add it up, can you?

Val and Molly kiss.

VAL. I'll be glad when this job's over.

MOLLY. Don't say that.

VAL. Well, you don't have a job, Mol. I'm a professional woman. I've got other things to think about. I'm in Chesterfield tomorrow.

She gets into her car as they go back to theirs.

MOLLY. *Yes?*

HAROLD. Nothing.

29. Interior. Ward or corridor. Day.

Mr Wyman sits in a wheelchair at the window, staring out at the wall.

WYMAN. Donald.

DONALD. What?

WYMAN. How are his beans?

DONALD. Coming on.

WYMAN. Frost. That's the bugbear.

30. Interior. Assembly hall. Day.

Pam and a mixed group of old men and women, as before.

VARIOUS VOICES. Cricket.

PAM. Cricket, yes.

VOICE. Tennis.

PAM. Tennis, yes.

VOICE. Table tennis, yes.

PAM. Table tennis, very good, Connie.

RISCOE. Snogging.

PAM. Ignoring you, Mr Riscoe.

VOICE. Badminton.

PAM. Badminton, yes.

RISCOE. Shagging.

MISS MUSCHAMP. Bridge.

PAM. Bridge did you say, Miss Muschamp?

MISS MUSCHAMP. Bridge. Chess.

PAM. Chess, yes.

MISS MUSCHAMP. Croquet. Bezique.

VOICE. We can't win if she plays.

PAM. Well you've got to think, Clifford. Compete. That's the name of the game. What about football? Nobody's mentioned football.

ALICE. Football.

PAM. Good, Alice. Football.

CONNIE. Blow football.

PAM. Blow football. Very good, Connie.

RISCOE. Love.

Pam ignores this.

VIC. Mr Riscoe says love.

PAM. Love isn't a game, Mr Riscoe. We can't give him love, can we
girls? (*To Vic*) I think you encourage him.

*Mr Wyman is sitting as usual by the window, but for once he isn't looking
out of it. Cut to outside the room, as Pam starts them up on a song: 'Bye,
Bye Blackbird'. Outside a labourer comes by with a wheelbarrow. Bricks.
The sound of singing from inside.*

31. Exterior. Wall.

32. Assembly hall. Day.

*Back in the recreation room Mr Wyman has seen the labourer with the
wheelbarrow and the bricks. He gets himself to his feet and tries to see out of
the window down the wall.*

WYMAN. They're doing something to the wall. (*His neighbours take no
notice as they sing and follow Pam in the actions to 'Bye, Bye, Blackbird'.
Mr Wyman stands up and addresses the room:*) They're doing something
to the wall! (*Only Donald takes any notice.*)

33. Interior. Corridor. Day.

*Cut to the old men trailing back along the corridor. Donald wheels Mr
Wyman.*

DONALD. Yes, I'll find out. Stop nattering about it.

*Vic is pushing someone in a wheelchair and singing 'You Made Me Love
You', waltzing him from side to side in the chair. Matron comes along,
overtakes Donald and walks behind Vic.)*

MATRON. Nurse. You won't get your grading that way, nurse.

*Vic stops. Matron gives him a black look and goes on. Donald catches up
with Vic.*

VIC. (*Ruefully.*) Go to Gaol. Go directly to Gaol. Do not pass Go. Do not collect two hundred pounds.

The procession continues.

34. Interior. Treatment room. Day.

At the wall outside we see bricklayers at work. Mr Wyman is having his foot treated by Donald. So that when Donald talks about the decay of the wall he is actually dealing with the decay of the foot.

WYMAN. What sort of repairs? What for?

DONALD. Re-pointing. The stone's been eaten away. The mortar's crumbling. It's sagging in parts. Like me.

WYMAN. If it's sagging they'll have to take it down. (*Donald says nothing.*) I'll maybe see the little house. (*Donald says nothing.*) Donald.

DONALD. What?

WYMAN. I'll maybe see the little house.

DONALD. How does that feel, Joey?

WYMAN. Champion. Champion.

35. Interior. Ward. Day.

Val, Molly and Harold are talking to Donald.

VAL. Can you give us some sort of timetable? It's only so we can plan ahead. There's a possibility I may have to go to Milan.

MOLLY. And Paul's got his 'O' levels coming up.

HAROLD. Yes, only that doesn't matter.

MOLLY. Well, we don't want him upsetting.

DONALD. He's been a bit better these last few days. His foot's improved. It seems to have stopped spreading.

VAL. I'd prefer to see a doctor. I don't think I ever have seen a doctor, in all the time we've been coming here.

DONALD. He comes round in a morning. He won't be able to tell you any different.

They go and Donald goes back into the ward. Mr Wyman is sat looking out of the window.

WYMAN. Getting nearer.

36. Exterior. Day.

Men at work, shot through foreground window.

37. Interior. Ward.

Donald and his girl, sat at the night table.

JENNY. There's one big room and one little room that would do as a bedroom. Then there's the kitchen.

She draws him a plan.

DONALD. Three rooms. Where's the bathroom?

JENNY. The bath's in the kitchen. Under the draining board. It like lifts up.

DONALD. Where's the lav?

JENNY. Across the landing. She seems a nice enough woman. She said she appreciated the plight of young married couples and was prepared to make an exception for us on that basis.

DONALD. We're not married.

JENNY. We will be.

DONALD. What's she? Widow?

JENNY. Divorced.

DONALD. She say anything about children?

JENNY. I didn't ask her.

DONALD. Why?

JENNY. I didn't dare. (*Donald makes a gesture of despair.*) You don't know what it's like. Rushing to be first with the paper. Trailing round day after day. Ringing up and it being engaged. I've had it all to do.

DONALD. We swore we wouldn't rent.

JENNY. We can't buy. What else can we do?

DONALD. I don't know.

JENNY. Come into the office.

DONALD. No. It'll just eat away everything we've got saved up. Even if it's me gets the grading it'll eat it all away.

38. Interior. Ward. Day.

Mr Wyman is in bed. Molly sits on the bed. Harold plays with a walking frame.

MOLLY. A bit better again today. He looks better. You look better, Dad. How's your Lucozade? (*She opens his locker.*) Still got quite a bit in hand. (*She takes out the leather folder of snaps.*) This belongs on top of your locker, Dad. We want to be where you can see us, love. (*She puts it on the locker. Pause.*) Our Melanie's discovered boys. (*Pause.*) I suppose it was only a matter of time. (*Pause.*) And Paul's limbering up for his 'O' Levels. (*Pause.*) Stephen's got a verucca. No more lifesaving. Confined to dry land for the time being. They'll just have to drown. Harold, stop playing about with that thing and come sit down. (*Donald goes by.*) Bit better again to-day.

DONALD. That's right.

Val comes in, limping, her shoe in her hand. Mr Wyman has his eyes closed.

VAL. I've just gone over on my heel. That path's a quagmire. Forty quid.

HAROLD. You want a drop of that superglue.

MOLLY. Bit better again today.

VAL. Is he?

MOLLY. Asleep.

VAL. Better; no better. It's just a prolongation. I'd just like to hear an authoritative statement from somebody. That nurse knows nothing, you can tell.

WYMAN. (*Opening his eyes.*) Are you the married one?

MOLLY. No. I'm the married one, Dad. That's Val.

VAL. He knows perfectly well.

MOLLY. He doesn't. He gets confused.

VAL. I thought you said he was better.

MOLLY. Try and have a bit of understanding. Val's in ladies' gowns, Dad. She's the career girl.

VAL. What's that supposed to mean, career girl?

Harold is still playing with the walking frame.

HAROLD. The man that invented these deserves a medal. Light as a feather. I'm looking forward to having one of these, Dad. I can't wait.

VAL. I only did what Mam wanted me to do. She wanted me to get on.

MOLLY. Yes, but she thought you'd look after them when the time came. Instead of that, I was the one.

VAL. I did my share. I'd have been in London now if it hadn't been for him.

MOLLY. I bore the brunt. And I've got a family of my own.

VAL. I've sacrificed. I've sacrificed all down the line. I could have been married. I could have been in London. I could have been a buyer for C & A.

MOLLY. Married? You've no need to get married.

VAL. What does that mean?

MOLLY. Little trips to Manchester. Blackpool. Mr Stillman this. Mr Stillman that. What does Mrs Stillman think?

HAROLD. Nay, Mol.

VAL. She doesn't think anything, because I'm a friend of the family. She tells me all sorts. They've got a son at York University. The idea. I helped her choose some curtains.

WYMAN. Shut up, fratching.

VAL. Little trips! It's work.

WYMAN. Stop it. The pair of you. (*Pause.*) I loved your mother.

VAL. You'd a funny way of showing it.

HAROLD. No. No. Shut up. Shut up.

MOLLY. Valery Wyman, what a thing to say to your own father.

VAL. Hitting her.

MOLLY. He never hit her.

WYMAN. I hit her once.

VAL. You hit her more than once.

HAROLD. No. Please. Stop it.

VAL. On her breast. That's where you hit her. That's what started it all.

MOLLY. Nay, it never is. Doctor Roberts said that was all rubbish.

VAL. Mam didn't think so.

Mr Wyman is crying.

MOLLY. You've made him cry.

VAL. He wants to cry.

HAROLD. No.

VAL. He should have cried years ago. Me and Mr Stillman. I put in eighteen hours a day at the Northern Fabrics Fair. And you want to ask Mrs Stillman who helped get rid of her sinus. You always had a small mind, Maureen Wyman.

Val stalks out, her exit somewhat spoiled by the fact she is still only wearing one shoe.

HAROLD. Dear oh dear.

MOLLY. I might as well not be married. You wet hen. You're supposed to stick up for me. That's what marriage means.

39. Interior. Ward. Night.

Donald is sitting by Mr Wyman's bed, holding his hand. Jenny comes in and tiptoes down the ward and stands at the end of the bed. Donald smiles.

DONALD. I won't be a sec.

She smiles. Walks back up the ward towards the orderly's room.

WYMAN. Have they got kiddies, that couple?

DONALD. What couple?

WYMAN. Over the wall.

DONALD. Not yet. I shouldn't be surprised if they do though. Little house, garden. Just right for kiddies. They've got a dog.

WYMAN. Dogs are all right. Do you know them? (*Donald hesitates.*) Will you tell them something?

DONALD. What?

WYMAN. They mustn't have children.

DONALD. Why not?

WYMAN. No children.

DONALD. Don't be so daft, Joey. What sort of a thing is that to say to anybody. Don't have children. They're young. They're just at the beginning. They've got all their lives. (*Wyman has hold of Donald's arm.*) Let go.

WYMAN. Tell them. No children.

DONALD. I won't. You silly daft sod.

WYMAN. Donald.

DONALD. Lay off. (*Mr Wyman releases his grip on Donald's arm and slumps back on the pillow. Donald tucks him in.*) Oh Christ. What have you done?

WYMAN. I'm sorry.

DONALD. Don't say you're starting on this game now. You were supposed to be different. You've spoiled your record, you.

He goes up the ward.

40. Interior. Orderly room. Night.

Donald goes into the orderly's room. Jenny is sitting there. He shakes his head, but doesn't say anything, and gets a sheet out of the cupboard. Camera stays with her.

41. Interior. Ward. Night.

When we go back to the bed the sheets have been changed.

DONALD. All right?

Wyman nods. Donald checks one or two other patients then goes up the ward towards the lighted doorway of the orderly room. Donald goes in. Cut back to the bed where Wyman is still awake. Eyes open. Camera goes slowly up the ward, pausing at the door of the orderly room, now half closed.

42. Interior. Orderly room. Night.

Donald is kissing Jenny. He breaks off suddenly and listens. She watches him, listening, and listens too. Then he looks down and we hear his trouser zip.

43. Exterior. Hospital grounds. Late dusk.

A shot of the lighted windows of the corridor. The door leading out of the corridor into the grounds is open. We see Matron coming down the corridor. She stops at the open door, comes out and looks round. Finding nothing, she goes back inside, closing the door.

44. Interior. Corridor. Night.

Matron comes down the corridor. There is a line of light from the orderly room, which she passes, going straight into the ward.

45. Interior. Ward. Night.

There is no one at the night table at the end of the ward. She walks round the beds. Wyman's bed is empty.

46. Interior. Orderly room. Night.

Donald is making love to Jenny on the floor of the orderly room. The door is pushed open, but is stopped by Donald's leg. He looks over his shoulder up at Matron standing in the doorway.

MATRON. When you've finished that, nurse, you might just glance in the ward. One of your patients seems to have gone for a walk.

47. Exterior. Grounds by wall and canal. Day.

A high angle shot of an ambulance drawn up on the drive, in front of where the wall is being rebuilt. Two attendants are stepping through the gap with a stretcher on which is a sheeted figure. Beyond, by the bank of a canal, is Donald, and a couple of policemen and a man in a wet suit.

48. Exterior. Grounds by wall and canal. Day.

Reverse shot of Vic watching from a first floor window.

49. Interior. Corridor outside Matron's office.

Matron is just showing Molly and Harold and Val out.

MATRON. . . . Yes. Of course, they do wander at that age. And as I say we can't lock the doors. Not unless they're violent.

VAL. He was never violent. He was much more sweet-natured.

MOLLY. The tragedy is he just seemed to be picking up. His foot was better, he . . . anyway.

MATRON. Yes. Though, it's all downhill one way or another. At this age.

HAROLD. Quite. My mother fell down the cellar steps. All over in two minutes. I think that's the best way.

The camera draws back and we see them shake hands with the Matron. Then they come towards the camera on their way along yet another corridor out of the hospital.

VAL. Nice woman. Get them in a uniform and they have a lot of dignity. Very professional, but caring. Whereas we've never even had an apology from that male nurse. What was he doing?

MOLLY. They're shorthanded.

HAROLD. I couldn't blame him. They deserve a medal. I hope he'll not be sacked.

VAL. Why? Only he won't be. Nobody's sacked. Not in this day and age.

50. Exterior. Grounds by wall and canal. Day.

They are outside, passing the hole in the wall. A bricklayer is at work patching up the hole.

MOLLY. I don't know what all that was about, him wanting to know what was the other side.

VAL. He knew what was the other side. I've told him a time or two. Just staring and staring and not talking. I got fed up of it. I said, 'I don't know what there's to stare at. There's a wall. And a canal, and beyond it's the cemetery.'

MOLLY. He'd be confused, bless him.

VAL. They ought to cater for that. (*They are walking out of earshot towards the car park.*) A hole there. Its a standing invitation. Somebody wants reporting. But they won't be. You bet.

HAROLD. They can't think of everything.

51. Exterior. Car park. Day.

They are standing by Val's car.

MOLLY. He's at peace now, anyway.

She blows her nose.

VAL. I mustn't linger. I'm due in Bradford at three to look at some slip-overs. It never stops.

MOLLY. Paul's taking part in a demonstration to-night. So we've got to be on parade. Rescue and Resuscitation in Sub-Zero Temperatures. He gets wrapped up in tinfoil, apparently.

VAL. Ring anyway. We can liaise about the funeral after the inquest. Mr Stillman knows someone in the Lions who's an undertaker, and we can both chip in over the eats. (*She leans out of the car.*) I've got an Answerphone now, so you can give me a tinkle anytime and put it on tape. You speak after the tone.

She drives off. They walk to their car, get in and sit for a moment, before Harold starts the engine.

MOLLY. Tell me something.

HAROLD. What?

MOLLY. Why is it we always see her to her car and not the other way round?

Harold shakes his head.

HAROLD. We shan't be doing now, anyway, shall we. We shan't be coming again.

MOLLY. That's not the point I'm making.

He starts the engine. Another car meanwhile has arrived and a woman and her husband get out with an old man. As Molly and Harold drive off, the new trio are going up the steps of the hospital, as Matron comes out. And we hear her say:

MATRON. Do you know, you're our first Kevin. We've never had a Kevin before.

52. Interior. Ward. Day.

Donald is busy with the new old man. An Asian doctor is on his rounds, followed by Matron and Vic, who now sports the tabs of his higher grading. He also carries a clipboard. The party stops at the new arrival's bed.

VIC. Could you see to this, nurse?

Vic walks away down the ward as Donald draws the curtains round the bed for doctor's examination of the new admission. It is plain that Donald has not been upgraded. The doctor and Matron wait as Donald pulls back the sheet from the old man for the examination. Overhead shot of the old man lying flat on his back, naked. Music.

Marks

MARJORY   Marjorie Yates
LES   Ian Targett
DAD   Charles Lamb
LILY   Dandy Nichols
NORA   Diana Rayworth
LESLEY   Tracylynn Stephens
MARGARET   Colette Barker
PHOTOGRAPHER   Ojah Maharaj
VICAR   Nicholas Denney
DENISE   Frances Ruffell
A DAD   Sydney Golder
A MOTHER   Helen Keating
A BROTHER   Peter Acre
HUSBAND   John Fowler
BABY   Claire Cowell

Produced by Innes Lloyd
Directed by Piers Haggard
Designed by Oliver Bayldon
Music by Geoffrey Burgon

1. Interior. Church. Day.

A church. The font where a baptism is taking place. The camera begins with the sign of the cross being made on the head of a baby by a youngish vicar with a beard.

VICAR. In the name of the Father, and of the Son and of the Holy Ghost. Amen.

The camera takes in the young parents who are seventeen or eighteen. The relatives of the young parents are gathered round the font in two distinct groups: the relatives on the father's side, who are jolly, a bit over-dressed and have had a drink or two; and the young mother's relatives, who stand a little apart – the girl's mother, Marjory, who is about 45, her son Leslie, who is fifteen or sixteen and another woman, Nora, Marjory's friend. Marjory looks fed up, Leslie is expressionless. Of the three of them, only Nora looks at all happy. Cut to the end of the ceremony. The congregation is filing out, the young mother, Margaret, carrying her baby. She pauses by her mother.

MARGARET. Happy? (*Meaning 'satisfied?'*)

Marjory says nothing. She puts her arm through Leslie's, who looks uncomfortable.

2. Exterior. Church Steps. Day.

A photographer is posing them all on the steps. Marjory is still unsmiling. There is a definite sense that the family on the young father's side is a bit common. Lots of banter.

PHOTOGRAPHER. Close in a bit.

FIRST VOICE. Yes, budge up.

SECOND VOICE. Give over, Denise.

THIRD VOICE. Any closer and we shall be here again in nine months time.

FOURTH VOICE. (*Woman.*) Wilfred!

SECOND VOICE. I'm being assaulted here.

THIRD VOICE. Change places with me then.

FOURTH VOICE. You've clicked my stocking now, Wilfred, arsing about.

FIRST VOICE. Mind the bloody baby, I mean.

PHOTOGRAPHER. Come on everybody. Lady in the blue hat, smile love please.

LES. Come on, Mum. Crack one.

Marjory forces a smile.

THIRD VOICE. (*Whispered.*) Hey. 'She gave a grim smile.' (*Titters.*)

PHOTOGRAPHER. One for the mantelpiece now.

3. Exterior. Terrace of houses. Day.

Establishing shot.

4. Interior. Marjory's home. Day.

Ordinary terrace house. Nora and Marjory talk, Nora has her hat and coat on, so it is plainly not her house. Leslie has headphones on, plugged in to a cassette recorder and occasionally sings a phrase or two in a toneless unintelligible way.

NORA. It was you wanted her christening.

MARJORY. Not with a name like that.

NORA. It's a nice name.

MARJORY. Kimberley? Kimberley? It's the name of a place.

NORA. No, that's Camberley.

MARJORY. Kimberley. It's in Australia. It's where that diamond came from.

NORA. Well, she is a little jewel.

MARJORY. Saddled with a name like that. She's marked for life. She's no taste, Margaret. She takes after her Dad. Kimberley.

Les takes his earphones off for a second.

LES. I like it.

MARJORY. What?

LES. Kimberley.

NORA. Give us a listen. (*She puts on the earphones and listens happily, saying, in a too-loud voice.*) Turn it down.

MARJORY. He ought to have put her off it, that vicar. Advised her. You'd never think he was a vicar outside. One of these, 'We're just the same as you are' brigade. Only I bet his daughter's not called Kimberley. She'll by Polly. Or Jane. Proper names. I just wanted her called Susan. Something ordinary.

Nora takes them off.

NORA. It's like you're somewhere else.

LES. Try it. (*Marjory shakes her head.*) Live a bit.

MARJORY. How? I'm a grandmother. Imagine calling her in on a night. Kimberley! Kimberley!

Les has got his earphones on again.

NORA. You've still got one. (*Meaning Les.*)

MARJORY. Yes. Margaret was always a big Dad fan anyway. I don't know what he's going to do. (*They are free to talk about Les because he has his earphones on and is oblivious.*) Schools, they do it on you. He's had satisfactory reports all the way through. Marks good. 'Does well.' 'Up to standard.' I knew he couldn't spell, but I thought 'Well, the school will know,' compared with the average. Then the letter comes. Failed everything. CSEs. Whole bloody lot. Not even graded. I go down there and his teacher says they never expected him to pass. I said to him 'So what does 'up to standard' mean?' And he says, 'Well, you know, he's a nice enough lad.' What's that got to do with it? It's a fraud, schooling now. If they're clever they keep them back. If they're not they pretend they are. Nobody lays it down. Then it's too late. I could spell.

NORA. You write a grand letter, you always have.

MARJORY. Sums. All that.

NORA. They have these calculators now. Still he's lovely-looking. And he's shy. I always think that's nice.

5. Interior. Kitchen. Day.

Marjory and Les are washing up. Nora has gone.

MARJORY. Seventeen.

LES. Don't keep saying seventeen. You just don't like being a grandmother.

MARJORY. Promise me you won't ever get yourself into that boat with a girl. (*Les reaches for his headphones. She stops him.*) Promise me.

LES. Mum. Girls don't like me. I don't say the right things.

MARJORY. If it's what he said to Margaret, good job. And any girl that doesn't like you wants her head examining. You're lovely.

She touches him. He pulls away.

LES. It's the girl's responsibility now, anyway.

MARJORY. What?

LES. Birth control.

MARJORY. You seem to know a lot about it.

LES. We did it at school.

He puts the headphones on.

MARJORY. School. They get that into your heads. You can't spell, but you know all about birth control. Birth control's not going to get you a job. You can't say that at your interview. 'What qualifications have you?' 'I know about birth control.' Margaret can't even say that. She must have been looking out of the window. (*She looks at herself in the mirror.*) Forty-three.

LES. What?

MARJORY. I'm a grandmother.

LES. Well *she* was, that German bag. And she did all right.

MARJORY. What German bag?

LES. I don't know. That German bag. With the nice legs. Maureen somebody.

MARJORY. Maureen? Maureen? *Marlene*. Marlene Dietrich. Maureen Dietrich. How are you ever going to get a job, you don't even know Marlene Dietrich.

They both laugh.

6. Interior. Kitchen. Day.

Marjory is ready to go to work. Les is having his breakfast.

MARJORY. Do you read any newspapers?

LES. No.

MARJORY. I'm testing you.

LES. The Sun.

MARJORY. Say the Mail. The Mail's better. It's classier.

LES. Today's only a formality, Mam. He's not going to give me a job. He'll just put me down on the register.

MARJORY. You don't know what tips the balance. What do you do in your spare time?

LES. It's all spare time.

MARJORY. Say you were in full employment. (*Les studies.*) Try, Les. (*Nothing.*) You listen to music, don't you?

LES. I listen to music.

MARJORY. Pop or classical?

LES. Rock.

MARJORY. Say some classical.

LES. What if he asks what?

MARJORY. Say . . . say Tchaikovsky. You've got to push yourself, Les. You can't just trot out the Top Twenty. They'll all do that. Show you're different.

LES. I'm not different.

MARJORY. Isn't there some respectable pop now? Serious. Elvis Presley's serious, isn't he, now he's dead? We used to like Buddy Holly. Hasn't he come round again?

LES. It'll just be somebody that takes your name down.

MARJORY. But you don't seem to know anything.

LES' *You* don't know anything. It doesn't matter.

MARJORY. Something matters. Something's got to matter. (*Getting a bit of paper out of her bag.*) Promise me something?

LES. What?

MARJORY. Don't go in your jeans. (*She reads the scrap of paper.*) I cut this out at work: 'When to an interview you do go Dress carefully, but without show, Arrive on time, don't chew or smoke Or else they'll choose the other bloke'. (*It has no noticeable effect on Les.*) I think you should look in these newsagents' shop windows. Cards. That's where the jobs are. At grass roots level. Give us a kiss. (*She is just going when she stops.*) And if you have to fill in any forms, your father's dead. (*Les says nothing.*) Do you hear? Dead.

LES. He's not dead. He's living in Bristol.

MARJORY. Your father is dead.

She goes. He reaches for the earphones.

7. Interior. House. Day.

Montage of Les doing housework with earphones on. Hoovering, emptying ashtrays, washing up.

8. Exterior. Job Centre.

Establishing shot.

9. Interior. Job Centre. Day.

A youngish, bearded man at a desk interviewing Les. They are in a cubicle closed on three sides. In another cubicle sits another interviewer. One should be able to see both interviewers in the same shot if need be. Though they cannot see one another.

BEARD. Hang gliding? *Hang gliding?* Cost you, hang gliding. Where do you get the money to go hang gliding?

LES. I sometimes go to watch.

BEARD. (*Wearily.*) Then it's not a hobby, is it. Spectating is not a hobby. (*He raises his voice, addressing Des in the other cubicle.*) It's like sport, Des, all these jokers, you ask them for a hobby and they say football. Only they don't play. Doing lad, that's what we're after. Doing. Not watching. (*He writes something down.*) What gives, Des?

Des is sitting in his cubicle staring into space.

DES. As of now, Dave, nothing. A slight hiccup in the never-ending procession of square pegs desirous of being inserted into round holes.

Les sits expressionless throughout this.

BEARD. All right for some. (*There is a thick folder and a thin folder on his desk.*) Jobs required. Jobs available. We're in a loaves and fishes situation here. Do you fancy being a lavatory attendant?

LES. No.

BEARD. Private Secretary to a Nobel Prizewinner?

LES. N-no.

BEARD. Right, well we've established the parameters. (*Pause while he looks at Les's form.*) Aren't you interested in anything?

LES. I'd like to travel.

BEARD. Louder. I didn't hear.

LES. (*Louder.*) I'd like to travel.

Beard lifts his hand, as if giving a cue and promptly Des, without amusement or interest says,

DES. What in?

BEARD. Why do you want to travel?

Leslie says nothing.

DES. Broadens the mind.

BEARD. I travel, don't I Des? (*Des says nothing. They have obviously done this routine many times.*) Every day between here and Fordyce Road. Never broadens mine. (*At which point the office door opens and a pretty but expressionless girl comes in with two coffees and biscuits for Beard and the other man.*) All hail, Christine. It is the hour of custard creams.

CHRISTINE. Fig rolls.

BEARD. You have a nice bum, Christine. (*Christine looks used to this.*) It is the only thing that keeps me going is your bum. Faced with a character with no O Levels, no CSEs, no ideas and no ambitions I think, 'Well we have always Christine's bum.' When you get a job . . . what's your name . . . Leslie. (*He looks at Les's form.*) . . . if you get a job, whether you are digging a septic tank or are Personal Assistant to the head of the CBI, job satisfaction will not consist in any work that you are employed to do. It will consist in incidentals. Like Christine's bum.

DES. And Maureen's tits.

BEARD. Goodbye bum.

Christine goes out, unmoved.

LES. I wondered about the army.

BEARD. Ever feel you've been here before, Des?

He reaches behind him without looking and takes a leaflet from the rack behind him. There is silence in the office. Les looking at the Army form. Beard bored. Other man staring into space.

10. Interior. Marjory's living room. Day.

Les is in his underpants, ironing a shirt.

MARJORY. You have got skills. Ironing's a skill. Hoovering's a skill. Looking after the house, that's a skill. Look at your Dad. He couldn't make a cup of tea. (*Les goes on ironing.*) You could be a butler. A Gentleman's Gentleman. All that's at your fingertips. (*He goes on ironing. She watches him.*) You're a lovely looking lad, Les. The one that gets you is going to be lucky.

He doesn't look at her, but says:

LES. Don't, Mum.

MARJORY. Don't what?

LES. Don't look at me.

MARJORY. I'm your mum. I'm allowed to look at you.

LES. You want to find yourself a chap.

He puts on the shirt he has been ironing.

MARJORY. I don't want a chap. Even part time. What do I want with a chap? I had a chap. I had my bellyfull with a chap. Twice.

LES. Your life's not over.

MARJORY. That part of it is.

LES. There'd be some fellers jump at you.

He goes upstairs.

MARJORY. (*Calling after him.*) Bring your jeans down and I'll wash them.

11. Interior. Les's bedroom. Day.

Les is ready to go out. He gets out a small printing outfit with four or five different stamps. He carefully stamps a star on his palm. A square on the back. Another two signs on his left hand. Tries them out. Bunching his fist, the sign showing. It should be plain what he is doing, but not what he is doing it for.

12. Interior. Living room and hall. Day.

MARJORY. Your jeans.

LES. They're upstairs.

She kisses him. The lipstick leaves a mark.

MARJORY. I've lipsticked you.

She rubs it out.

LES. Mum!

Marjory shrugs. Les goes. She irons a wrinkled shirt, then goes to the mirror and smooths out the unironable wrinkles on her neck; then goes upstairs.

13. Interior. Les's bedroom. Day.

Marjory puts one or two items straight in his bedroom, then picks up his jeans. She takes a handkerchief out of the pocket, some coppers, which she puts on the mantelpiece. In the back pocket are the leaflets about the Army from the Job Centre. She sits down on the bed looking at them.

14. Interior/Exterior. School Entrance and Playground. Early Evening.

From inside, the sounds of disco music. At the door, a man is taking money as kids go in. Two girls come out, one with a boy. The man stamps their hands for a pass out.

SECOND GIRL. (*To First Girl.*) Don't be long.

The boy gives a dirty laugh as they go off together. Second Girl is left. Possibly the whole of this scene could be played on roller skates. Second Girl skating disconsolately round the yard. Les eyes the girl for a bit.

LES. Hey.

SECOND GIRL. What?

LES. Can I look at your stamp? (*She looks at him, but says nothing.*) Can I look at your stamp?

SECOND GIRL. What for?

LES. I just want to see it.

SECOND GIRL. What for?

LES. Go on. Show us.

SECOND GIRL. Do I know you?

LES. Is it like this?

He shows her his hand, which she looks at without interest.

SECOND GIRL. No.

LES. This?

Showing her another mark.

SECOND GIRL. Could be.

LES. That?

SECOND GIRL. No.

LES. That?

SECOND GIRL. (*Pityingly.*) No.

LES. (*Certain.*) That?

The girl's face changes.

SECOND GIRL. No.

LES. It is.

SECOND GIRL. It isn't.

LES. Show us then – go on.

He makes grab for her wrist.

SECOND GIRL. Leave off, you.

She shows him her hand. It has a mark stamped on it like one of his.

SECOND GIRL. I could report you. (*She is looking at the Chucker Out.*) He's merciless, is that one. I know his sister. He has a caravan and an alsatian dog. It's not fair on other people. Let's have another look. It's uncanny. Would you do it for me? Say I got to know you?

LES. If you want.

SECOND GIRL. I was supposed to make a useful contact today. It said in my horoscope.

LES. Here goes.

They go in. The Chucker Out scarcely glances at the mark.

SECOND GIRL. Jammy bugger.

LES. (*Disappointed.*) He never even looked. (*She takes Les's hand.*) I don't dance.

SECOND GIRL. What you come in for?

LES. Watch.

15. Exterior. Terrace of houses. Dusk.

LES. You can't come in.

SECOND GIRL. I don't want to come in. Why?

LES. My mum.

SECOND GIRL. She poorly?

LES. No. Narrow minded.

SECOND GIRL. Mine isn't. She's got a chap. Come in there.

LES. Where do you live?

SECOND GIRL. Crossfields.

LES. I'm not trailing all that way.

SECOND GIRL. Well, I've got to.

LES. You can come round tomorrow. In the daytime. She goes out to work.

SECOND GIRL. In the daytime? What for?

LES. How do you mean, what for?

SECOND GIRL. What do you want me to come round for?

LES. I don't, particularly.

SECOND GIRL. What time?

LES. Anytime.

She is going.

SECOND GIRL. You never asked me my name.

LES. It'll keep.

He is going in. Marjory is sitting at the table. She has the Army brochures in front of her.

16. Interior. Marjory's bedroom. Morning.

Les comes into his mother's bedroom in his pyjama trousers and a shirt with a cup of tea. Marjory is in bed facing away from him.

LES. Mum, Mum. I've brought you some tea, Mum.

MARJORY. (*Not turning round.*) What's the time?

LES. After half past. (*She turns round unsmiling, and takes the tea.*) Mum?

MARJORY. What?

LES. They were only leaflets. I didn't sign anything.

MARJORY. Do what you want. Go back to bed.

Marjory starts to get up. Les waits for a moment.

LES. Mum?

Marjory won't speak.

17. Interior. Les's bedroom. Morning.

He is lying in bed. He hears the door bang as shoe goes to work. Looks at the clock. Gets up.

18. Interior. Sitting room. Morning.

Les is tidying the room up, headphones on.

19. Interior. Les's bedroom. Morning.

He looks at the sheets; switches them round. He has just finished when the bell goes downstairs. He gives the bedroom a last look.

20. Exterior. Terrace. Day.

Marjory and Nora walking home.

MARJORY. Shortfall. What's shortfall got to do with us? We're canteen. Canteen can't have a shortfall. It's wicked. No notice. Nothing.

NORA. It's better than being finished. Three days a week is better than being finished.

MARJORY. I can't see how we're going to manage. Are you coming in?

She does.

21. Interior. Kitchen and living room. Day.

Les is in the kitchen in his shirt filling the kettle. Marjory and Nora's arrival startles him.

LES. Jesus. What's matter?

MARJORY. Just getting up? I thought you were going round newsagents' windows. What's matter?

LES. Nothing. What are you doing home?

MARJORY. Sacked.

NORA. We haven't been sacked. We're on short time.

MARJORY. Then you'd have to find a job, if I was sacked. What's *matter*?

LES. Nothing.

MARJORY. What've you been doing? (*She finds a coat on the settee.*) Whose is this? (*Les goes upstairs quickly and without speaking. Marjory calls up after him.*) Les. Leslie.

Marjory holding the coat looks at Nora.

NORA. I'll go. (*She is going.*) It's normal nowadays.

Nora goes. Les comes down with his trousers on.

MARJORY. So this is what you do, is it?

LES. No.

MARJORY. No wonder you're not busting to find a job if this is what you do.

LES. I don't.

MARJORY. You don't? You do.

LES. It's the first time.

MARJORY. I don't want to know. Just get her out of the house. Who is she?

LES. She's nobody. (*The girl has appeared in the doorway.*) I just met her last night.

MARJORY. I thought you were the shy one. I thought you were the one couldn't talk to girls.

LES. I can't.

MARJORY. I suppose you haven't had much talking to do. (*Marjory catches sight of her, stood in the doorway.*) What's your name?

GIRL. Lesley.

MARJORY. Your name, not his name.

LES. Her name's Lesley.

MARJORY. His name's Leslie.

GIRL. Yes.

MARJORY. That's disgusting.

GIRL. It's spelled different.

MARJORY. I don't care how it's spelled. What the hell difference does it make how you spell it? And what were you doing, how's that spelled?

GIRL. I didn't want to come here. We could have gone up home. My mum doesn't mind.

MARJORY. Well she bloody well ought to mind. How old are you?

GIRL. Fourteen?

MARJORY. Fourteen.

She starts to cry.

LES. Mum.

GIRL. I'll go. It's funny. My mum never turns a hair.

She goes.

LES. Mum.

MARJORY. Go after her. She's your girl.

LES. She isn't.

MARJORY. You've been to bed with her. Go after her. What do you think she feels like?

LES. She won't mind. I didn't even like her.

MARJORY. You should like her. That's what it reckons to be about.

LES. Not these days.

MARJORY. You haven't even got started. You haven't even found your feet and you're off on that game. You're never going to get anywhere now. It makes up for everything, does that.

LES. What?

MARJORY. That. And drink. It's why nobody gets anywhere. Same as Margaret. You start on that game, you wake up one morning, you're thirty-five, you've got two kids and you're nowhere. You want to get somewhere before you start fetching girls home.

LES. You can't do stuff in order. I might not have a job for years.

MARJORY. You haven't looked. I tell you. Go round knocking on doors. Looking at adverts.

LES. All right. I'll go this afternoon. But I know it's no good.

Pause.

MARJORY. Funny her having your name. Is that how you got talking?

LES. No. I only asked her name when we got upstairs. It put me right off. Lesley.

MARJORY. It's a nice name. In a boy. She wasn't a patch on you anyway. Fetch your sheets down. I'll wash them. (*He goes for his headphones.*) Did you do that in headphones? (*He grins.*) I expect they will be doing before long.

22. Exterior. Street. Day.

Les looking in shop windows at cards. (Say two shots.) He looks closer at one card and copies down an address.

23. Exterior. Council estate. Day.

Les approaching a concrete council block. He climbs a staircase. We see him ring a doorbell. A woman of about sixty opens it. We see her shake her head before beginning to hear the conversation.

LILY. No. Not here.

LES. Fifty-five.

LILY. I don't care. It's not here.

While she is talking to him she is looking behind him and around to make sure no-one is watching.

LILY. No.

DAD. (*From behind the door.*) What's he look like?

Lily is still casing the landing and stairs.

LILY. Youngish. Sixteen. Are you genuine?

Les is puzzled.

LES. What?

LILY. Come in.

DAD. (*Behind door.*) Sharp.

24. Interior. Flat. Day.

Lily pushes door open, and they bundle Les inside. Dad is older than Lily and more frail.

LILY. Now then. Where did you find the address!

LES. In a window.

DAD. Which window?

LES. Down Lorrimer Road.

DAD. It is down Lorrimer Road.

LILY. I don't know. What do you think, Dad?

Dad has been running his hand over Les's arm. There is a tattoo on Dad's hand.

LES. You've got a tattoo.

DAD. I've got a tattoo, yes.

LILY. What does that prove? Doesn't prove it's a tattooists, does it? A tattooist's'd have pictures on the wall. Designs. There'd be machines, needles. Paraphernalia. This is just an ordinary home.

DAD. He's got an earring.

LILY. Earrings don't mean nothing. They all have earrings. Police have earrings.

LES. They don't.

DAD. He's only young.

LILY. That might be part of it.

LES. I'm off.

DAD. Why?

LES. I've changed my mind.

DAD. Supposing I did them, what sort of tattoo were you thinking of.

LES. 'Mother'. Just 'Mother'.

DAD. Whereabouts.

LES. My arm.

Pause.

DAD. He's not from the council. You're not from the council. They don't wear earrings on the council.

LES. Why should I be from the council?

LILY. Rates. We're domestic rated. Council finds out he's running a business, they could have us out.

DAD. I'm not running a business. I do it more as a favour. One here, one there.

LILY. Feller on the end, started selling tropical fish from his front room. Just odd ones, now and again, to bona fide fish fanciers. Six o'clock one morning, knock on the door. Out. Fish tanks stuck on the pavement. Heartbroken. And she was just getting over shingles.

DAD. Take your coat off.

LILY. Take your coat off. He did have premises once upon a time.

DAD. Up till two years ago.

LILY. Two years ago. On Station Street. He was famous wherever tattooed people foregathered. Signed photographs in the window. Johnny Ray, Frankie Vaughan. Only he's had one or two setbacks health-wise.

DAD. I had a stroke.

LILY. You didn't have a stroke. Not a full-blown stroke. His speech was affected. Nothing else. I'll never be convinced it was a stroke. And even his speech wasn't bad. I could always understand, couldn't I, Dad? No, you're in safe hands here. (*But Dad has a definite tremor in his hands.*) Lifetime of experience.

DAD. Get my book down.

LILY. I'll get your book down. (*She opens a cupboard and takes out a big book, carefully wrapped up. Old and battered, it is his book of designs.*) This is the Bible. (*Dad smiles.*) And it was 'Mother'?

LES. Yes.

DAD. There's lots of Mothers. There's half a dozen Mothers. Show him Mothers, Lily. (*She is turning over the pages.*) Flags, Jesus, Mary, Mermaids. Give it here, Lily.

    He takes it.

LILY. No, Dad you've passed Mothers. (*Dad has some difficulty separating the pages because of his tremor.*) There, see. You glance at those while I take out his equipment. He can be glancing at those while I take out your equipment.

Les looks at them.

DAD. We'll want a clean cloth, Lily.

LILY. Oh yes. A clean cloth. (*Lily gets out a tray cloth and spreads it on the table.*) Came from Hong Kong, this cloth. He was always very particular. That parlour in Station Street, it was spotless. It's clinical, tattooing. It's like a surgical operation.

DAD. It doesn't hurt.

LILY. I didn't mean it hurt. I meant from a hygiene point of view. It's like a surgical operation from a hygiene point of view.

DAD. Shut up. Talking about operations. You'll frighten the client.

LILY. You're not frightened, are you?

LES. No.

LILY. He's not frightened, Dad. The client's not frightened. (*Lily takes out a box.*) These are his needles. They have to be sterilised. I boil them up in a bit of Dettol, personally. It's the boiling that does it. The Dettol's optional. (*She takes them into the kitchen, puts them in a pan and pours some water from a kettle over them, then switches the gas on. While she is waiting for them to boil, Dad comes in, opens the kitchen cupboard, and takes a nip from a bottle of whisky. She tactfully ignores this. She eats a bit of chicken from a Kentucky Fried Chicken Box.*) I'm eating this bit of chicken.

Les sits in the living room, waiting. He is uneasy. Dad comes back.

DAD. I generally let her do the preparations. Marriage, you help each other. Have you chosen?

LES. I think I'll have this one.

DAD. Oh yes. I like that one. That's one of the ones I like.

LILY. You chosen? Oh yes. I like that one. He'll do you a beautiful job on that one, you'll see. (*She takes the shade off an ordinary table lamp and puts it on the table, having first of all drawn the curtains, and looked out.*) 'All clear'. This was a wedding present, this –

She goes out again. The cloth is spread on the table. The lamp is by it. It should look almost like a mass. Lily comes back with the needle.

DAD. Do you want it on your forearm?

LES. I think so.

DAD. Not your bicep?

LES. No. My arm.

LILY. I thought forearm. Since it's his first. Shouldn't run before you can walk.

DAD. Shut up, Lily, and give me the razor.

Lily hands Dad the razor, a cut-throat, while she puts some lather on Les's arm with a stubby shaving brush. Dad's hand is noticeably shaking as it holds the razor.

LILY. I could do the shaving, if you want.

DAD. I don't want.

LILY. Naught much to shave really.

DAD. It has to be smooth.

LILY. Oh yes, it has to be smooth. Only it is smooth. I don't like a man with too much hair.

Dad finishes the shaving.

DAD. Beautiful.

LILY. Beautiful.

Dad now applies a transfer of the design to Les's arm. He is about to start.

DAD. It might just hurt a bit to start with.

LILY. Just a bit to start with.

DAD. It's only like a tingling.

LILY. A tingling.

DAD. Shut up, Lily.

He is about to start.

LILY. Dad.

DAD. What?

LILY. Disinfectant, Dad.

DAD. Oh ay. It's you, you know, going on. You're putting me off. I never had her down at Station Street. (*He swabs the arm with some stuff from a little bottle.*) Here we go.

Dad starts the needle, and puts it on Les's arm.

LES. (*At the pain.*) Oh *Mother.*

DAD. Steady as she blows.

LES. Jesus.

Dad tattoos in silence for a bit.

LILY. There you are, Dad, you see. It's all right. (*She smiles at Les.*) The boy's more nervous than you are.

DAD. (*Suddenly angry.*) Go next door, woman. It's not for you, this. It's a man's job, this.

She goes out and sits in the kitchen. Camera stays with her in the kitchen, sitting listening to the sound of the tattooing.

LILY. (*Calling.*) All right?

DAD. All right. Flesh has textures, you know. It can be like paper, it can be like cloth. The grain is different. This is a fine skin. It's like a girl's.

Les watching Dad tattooing his arm.

LILY. (*Calling out.*) You can talk and do it, Dad, you see. I told you.

DAD. Take no notice. You'd be surprised at the people that has tattoos. Film stars. Trade Union leaders. Royalty. The Prince of Wales had one.

LES. Which one?

DAD. Which Prince of Wales, Lily?

LILY. (*Calling.*) Him that died.

DAD. A man that has a tattoo is a free man. He's someone that's taken a decision. All the rest of you is what you got given. Got from your parents. You take after your mother or you take after your father. But this, this is you, setting your mark upon yourself. You're grown up now. A man.

In the kitchen, Lily blows her nose.

25. Interior. Marjory's home. Day.

Marjory is ironing the sleeve of one of Les's white shirts. She finishes, puts it on a hanger and hangs it up, smiling slightly. She runs her hand down the sleeve of the clean, white shirt. She looks happy.

26. Interior. Flat. Day.

A little later. The sound of the tattooing needle stops.

DAD. Lily.

LILY. What?

DAD. It's done.

Lily comes into the room with some tea.

LILY. There. I knew it would be all right. Doesn't that look lovely? Once it's healed up it'll be something to be proud of, and a real talking point.

LES. I didn't tell my mum.

LILY. Well she can't complain about that, can she? Mother. You must be fond of her.

LES. Yes.

LILY. I like a boy that's fond of his mother.

DAD. It's quite usual.

LILY. Not these days.

DAD. It's one of the ones I used to get asked for most often.

LILY. Not 'Father', though. I don't think I've ever seen anybody with 'Father' tattooed on him.

DAD. No. I've never had to do 'Father'. But 'Mother' – oh, every day of the week.

LILY. Show him mine, Dad.

Dad rolls his sleeve up and shows him 'Lily' tattooed on his arm.

That was done before we were married. I'll put you some stuff on it.

DAD. I'll do it.

LILY. No holding him now, is there!

DAD. It's an art form, is this. They've woken up to that in America.

LILY. America. And Japan.

DAD. And Japan. Not in the UK.

LILY. Dragging our footsteps as usual.

DAD. But remember, if you ever want to start an interesting conversation fetch it round to tattoos.

He binds up Les's arm.

LILY. It's coming back into fashion again. It tailed off a bit after the war, but it's due for a boom. (*Lily helps Les carefully on with his jacket.*) Course the rundown of the armed services hasn't helped.

LES. I might go in the army.

DAD. Oh well. This'll stand you in good stead there, this. Give you some status with your mates. Marks you out, straightaway.

LES. How much do I owe you?

DAD. How much, Lily?

LILY. Well, now then.

DAD. It used to be five pounds, did that.

LILY. But the cost of raw materials have gone up. And electric's wicked.

DAD. Still I think five. For old time's sake. And you're only a boy.

LILY. He thought you were from the council.

They laugh. Les goes. They sit for a moment of two.

DAD. Nice lad.

LILY. Lovely.

DAD. I never shook once, did you notice? Soon as I got hold of the needle I never shook once.

LILY. I knew.

DAD. Steady as a rock.

LILY. It's not been a stroke. I told you.

DAD. Shaking now though. Look. There's something not right.

LILY. But you haven't lost the knack, that's the main thing.

She holds his shaking hand.

27. Exterior. Landing of council flat. Day.

Les going home. Tentatively feeling his arm. He shouldn't look apprehensive: simply that he has a secret.

28. Interior. Marjory's. Day.

Les is eating a meal with his fork in his right hand. Marjory not eating.

MARJORY. Maybe we're attacking this from the wrong angle. I don't want to go on working at the canteen all my life. And we both get on. I wondered, if I could scrape up a bit of money . . .

LES. What?

MARJORY. Personalised catering. In the City. Boardrooms. Functions. Business lunches, where they finalise deals. I could cook and you do the waiting.

LES. Me a waiter?

MARJORY. It's not complicated. You'd want a white coat. Some black trousers.

LES. (*Eagerly.*) I've got some black trousers.

MARJORY. That's right. We're half way there. And it's simply a case of saying, 'Red or white?' Though some people now prefer a soft drink, the trend is away from alcohol, I was reading.

LES. What would they eat?

MARJORY. Salads with raisins. Quiches. It's every week in these magazines. Just fork things. We could, Leslie.

LES. Yes?

He is having difficulty eating something with just his fork.

MARJORY. Use your knife, love. And once we'd done one or two and the word got round, it would snowball. Cut it up.

LES. Do you reckon?

MARJORY. *Yes.* What's the matter with your hand?

LES. Nothing. When? When could we start?

MARJORY. We'd have to go into it all very carefully I can get a book out of the library. Oh, Les, just think. Is it sore?

LES. No. What else could they eat?

MARJORY. Sausages. Little, refined ones. Eggs scooped out. You've not been in a fight?

LES. *No.* What else?

MARJORY. Vol au vents. Does it hurt?

LES. What's that?

MARJORY. Little tarty things with stuff in. It is sore.

LES. No. What else?

They are both now enthusiastic.

MARJORY. Well, anything.

LES. Could we do it? Just the two of us?

MARJORY. Yes, I'm sure we could. Honestly.

She takes hold of him and he cries out.

MARJORY. What's up? What have you done?

LES. Nothing.

MARJORY. Have you hurt yourself?

LES. Mum. I'm having my tea.

MARJORY. Roll your shirt up.

LES. Mum, it's nothing. (*She goes into the scullery. As soon as she is out of the room he eats with a fork in his right hand.*) I met two nice people to-day.

MARJORY. (*In the kitchen.*) Where?

LES. When I was going round. A couple. Old. Husband and wife. They kept a newsagents. He hadn't been well. She was helping out. He's had a stroke. What is a stroke?

MARJORY. (*Coming back.*) Why?

LES. This old man had had one.

MARJORY. What old man?

LES. I'm telling you.

MARJORY. Les.

LES. What?

MARJORY. You're not still thinking about the army.

LES. *No.*

MARJORY. You've not been getting yourself vaccinated?

LES. *No.* I want to tell you about this couple. Listen to me about this couple. This husband and wife.

MARJORY. I'm not interested in husbands and wives.

LES. Tell me about catering.

Pause.

MARJORY. No. What have you done?

LES. You're *terrible.* It's a present. Only it's not ready yet.

MARJORY. A present. You've hurt your arm. How can it be a present?

LES. Turn around. And promise not to say anything. Because it's not right yet. (*He takes off the gauze pad.*) All right.

MARJORY Leslie!

LES. It won't look like this. It's with it just having been done.

MARJORY. *Leslie.*

LES. He's given me the name of some stuff to put on. Can you see what it says?

MARJORY. Les.

LES. 'Mother'.

MARJORY. You stupid little fool. You silly, stupid barmy little sod. What have you done?

LES. I haven't done anything. I did it for you.

MARJORY. For me? But there was no need to do anything for me. You were lovely. You were perfect. You didn't have to do anything for me. You were mine as you were. You were perfect. Now you're not perfect.

LES. If all that makes me not perfect is having your name on my arm I don't mind. What will we call this firm?

MARJORY. What firm?

LES. Our firm.

MARJORY. You little fool. (*He tries to get hold of her.*) Get off me. My name. It's not my name. You don't call me Mother. You call me Mum.

LES. I thought 'Mother' was more classy. You're always wanting to be classy.

MARJORY. You don't understand a thing, do you? Not a bloody thing. Did you really think I'd be pleased? Did you honestly think so? 'Mother.' That's not me. That's him. Father. That's what that says. Not Mother: Father. He had a tattoo. That's the kind of man he was.

LES. Mum, it *hurts*. It hurts me now.

MARJORY. It hurts *me*. It'll never come off. You're stuck with it. It's indelible, is that. It's like a bruise. A bloody great ornamental bruise. It's like my varicose veins, that blue. Is that what you wanted?

LES. It isn't.

MARJORY. Writing on your body. You can't even spell and you go writing on your body.

LES. Lots of lads have them.

MARJORY. Lads. Your dad used to talk about lads. Me and the lads. You've never been one of the lads. I hate the lads. (*Marjory sits down and starts smoking. Les goes upstairs. She gets up and shouts up the stairs.*) You'll never be able to take your clothes off in front of better class people. (*She is coming back, then goes back to foot of the stairs.*) Who did it? Did he know how old you were? He wants reporting.

Les angry and at the top of the stairs.

LES. They were nice.

MARJORY. He ought to be ashamed of himself.

She is going back to the fireplace when she suddenly rushes upstairs into his bedroom.

29. Interior. Bedroom. Day.

MARJORY. I'll show you something. I'll show you my marks. (*She pulls up her skirt and pulls down her knickers.*) These. Do you see these marks. Stretch marks. You made them. That's your tattoo on me. You and Margaret.

LES. Mum I don't want to see you. I don't want to see you.

MARJORY. Look.

30. Interior. Living room.

Les runs downstairs. Puts on his headphones and sits by the fire. Marjory follows him down after a moment or two.

MARJORY. I'll tell you one thing. You'll never get a job now. Except a labouring job. And it's no good hiding your head in that stuff. Music. That won't get you anywhere. It's the same as sex: you're no further on when it stops. You're ruined, you. Finished.

He can't hear, but he says very loud because of the headphones:

LES. Shut up.

MARJORY. (*Shouting.*) Finished, you. Done for. (*She snatches the headphones off.*) Finished. Finished before you've even started.

She chucks them in the fire. Or breaks them.

LES. You stupid cow. You silly stupid cow. (*Les hits Marjory in the face.*) Oh, hell.

MARJORY. You'll have marked me now.

LES. Bathe it. Come on.

MARJORY. Bathe that thing too. (*She gets a bowl and puts in on the table. She is smoking.*)

LES. You shouldn't smoke, Mam.

MARJORY. You make me smoke.

LES. Here. Let's see.

Marjory lifts her face to the light and he bathes it. She wipes it with a towel.

MARJORY. Maybe we could have it removed. I could save up maybe. They have skin grafts.

Camera should pull away from them both during this.

31. Interior. A dark room.

A man (unfeatured) lying naked on his front on a bed. He is Les, older.

VOICE OVER. But he never did have it removed. And in years to come when he looked at the tattoo it did always remind him of his mother, though not in the way it had been meant to. He remembered only her anger and her grief, and how she had wept to see him spoiled. It that sense the tattoo had served its purpose. It was a badge, an emblem. A mark that he was hers. It was as if she had engraved it herself.

A male hand strokes the tattoo.

A MALE VOICE. Oh. You've got a tattoo. Tattoos always turn me on.

Say Something Happened

MAM	Thora Hird
DAD	Hugh Lloyd
JUNE POTTER	Julie Walters

Produced by Innes Lloyd
Directed by Giles Foster
Designed by Austin Ruddy
Music by George Fenton

Interior. Living room. Day.

The living room of a semi-detached house. A couple in their sixties are sitting there, the man in an easy chair, the woman gazing out of the window. Pause.

MAM. More leaves coming down. (*Pause.*) Straight onto our path. (*Pause.*) I could be in and out all day. (*Pause.*) It's not right. It's her tree, yet somehow they're our leaves.

DAD. I might get down the atlas in a minute. (*Pause.*) Try and spot Helsinki.

MAM. I'm just wondering if I ought to wash one or two stockings. Don't upset. (*Dad is getting up to get the atlas.*) I've just this minute sat down. (*Pause.*) I shouldn't know where to look.

DAD. Helsinki? Oh yes. It's the capital of Finland. It was a station on the little wireless we had when we were first married. Hilversum. Helsinki. Droitwich. No end of different places.

MAM. All radio this that and the other now.

DAD. It won't be so warm. Getting on for the Arctic Circle.

MAM. It's to be hoped she takes them little bootee things we bought her. They'll be just what the doctor ordered in the Arctic Circle.

Dad is turning over the pages of the atlas.

DAD. It can't be so far off Russia.

MAM. (*Alarmed.*) Russia?

DAD. She's a sensible girl. Russia won't worry our Margaret. (*He reads out the statistics from the atlas.*) 'Helsinki. Seaport and capital city of Finland. Population 2.7 million. Chief industries: carpets, sugar, paper-making . . .(*The doorchimes go*) . . . fisheries.'

MAM. I hope this isn't next door. (*She stands up and looks out of the window.*) It's a young woman.

DAD. What sort of a young woman?

MAM. Educated. Got a brief-case. You go. Only, Dad . . . (*Dad has got up and is going out into the hall. He pauses.*) Put the chain on.

In the hall Dad puts the chain on and opens the door. We don't see the young woman.

DAD. Hello.

JUNE. Mr Rhodes?

DAD. Yes.

JUNE. June Potter. I'm from the council. The Social Services Department.

DAD. Yes?

JUNE. You had a leaflet.

DAD. What leaflet?

JUNE. You should have had a leaflet. Put through.

DAD (*calls*.) Mam. Have we had a leaflet?

Mam comes out into the hall.

MAM. What about?

JUNE. The register. Old people in the Council area.

All this is spoken through the open crack of the door.

MAM (*mouthing to Dad.*) I threw it away. (*Pause.*) We're not Council tenants. You've got mistaken.

JUNE. Hullo?

DAD. Yes?

JUNE. Rhodes, Arthur. Rhodes, Elizabeth Mary.

DAD. Well?

JUNE. It's not confined to Council tenants. It's all senior citizens in the Council area. We have you down as pensioners.

MAM (*mouthing.*) Ask her for her card.

DAD. She looks right enough.

MAM. She should have a card. There was a woman at Bramley gagged with her own tights, and they said they were gasmen.

Suddenly the card is held round the door and moved up and down. Dad takes it and hands it to Mam. He then unchains the door. It is a girl in her early twenties wearing a cape.

Does this reckon to be you? June Potter?

JUNE. Yes.

MAM. The hair's different.

JUNE. I wasn't in Social Services then. I was Transport. I had it frizzed out. They tend to be more relaxed in Social Services.

MAM. It's not the same colour.

JUNE. I'd just got back from Torquay.

DAD. It is her.

JUNE. I might have had it dyed, then. I can't remember.

MAM. Dyed?

JUNE. A cream rinse.

MAM. I thought you said you worked for the Council. My uncle worked for the Council, and you'd never see him without a collar and tie.

DAD. They all dye their hair nowadays. Lads. Everybody.

MAM. He wore a suit every day of his life did my uncle.

JUNE. Social Services they make us wear what we like.

MAM. That's one of them poncho affairs, isn't it?

DAD. Well, I've seen Princess Anne in one of them.

MAM. Not since she got married.

JUNE. It's just a matter of one or two questions.

DAD. Fetch her inside. She's only young.

MAM. You keep saying that. Youth's no guarantee nowadays. There was a woman attacked in the Grasmeres and it left her a vegetable. Wipe your feet. (*June comes in and they go through into the living room, as Mam says:*) If you want to come waltzing into people's houses you ought to get yourself a little costume. You'd look heaps better in a two-piece, and you'd find people much more forthcoming. She wants to take a leaf out of our Margaret's book.

DAD. They can't all be like our Margaret.

MAM. That's a change, coming from you. Sit down. Do you want some tea?

June nods and Mam goes out to the kitchen.

Sending out questionnaires. They want to do something about public toilets. Stuff written up on walls. Them little rings from beer cans you see lying about everywhere – never mind questionnaires.

Dad has been embarrassed by all this, and is more anxious to put June at her ease.

DAD. She's hyper-careful, is Mam.

JUNE. No, full marks. There are very few people your age know how to answer the door. I wish I could show her to Mr Farquarson. At night I walk down the middle of the road.

Pause.

DAD. I like those poncho things, personally.

JUNE. Mr Farquarson tells us not to dress up. Otherwise we get into an 'us' and 'them' situation. (*Pause.*) These are in fact old ski pants.

Dad nods. Pause.

DAD. Not them jogging things?

JUNE. No.

Pause.

DAD. Not a jogger?

JUNE. No fear. (*Pause.*) Thin enough!

June prepares her interviewing kit – clipboard, form, pencil – very methodically.

DAD. What's it to do with, this questionnaire?

JUNE. No. (*She reads from her notebook as if talking to a child.*) 'Where possible, interviewer should endeavour to see all members of the household together.' I've never done this before, so I have to stick to the book of words. (*Pause.*) You know . . . structured.

DAD. Don't want telling two different tales. (*Pause.*) Tip-top job, now, working for the Council.

JUNE. They took me on to do discs. Controlled parking.

DAD and JUNE (*together*). Transport.

JUNE. Then the inevitable happened. Computers. I went and saw Mr Stringfellow and he said, 'My advice to you, June, is to do a bit of a sideways jump and get yourself into the S.S.' Social Services.

DAD. We don't have a parking problem. We don't have a car.

JUNE. I prefer working with people to cars. They're more unpredictable but they're more rewarding. With me people come first. Old people specifically. Old*er* people.

Pause.

DAD. They are a problem.

JUNE. Yes.

DAD. Where to put them. They have to be put somewhere.

Pause.

JUNE. Old people?

DAD. Cars. I've often thought, if we had one I could put one of those carport affairs inside the front gate. There's room.

JUNE. As I see it, young people have a lot to give old people, and old people have a lot to give young people. You know . . . *caring.*

DAD. I agree. With a car our daughter can run us to Ilkley. Or Knaresborough. Will you be motorised?

JUNE. I've got my trusty moped, only the clutch has packed in, so I'm sampling public transport.

DAD. Your parents'll have a car?

JUNE. Split up.

DAD. Oh. (*Pause.*) That's on the up and up.

JUNE. What?

DAD. Divorce.

Mam returns with the tea things.

MAM. How do you like your tea? We like ours strong.

JUNE. Weak, please. No milk.

MAM. No milk?

JUNE. No milk.

MAM. Whatever for?

DAD. Because that's how she likes it.

JUNE. I generally have lemon. I don't want lemon but that's what I have.

DAD. I've seen our Margaret have lemon.

MAM. Only in a cafe. We haven't got any lemon.

DAD. We've got one of those plastic squirters. Lemon juice.

JUNE. That'll do.

Dad gets up to go into the kitchen.

MAM. And Dad. Some little plates. (*He goes.*) All that's come in now. Lemon in your tea. Yogurt. Carrying babies on your back. We weren't brought up to any of that. I was thought a bit revolutionary for having prunes. (*Dad returns with the plastic lemon and plates.*) Not them plates, Dad. The *side*plates.

She goes out.

DAD. You're not bothered about sideplates? (*Calling.*) She's not bothered about sideplates.

MAM. (*Calling from the kitchen.*) She wants a scone.

JUNE. (*To Dad.*) I don't want anything to eat.

DAD. (*Calling.*) She doesn't want anything to eat.

MAM. (*Returning.*) You'll have a scone?

JUNE. No. I'm on a diet. I get migraine.

MAM. From scones?

JUNE. It's a special-type non-gluten diet. They've only just pinpointed it. I haven't to have flour.

DAD. It's a terrible scourge, migraine. Our daughter gets migraine.

MAM. Not from scones. It's chocolate with her. I've never heard of anyone getting headaches from scones.

DAD. Look at me. I can't do with tomatoes.

MAM. That's your bowels.

DAD. (*Embarrassed.*) Mam.

MAM. (*Poised with the plastic lemon.*) One squirt or two squirts?

DAD. Let her squirt it herself.

JUNE. One please. (*Mam squirts it.*) Now. Can we start? This is the leaflet you should have had and I will read it to you.

DAD. Mam threw it away.

MAM. I didn't throw it away. It got thrown away.

JUNE. (*Reading.*) 'In recent months there have been one or two mishaps involving old people, senior citizens who have become isolated within the community. Some genuine tragedies have occurred. Accordingly your council has decided to compile a register of all persons of pensionable age within the council area. The establishment of such a register will . . .'

MAM. Hypothermia. (*June stops.*) Is that it? Hypothermia? Not us. (*She points.*) We've got a Dimplex. Background heating.

DAD. Plus a fire.

MAM. Dimplex and a fire.

DAD. For company.

MAM. The fire's company. The Dimplex isn't company.

DAD. I didn't say the Dimplex was company.

JUNE. Anyway. That takes care of question seven: source of heating. Any heating in the bedroom?

MAM. Him.

DAD. Mam.

MAM. This is old people. It's not us. You want Miss Venables over the road. She has a pacemaker and her friend comes in from Bramley.

June has been told to expect such a reaction, and covertly consults her notebook.

JUNE. Hang on . . . 'the refusal to recognise the approach of old age and the possibility of infirmity is entirely natural . . . and in its way commendable.' That was Mr Farquarson, last week. (*She laughs in a stilted way.*) You are as old as you feel. But let me sketch out a possible scenario. You're not feeling too clever; you're in bed. Mr Rhodes goes to fetch the milk, it's slippy and bang, that's his hip gone. Hearing a shout you get up, go downstairs and try shifting him. You promptly have a dizzy do and bang, that's two of you lying on the path in sub-zero temperatures. You won't last long.

Pause.

MAM. The point is, we don't want roping in for any get-togethers.

DAD. That's it. They put you on a register, next minute you're sitting round banging a tambourine.

JUNE. (*Reading again.*) No. 'When your council has compiled the register a number of Old People's Wardens will be appointed, whose job it will be to keep track of all old people in the area, particularly those who are "at risk".'

MAM. Oh. It's 'at risk' is it? That's something else that's come in, 'at risk'. There never used to be that, did there, 'at risk'. It's all 'at risk. now. Battered babies, battered wives . . . are you sure you won't have a scone?

JUNE. No.

DAD. You do read some shocking stories. There was an old lass at Moortown got eaten by her own alsatian.

MAM. Her own silly fault. I wouldn't have an alsatian. They always revert. We don't want pestering to go to bingo. Joining in. That's what choked us off with church.

JUNE. This isn't bingo, Mrs Rhodes. This is survival.

Pause.

DAD. We aren't good mixers, that's the trouble.

MAM. You're not. I am. I used to be a right good mixer.

DAD. You never were.

MAM. I went to the Fellowship.

DAD. When they lassooed you first. We're neither of us anything in the mixing line. We were when we were first married but you lose the knack.

June makes a note.

MAM. What is it you're writing down?

JUNE. Nothing.

MAM. What did we say?

JUNE. Nothing. (*There is a silence. June doodles embarrassed on her pad, then talks while she's doodling.*) Mr Farquarson said that the survey would be a chance for us to do a little ad hoc assessment. Part of our training. You know, fieldwork. Only I'm not supposed to tell you that.

MAM. We're guinea pigs.

DAD. She has to learn.

MAM. Not on us she doesn't.

JUNE. I was just noting you both seem very alert mentally.

DAD. There you are.

MAM. Mentally?

JUNE. And you quarrel. That's another good sign.

MAM. We never do. We never have a wrong word.

JUNE. You don't agree always. You *spar*. Look on it as a sign of life. Vitality. On a scale of 1–10 you've got 8.

MAM. Why not 10?

JUNE. Nobody gets 10. The Queen Mother wouldn't get 10. This is the joy of the job for me. I did surveys in Transport . . . traffic projections, long haul or short haul, purpose of trip . . . only there was no feedback. The beauty of this is . . . it's people. This is what they call interaction. (*A long pause with interaction notably absent.*) What were we saying? (*Mam won't speak.*) You were talking about church. How you used to go to church.

DAD. They got this new young vicar.

MAM. (*Reluctantly.*) It was the singing we liked.

DAD. He kept wanting these discussions. Forums. Race. Religion. Current affairs. We stopped going.

JUNE. That's a pity.

MAM. Why, do you go to church?

JUNE. No.

DAD. That's with you being educated. God's always the first casualty. One time he had us all talking about Buddha. Well Mam doesn't know anything about Buddha. And I don't know anything about Buddha. And the Third World.

MAM. I don't even know where that is. We just haven't been educated.

DAD. No dog collar. Always wore civvies. It's as if they're ashamed of it.

MAM. Last time we went to church, in the middle of the service he suddenly gets up and says, 'Now, I want you all to shake hands with the person on either side of you.' Well Dad was all right because he was sat on the aisle, so he'd only to shake hands with me, but I got a right common woman in a leopardskin coat. I'd never seen her before in my life.

JUNE. But that's good, isn't it?

MAM. Yes I can see you're in the same brigade.

JUNE. Isolation, that's the bugbear.

MAM. We don't mind a bit of isolation. It's the other *we* don't like. He had a couple kissing on the front of the parish magazine. Christian Love. I'd prefer little kiddies with rice bowls, I would.

DAD. I don't see that God is to do with mixing. Too much God, and it puts the tin hat on it.

MAM. What about you, do you mix?

JUNE. I tend to run across people at work. I'm not at risk. I'm not old.

MAM. Old, old. There's risks with youth. You might commit suicide. That's snowballed.

DAD. Mam.

MAM. Well. How old are your parents?

DAD. Nay, they've split up, haven't they?

MAM. Split up? Are you married?

JUNE. No.

MAM. Where do you live?

JUNE. Kirkstall.

MAM. They've knocked most of it down. Is it a flat?

JUNE. A bedsitter.

MAM. A bedsitter? Child of a broken home, living in a bedsitter in one of these inner city areas: you're the one that's at risk. You want to get *yourself* on a register. Coming round telling us. Isolated. We like being isolated. We're like that. It's the same as the radio now, every programme you turn on, it's folk ringing up. And they make out you're all friends. Everybody friends. Well we're not friends. We've got each other, and that's enough.

JUNE. But that's it. You won't always have each other.

MAM. Oh, hell and damnation. Do you think we don't know that? Youth.

JUNE. I'm not youth. Don't call me youth. I wish I was youth.

DAD. (*Comfortingly.*) You are youth.

Pause.

JUNE. Can I have that scone?

MAM. Go on.

June eats the scone slowly.

DAD. Some more tea?

He gets her it. June has got out an exercise book and is looking through it.

MAM. What's that?

June is on the edge of tears.

JUNE. My notes. 'Conduct of Interviews' . . . I've gone wrong somewhere . . . it's my fault . . . we're in a confrontation situation now . . . well you shouldn't get into a confrontation situation, Mr Farquarson says, you get into a confrontation situation you've slipped up . . . Cars – it's much more open and shut. It's just a case of, 'Do you mind telling me your ultimate destination. Thank you. Drive on.' I'm maybe not suited to people.

She blows her nose.

DAD. You are. I'm sure you are. You're doing champion. We're not good at interviews, probably, are we Mam?

MAM. Have this other scone. (*June takes it and eats it quickly.*) That's right.

JUNE. Transport, I was in a rut. Mr Stringfellow said 'Take this sideways jump, June and there'll be so many more doors open to you'.

DAD. Listen. You did right. We've got a daughter. *She's* ambitious. 'Life is for living.' That's her motto.

JUNE. Well, let's have another go. (*She takes up the clipboard again.*) This is Margaret, is it?

MAM. Yes.

JUNE. That's question four. (*She reads again.*) 'The council does not aim to replace family responsibility, only to supplement it, particularly in cases where senior citizens are childless.' So you're not childless. You've got a daughter. (*She writes down 'Margaret'. Mam and Dad look at one another.*) Any other siblings? I didn't know that either. It means brothers and sister. No?

Mam looks at Dad again.

DAD. (*Firmly.*) No.

JUNE. Is Margaret married?

MAM. No. Are you married?

JUNE. No.

DAD. She could have been married. Married three or four times over if she wanted.

MAM. You'll have boy friends?

JUNE. Oh yes. And lives where?

DAD. London. Where else?

MAM. She has a flat.

DAD. She's a personal secretary.

JUNE (*Writing.*) A secretary.

DAD. No, not a secretary. A personal secretary. Her boss is to do with this ceramic heating.

JUNE. I've not heard of it.

DAD. We hadn't heard of it. It's these heated pottery panels. Set in. And being pottery it retains the heat without running up lot of expenditure on electricity. I've got a lot of literature about it if you're interested.

MAM. She's not interested, Dad. It's only with it being our Margaret that she's interested. Ceramic heating!

DAD. She could have gone to university if she'd wanted. But she said, 'Dad, I want to get on with life.' So she took a secretarial course and started off at Brunskill's in Cardigan Road. It was just an ordinary job in the office, with no responsibility. But as Margaret says, 'You make your own responsibility.' It was old Mr Brunskill picked her out, saw she wasn't like half the girls in offices, just marking time till they find the right man. She's never been all that interested in the opposite sex, our Margaret.

MAM. It was always, 'What does he do? Does his work take him to faraway places?' She had a passion for geography. It was always, 'Get out the atlas, Dad. Show me Perth. Rio de Janeiro.' I said to her last time she was home, Did you ever dream you'd be in Valparaiso? But she's very modest, just laughed.

JUNE. I'd like to travel. I never go anywhere.

MAM. Daughters, they used to live round the corner. All that's gone.

DAD. She comes up to see us whenever her schedule permits. She flies to Leeds sometimes. Takes air travel in her stride. More people are killed on the roads. It's a new breed.

JUNE. When did she come up last?

DAD. When did she come up, Mam? It's only a week or two since.

MAM. March.

DAD. As long as that? It's with speaking to her on the phone.

JUNE. Question three. (*She ticks it off.*) So you're on the phone.

DAD. Margaret made us have one installed so she could keep in touch.

MAM. It was for her convenience. She has to have the phone when she's here anyway. Last time her boss rang up in the middle of the night wanting her to fly to Dusseldorf.

DAD. She says the telephone is one of the tools of her trade. She won't be much older than you and she's on a five-figure salary.

MAM. You won't be badly off, will you, love? The council, it's a good job these days. My uncle worked for the council.

DAD. It's not like the private sector.

MAM. You've got the satisfaction, though, haven't you? Helping people.

DAD. I noticed you didn't take sugar. Margaret doesn't take sugar. She has a bit of a struggle with her figure. Has to steer clear of the carbohydrates. It's all these business lunches. She could have whatever she wanted to drink but it's generally, 'May I please have an orange juice.' Left on her own she'd as soon have a bit of cheese and an apple.

MAM. You've got a better figure than our Margaret.

DAD. Has she? I'd 've thought they were about the same. (*He gets some snaps.*) This is her. Taken at Turin Airport.

MAM. She dresses very simply. Crisp white blouse. A few well-chosen accessories.

DAD. (*Showing her a snap.*) Amsterdam. She can look stunning but her aim is to blend in with the background. She says an ideal secretary should not be noticed, just taken for granted. (*Showing her another.*) Los Angeles.

MAM. Though she can tick people off. She put a woman in her place at Leeds and Bradford Airport. I was embarrassed. I don't know where she gets that from. Not Dad, anyway. He never speaks up. Have you travelled?

JUNE. Only Spain.

MAM. Everybody seems to have been to Spain now. Except us. They've been to Spain next door. They fetched us a little doll back. It was nothing. We like Scarborough.

DAD. Margaret goes all over. You'd be staggered if I told you her itinerary. I've got to know the names of airports just from listening to her converse. Paris: Charles de Gaulle. Chicago: O'Hare. Rome: Fiumicino. Her boss would be lost without her.

MAM. But that's all it is, purely professional. He's married with two grown up sons, one of them at veterinary college. Our Margaret's like a friend of the family. She's spent Christmas with them.

DAD. Only because she couldn't get up here.

JUNE. And you don't have a car?

DAD. No.

MAM. We could have done. We could just about have run to a car but Dad wouldn't learn.

DAD. It makes it more of a treat when Margaret comes up. Last time she ran us out to Fountains Abbey.

JUNE. So 'no car'.

MAM. You've got your poise back now, love, haven't you? Asking your questions. It's just a case of having confidence.

JUNE. Thank you.

A pause, before Dad reverts to his one topic of interest.

DAD. She's got confidence, our Margaret. She's quite at home in hotels. Can choose from a menu without turning a hair. And she knows all the vintage years. But when it comes to her, as I say it's, 'Can I just have an orange juice, please.'

MAM. Where have your parents split up to?

JUNE. Mam's in Armley. I don't know where my Dad is. I'm always going down home.

MAM. That's nice. Nice for your Mam.

JUNE. Nice for us both. This old people's warden will just keep a quiet eye on you. You won't even know he's there.

MAM. It's a him, is it?

JUNE. It could be a her, either.

DAD. That's the law nowadays, isn't it? Has to be a him or a her. When our Margaret was first starting there was none of that. She had to fight every inch of the way.

MAM. Oh, Dad. Not fight.

DAD. You don't know. We get postcards from all over. I've got booksfull. If we had grandchildren it would be a real geography lesson. Where's the one we had from Washington?

MAM. Upstairs. In my drawer.

JUNE. It doesn't matter.

MAM. No, let him. (*Dad has gone. June is on her feet ready to go.*) Sit down. (*Urgently.*) Sit down, love. (*June sits down.*) We've told a lie. We have two children. We had a son. After Margaret. Colin. Only he wasn't right. He's in a home near Otley.

JUNE. That's all right. I don't need to know that. Your daughter's the one that matters.

MAM. We never talk about it to anybody. We never talk about it to each other. We ought to do, only he won't.

JUNE. I won't write it down . . .

She is nonplussed, not really wanting to know, either, and hides her confusion by consulting her notebook.

MAM. We thought he was all right, only our Margaret could tell. She wouldn't play with him. Wouldn't have anything to do with him. In the finish we couldn't cope. We waited too long, I think. He was born after Dad got back from the war. We reckon to go once a month only they don't run enough buses. He knows us. We just go and sit out on a seat somewhere, weather permitting. He'd miss us if we didn't go.

JUNE. I don't know what to say. It's not to do with this, that. It's more . . . private.

MAM. He's like a child. I look at him and think, well if he was a proper lad he'd be married now, with grown-up kiddies. Margaret won't marry. She's not the marrying sort. She's happy, that's the main thing.

JUNE. I get the impression . . . correct me if I'm wrong: she wouldn't come back, Margaret. I mean, say something happened . . . to look after you.

MAM. I never said that.

JUNE. No. But . . . they tell us to listen to the things you're not saying. Mr Farquarson says that the things you're not saying are more important than the things you are saying.

MAM. What about this other?

JUNE. I don't know.

They sit, June smiling with embarrassment. Dad is coming back.

MAM. Don't say I said.

June shakes her head. Dad comes in with the postcard.

DAD. (*Sarcastically.*) Your drawer! It was in the scullery. Washington.

JUNE. Nice.

MAM. It'll be all cars, same as everywhere else.

DAD. I've been abroad a bit myself.

MAM. He was in Tunisia.

DAD. Not only Tunisia. Tunisia. Libya, North Africa, Sicily. I saw

Monty once. He came past in a jeep and waved. It's not many people can say that.

JUNE. One last thing. In the event of an emergency, say you're both ill, who looks after you?

DAD. Well we wouldn't both be ill, would we?

JUNE. I'm trying to look ahead.

DAD. We shouldn't want our Margaret coming back, would we? She's got her own life to lead.

MAM. We should just have to manage.

JUNE. Supposing the worst came to the worst. There was just one of you.

DAD. She'd come back. Only I wouldn't let her. I discussed it with her once. She said, 'Well, Dad. We all get older. Life is for living, that's my philosophy.' I don't think you should expect it of your children.

MAM. I looked after my mother.

DAD. You weren't a career woman.

JUNE. No close neighbours? Nobody who could come in.

MAM. Next door'd come in all right, given the chance. Don't put her down.

June makes a final note and closes her file.

JUNE. The only other thing is to give you this card. (*She fishes in her bag for a card, one of a bunch. She gives one to Dad. He looks at it. It says 'HELP!' in large red letters.*) It's just in case we have a winter like last year. If for some reason or other you can't get out. You pop this in the window and the warden'll know to call.

DAD. (*Reading the card.*) 'Help!' Bit stark is that, isn't it?

JUNE. It says it all, that's the point. You haven't got to be ashamed of asking for help, particularly now you're older. Everybody's getting them, the old, the disabled.

MAM. (*Drily.*) People 'at risk'.

JUNE. That's right.

They are in the hall.

DAD. It's been a nice change for us talking to you. We don't get many visitors.

JUNE. Don't thank me. It's you that's done me the favour. Helped me with my course. Mr Farquarson says, 'Sit and chat. Learn how to draw people out. Get them talking. That's your job.'

June catches Mam's eye and looks away, confused. She has turned them into guinea pigs again. Dad opens the door.

DAD. Good luck with your chosen career.

JUNE. You too. Well, your retirement anyway.

MAM. And think on, try and find yourself a man.

DAD. You do what you want. (*June lingers, not having mastered the art of leaving.*) Happiness, that's the main thing.

JUNE. Anyway . . .

And on this tentative note she closes the door. They go back into the living room. Dad sits down in the easy chair. Mam stands by the window. Pause.

DAD. She seemed nice enough.

Mam doesn't say anything.

MAM. She wants to find herself a chap.

Pause.

DAD. What do I do with this card, Help? What d'you think?

MAM. It's telling the whole street. We'll keep it, just in case. I'll put it in my drawer.

DAD. We won't let our Margaret see it. (*Pause.*) Makes you feel older.

Pause.

MAM. More leaves coming down. Mess. (*Pause.*) It never stops.

It is dusk and she begins to draw the curtains. We cut to the outside of the house. The lights are on in the room. We see her finish drawing the curtains and the last chink of light disappears.

A Day Out

ACKROYD   John Normington
SHORTER   James Cossins
WILKINS   Philip Locke
SHUTTLEWORTH   David Waller
MR TETLEY   Don McKillop
ERNEST TETLEY   Bernard Wrigley
GIBSON   David Hill
EDGAR APPLETON   Paul Greenwood
BALDRING   Paul Shane
BOOTHROYD   Brian Glover
CROSS   Paul Rosebury
MRS ACKROYD   Helen Fraser
MRS SHORTER   Maggie Jones
PLAIN GIRL   Rosalind Elliott
PRETTY GIRL   Sharon Campbell
FIRST BROTHER   George Fenton
SECOND BROTHER   Anthony Andrews
MOTHER   Dorothy Reynolds
FLORENCE   Virginia Bell

Produced by Innes Lloyd
Directed by Stephen Frears
Designed by Jeremy Bear
Music by David Fanshawe

First shown on BBC2 on
24 December 1972.
Filmed in black and white.

A Day Out (1972) was the first film I wrote, and the first of several that I
have made with the director, Stephen Frears. The original script bears
only a distant relation to the film as shot and edited; the dialogue
remains the same but the sequence of it is much altered. I've therefore
followed the transcript of the film as transmitted, while occasionally
including some of the stage directions from my original script. These
show how what was intended as a gentle Edwardian idyll with
intimations of the war to come had to be converted, on account of the
weather, into an altogether brisker piece. As I explain in the text, the
major change was the scrapping of a long, lyrical ending in favour of a
more pointed final scene. The following extracts from a diary I kept
during the shooting first appeared in *The Listener*.

1 May, Halifax

The first ten days of filming are in and around Halifax. Ten years ago
when I was last here, this area looked pretty much as the nineteenth
century had left it: villages huddled round the mill in the valley bottom,
rambling seventeenth-century farms on the tops. A line of gas-lamps ran
out into the country, stopping in the middle of the moors at the council
boundary. There were cobbled streets between green fields, boarded-up
chapels and black leaning cemeteries. Now many of the mills are pulled
down, the chapel is a carpet warehouse, the solid, sensible dwellings
have been tarted up with bow-windows to fetch them into line with a
Christmas-card view of the past. Flush doors, leaded lights, 'Monk's
House' on a glazed slice of log, and not a gas-lamp to be seen except as
salvaged to grace the drive of 'Four Winds' and its tastefully converted
frontage.

Shooting a period film in urban surroundings involves frequent and
costly shifts of location. You may find a nineteenth-century ginnel
intact, but pan 15 degrees and there's a cooling-tower. Here's a good
row of mill cottages, but pull out and there's a car-port. In colour,
anachronistic details are hard to lose, and the BBC is persuaded to settle
for black and white. Everyone is slightly surprised when they agree.
Even so, the production assistants and props boys spend the first part of
the morning shinning up walls, swathing concrete lamp-standards in
blackout material, draping 'a spot of dingle' (greenery) over the intrusive
bus-stop. And always a nagging feeling that somewhere in shot is
something so obviously wrong that no one has noticed it. At the first
rushes all I was looking for was lamp-standards.

2 May, Ackroyden Square, Halifax

A good start. The day dull and cold, but since we're not shooting in colour this is a possible light for early morning, when the club meets before setting off for the day. Because of traffic we don't shoot sound, so filming bowls along. Once in costume and on their bikes, the individual character of the actors takes over and they become fully-fleshed versions of characters only sketched in the script. In Hebden Bridge we do one shot when they all come down a steep hill on their bikes: Philip Locke as Wilkins, a shy chapel-ridden man, very sedate; Jimmy Cossins playing a pompous fool nervously running with his bike; David Hill, as Gibson, a lout stood up on his pedals; and David Waller as Mr Shuttleworth, the father of the club, bringing up the rear. Most of the cast know each other already. Several are from the RSC, some from the Royal Court where they were together in David Storey's *The Changing Room.* Bernard Wrigley, who plays an idiot boy, is a folk singer from Bolton, Paul Shane a club comedian from Rotherham. We are sitting in the hotel this evening and a football crowd is braying up and down the street. 'Oh God,' sighs John Normington, 'I knew Patience Collier would tell all her friends we were here.'

4 May, Oats Royd, Luddenden

In between takes while shots are being set up, we sit in the coach, drink coffee and eat bacon sandwiches. The actors do the *Times* crossword, tell stories, play the cinema game: 'In what film did Cedric Hardwicke star with Arthur Lucan and Bela Lugosi?' '*Old Mother Riley meets the Vampire.*' Sitting around like this is the most characteristic part of an actor's life. They swap anecdotes about the awfulness of the shows they have been in, the sadism of directors and the terrible things that have happened to them on the stage. My function here is not defined. I am called in if there's a problem about the script and I watch any scene that involves dialogue, but my main job seems to be to help jolly things along. If I want to make a suggestion about the acting of a scene, I'll generally ask the director, Stephen Frears, first, though relations are so easy it wouldn't be remarked on if I didn't. Since the film has been carefully cast, the actors are encouraged to fill out the characters themselves. Most of my suggestions are to do with pronunciation. I think anyone not brought up in the North finds it hard to get dialect pronunciation exactly right. If you say 'up at t'mill' as it's written, it comes over like a parody. The 't' shouldn't be sounded at all: it's a syncopation, not a sound. If you're not careful the whole thing sounds like the *Take it from here* take-off of *The Crowthers of Bankdam:*

'There's trouble at t'mill. T'workers are upset. They say they've too far to come to t'mill.'
   'Too far to come? Nay, but they've only three fields to cross.'
   'Ay, but they're Huddersfield, Macclesfield and Sheffield.'

Electricians' slang: 'An elephant': a small box to stand on. 'A pancake': a smaller box. 'Horse': electrician's assistant. 'Make it Chinese': give me just a slit of light. 'A pup with a snoot on it': a small light, shaded. 'Baby legs': small tripod for camera. 'Running all the way, Guvnor': I'll walk over to that light and switch it on.
   Sequence of calls before a shot. Production Assistants: 'Quiet. Going for a take. Standing by.' Director: 'Right.' Sound: 'Sound running.' Director: 'Turn over.' First Assistant: '245, Take 5.' Director: 'And remember it's tight on you, Paul. Action.' Then the take. Director: 'Very good. Now let's go once more.'

10 May, Mytholm Steps
After three days in London I come back to Leeds, arriving in City Square just as Leeds United begin their triumphal progress to Elland Road. At Halifax they are shooting the country-pub scene. It ought to be an idyllic country place, a lush pub garden with an earth-closet set in a bower of honeysuckle. Instead, it's a grim dark spot, with a few thin privet bushes and a tussocky garden set with sooty plants. It looks dismal and is bitter-cold. The bad weather which we've had consistently since we started has altered the character of the film. We'd decided to film in May because you can generally bank on a spell of fine, prematurely hot weather. But not this year, and each day is worse than the last. However, this natural disaster puts everybody on their mettle and the atmosphere of the slightly crisis-ridden unit is very good. Stephen Frears realises that the slow, dreamy piece I'd written won't work in this sort of weather: you can't film an idyll in temperatures of 45 degrees. So he shoots the script much more off the individual characters of the actors, and the story becomes brisker and, I think, stronger than I had imagined. Not figures in a landscape, but characters in relation to one another.
   This is the last sequence in Halifax and we move to Ripon. At the hotel there is chaos, partly endemic but also because of improvements being made against a visit by the Queen Mother. The manageress, a genteel Scotswoman, regards the BBC as a subversive organisation. 'No one has ever complained about that room before,' she says to Philip Locke. 'No one of normal size, that is.' It is a hotel straight out of

Feydeau with residents to match. On television in the Lounge, the Duke of Edinburgh remarks on the unemployment among young people on Teesside. 'Rubbish,' comes a voice from an armchair, 'they can work. They just don't want to.'

11 May, Fountains

The abbey is set in a deep wooded valley, so that you come upon it from above. What at first sight looks a plain squat tower, like a Norman keep, turns out to be only the last stage of the bell tower soaring above the valley-top to the level of the surrounding fields. Now it's encased in shining stainless steel scaffolding, so it's useless for our purposes. 'How long will it take, all this?' someone asks the foreman. 'I don't know. It'll last me out.'

As I am writing, we are waiting for silence. High up above Fountains, a young man leading a man's life in the regular Air Force idly loops the loop hour after hour. Stuart, the boom operator, who has seen it all before, explains that the offending plane is practising stall turns. Innes Lloyd, the producer, phones the BBC. The BBC phone the nearest RAF base, Leeming, but they say it's not one of theirs. He could be from Leuchars or St Mawgan. At his speed here is only ten minutes from anywhere. But there he is, two miles up with all England spread out below him.

Kay Fraser, the director's assistant, is putting a daffodil into her hat before writing up her continuity notes. Anne Ailes, the make-up girl, is cutting Laurie, the second assistant's, hair. James Cossins is doing the *Times* crossword. Stephen does the odd clue, then goes over the next shot. Bob, one of the grips, keeps an eye on the sky through a glass. Jimmy and Alf, the props boys, are changing a wheel on one of the bikes. Joan Hamilton, the production assistant, sits by the refectory wall ready to warn sightseers who might wander into shot. John Normington is doing an imitation of Bette Davis in *Mrs Skeffington*. Philip Locke is doing Marlene Dietrich going round to a friend's dressing-room to congratulate her after a terrible performance. Bernard Wrigley, Paul Rosebury and Don McKillop are playing football. Ray Henman, the cameraman, is handing round a pattern-book of shirt samples he can get cheap from Hong Kong. David Hill is making a daisy chain.

12 May, Sawley Hall
The shot is down an avenue of Wellingtonias at Sawley Hall ('used this last year for *Jane Eyre*,' the costume designer says drily). The sun casts long shadows across the path, trees are alive with birds, midges flickering in the sun. 'Oh dear. This is what the film was supposed to be about,' says Stephen.

Next day it is bitter cold again. On the lawn in front of the house, the tea-party scene is set up. There is a fierce east wind cutting across from the wolds. Dorothy Reynolds in a thin cotton frock pours tea, with the tablecloth weighted down against the gale. As soon as one shot is in the can, make-up and wardrobe rush out from behind a wall and swathe the cast in rugs and coats. On the lawn, Virginia Bell plays croquet. She is a great-niece of Virginia Woolf, to whom she bears an extraordinary resemblance. A fragile, transparently beautiful face, with sad downcast eyes, but underneath, I suspect, as strong and direct as her great-aunt. I sit in on this scene as an extra in blazer and straw hat, eating chilly little fancies at Dorothy's frozen elbow.

19 May, Laver Banks
The sex scene takes place by a stream in Winksley Woods above Fountains Abbey. A sex scene it is, too: not a love scene. Connie, the girl, lies passive and silent while Edgar unbuttons her blouse, searching her face for some reaction. When eventually he has her blouse open, he puts his hand quickly on her breast in a very odd way. It looks almost as though if he weren't quick the breast would take to its heels. We wait half an hour for a patch of sun, and I wander off into the woods and find a duck's nest full of cold blue eggs. Bad day for planes. There is an air display at Biggin Hill. At one point we wait ten minutes for an ancient Wellington droning its slow way from horizon to horizon.

23 May, Glaphay
Watched this afternoon by a long line of village children sat on a wall, including, on this May afternoon in the middle of Yorkshire, two little girls who are the great-grandchildren of Tolstoy. We film late sunset shots. The actors are fed up of their heavy black bikes, bumping over fields, humping them over stiles and always the chains coming off. Brian Glover who plays Boothroyd, an early socialist, is a wrestler as well as an actor, and at the end of these long days he drives off to Newcastle or Leicester to wrestle.

24 May, Ripon
Some of us talk over supper about fees. No one mentions any figures. I
have been paid £700. The leading performers, when expenses have been
calculated, will get about two-thirds of that. Stephen, since he's a free-
lance and his work editing and dubbing goes on until July, quite a bit
more. I feel slightly aggrieved, but fortunately our waitress, Maggie,
joins in the conversation. She has come on duty at seven that morning.
It is now 8.30 at night and she has had one hour off. She works six,
sometimes seven days a week. She is paid £9 plus her keep. 'And there's
folks queueing up in Ripon to do the job if I didn't.'

25 May, Halifax
The last day of filming. I drive to Halifax and shop in the covered
market. Cheese cut from the block, bacon from the roll, flowers and
good bread, all served with interest and friendliness, with none of the
aggression you get in London street markets with all their Cockney
cockiness and Bow Bells rubbish.

We film the last scene at the Memorial in Ackroyden Square, where
we started four weeks ago. Here, where the club foregathered at the start
of the day out in 1911, the survivors meet at an Armistice Day service in
1919. It's an afterthought on my part and doesn't quite work in the film
because of that. The filming ends with the whole units and a few
interested housewives standing on a street corner in the rain, singing
'O Valiant Hearts' for a wild track of the sound. And still bitterly cold.

Title Sequence.

*A northern mill town on a Sunday morning in Summer 1911. Deserted
mills, the double gates of the mills closed. Silent machinery through grimy
mill windows.*
'*Sunday May 17*' superimposed. [17 May, 1911 wasn't a Sunday. I had
several letters to this effect.]
*A stream tumbling into the mill dam. Dingy streets. The sound of the
five-minute bell of a church. A clock showing 7.55.*

1. Interior. Ackroyd's. Day.

*Close shot of mustard being spread thick on sandwiches. A sleepy, plump
young woman in nightgown, her hair down, is cutting the sandwiches and
wrapping them in paper. She pops a bit in her mouth. Behind her, two
young children are asleep in bed in a corner. The house is untidy, full of
objects, stuffed birds, pictures, books, butterflies. An upright piano.*

2. Exterior. Ackroyd's. Day.

*Ackroyd is outside feeding his rabbits and doing up buttons at same time.
His bike is in the yard by the rabbit hutches. He comes in.*

3. Interior. Ackroyd's. Day.

MRS ACKROYD. (*Whispering.*) Is two enough? And there's a bit of spice
cake.

> *Ackroyd, a sandy-haired, distracted, young-old man, has a little cap on
> and knickerbockers, his cycling gear. He kisses her.*

ACKROYD. Pipe.

> *He rummages round, and eventually she finds it down the side of the
> armchair.*

4. Exterior. Ackroyd's. Day.

*He sets off, butterfly net and panniers on his bike. She stands at the door
watching him go, then goes out into the little garden and closes the gate after
him, as eight o'clock strikes behind her . . .*

5. Interior. Shorter House.

. . . and strikes also over next shot: but it is a different clock. A cardboard box, open. Tissue paper being folded back to reveal a new knickerbocker suit and cap. The cap is taken out and tried on reverently in front of the mirror by Shorter, a middle-aged man in underwear. He fingers the badge on the cap. The Shorters' house is very spick and span. It gleams.

While Shorter is admiring himself in the wardrobe mirror, his wife turns down his stocking-tops, prinking and patting him.

MRS SHORTER. Grown men, gadding off on bikes. And on a Sunday. (*Shorter makes to go out.*) Where are you going?

SHORTER. I'm only going down t'yard.

MRS SHORTER. You're not going down t'yard in that. Take it off this minute. (*She makes him take off the cap and jacket.*) And be sharp.

6. Exterior. Shorter's.

We see him setting off on his bicycle, very upright, very neat, and the further away he gets from his wife, the more self-assured and self-satisfied he becomes.

7. Interior. Wilkins's house.

Wilkins, an old-fashioned young man tiptoes through the hall of his mother's house in his stockinged feet, carrying his boots. He tiptoes past the hall table on which there is a hymn book, a Bible and a neat pair of white gloves. His bike is standing in the vestibule. He puts his boots down, opens the door very quietly, and wheels his bike out. The wheel catches the door and he freezes. Then he comes back in for his boots. As he does so a woman's voice shouts from upstairs.

VOICE (*of Wilkins' Mother*) Gregory!

Wilkins freezes again, his boots in his hand, his hand on the door-knob. Silence from upstairs. Agonised look at hymn book etc. He goes out very carefully and quietly, closing the door behind him.

8. Exterior. Shuttleworth's.

Mr Shuttleworth is just edging his bike out of the passage by his shop, a

Men's Outfitters. An old youth brings out a chair to help him mount. Mr Shuttleworth is in late middle age, a figure of substance and some dignity. He is the chairman of the Cycling Club, to whom everyone defers: in fact he is a man of straw. He is mounting his bicycle rather unsteadily when Ackroyd wheels into view, so they ride off together.

ACKROYD. Morning, Mr Shuttleworth.

MR SHUTTLEWORTH. Good morning, Arthur.

ACKROYD. It's a grand day for it.

SHUTTLEWORTH. It is. It is that.

9. Exterior. Boothroyd's house.

Boothroyd is pumping up his tyres. Baldring bikes by very slowly.

BALDRING. Well I put t'larum on.

BOOTHROYD. T'larum! Keep going.

He mounts his bike and they ride off together.

10. Exterior. War Memorial.

The meeting place is at the War Memorial set up for the dead of the Boer War. Gibson is riding round and round in the road, watched by a small boy in a chatterbox cap, whom he occasionally pretends to run down. He pinches the boy's cap and rides off with it.

GIBSON. Here, got yer hat. Come on. Get yer hat.

Mr Shuttleworth is sat on the seat with Shorter, looking at a map.

MR SHUTTLEWORTH. It's a fair ride, Mr Shorter.

SHORTER. Easy stages, Mr Shuttleworth. Easy stages.

MR SHUTTLEWORTH. No, we won't overdo it.

SHORTER. And we've got all day.

BOOTHROYD. That is if we can get started. Saddle up, Mr Shorter.

There should be some friction between Shorter and Boothroyd, who is a Socialist.

MR SHUTTLEWORTH. Do you want to see the map, Percy?

Percy is Mr Baldring, who is fat and lazy.

BALDRING. No. No. I'll take it on trust.

SHORTER. Come on then, Percy, be sharp.

BALDRING. All in good time. All in good time.

MR SHUTTLEWORTH. Take it steady, lads. Shall you bring up the rear, Percy?

BALDRING. I expect so, Mr Shuttleworth. I generally do.

The two other members of the party are Mr Tetley and his son, Ernest. Ernest is simple. He doesn't talk in any distinguishable way, but roars incomprehensibly. On his account Mr Tetley tends to sit apart from the rest. He is an oldish man. He and Ernest ride a tandem.

MR TETLEY. Hold on a second. The lad's lace is undone. (*He gets off the tandem to fasten it, and Ernest lets go of the bike.*) Hold the bike, Ernest. (*Ackroyd tries to hold it.*) No. Leave him, Cyril, he can do it.

ACKROYD. Please yourself. (*Ernest roars.*) That'll do Ernest. Come on.

WILKINS. Wish we could get off. It's me mam.

ACKROYD. Don't worry, Gregory. We'll protect you.

GIBSON. Fancy being afraid of your mam at your age.

SHORTER. We're just lacking one of the full complement, Mr Shuttleworth. Mr Appleton.

GIBSON. (*Calling out from his bike.*) Who're we waiting on?

ACKROYD. Edgar.

WILKINS. He's happen not coming.

ACKROYD. Nay, he told me he wor coming.

SHORTER. We mun be off, I reckon. What do you say, Mr Shuttleworth?

Mr Shuttleworth is consulting his watch.

MR SHUTTLEWORTH. Ay. He'll happen catch us up.

SHORTER. Punctuality is the politeness of kings, that's what I say.

Shot of the setting off.

11. Interior. Edgar's room.

Edgar Appleton's digs. Untidy, clothes strewn about. He is fast asleep.
Young, handsome, a bit of a card. His landlady knocking softly at door, not
particularly anxious to wake him. She is blousy, and rather sweet on him,
and will linger slightly in the hope of seeing him dress. There is a cup of cold
tea by the bed.

LANDLADY. You haven't drunk your tea, Mr Appleton. It's after eight.
I've been shouting. You'll have to get your skates on.

Edgar shoots out of bed and dresses very quickly.

12. Exterior. Edgar Appleton.

Cut to Edgar pedalling off, down back lanes, carrying his bike down some
steps and over a field by a recreation ground. Cut to:

13. Exterior. Main party.

Main party pedalling through the town.

MR TETLEY. Don't be turning round, Ernest. You'll have us over.

Mr Shuttleworth leading, flanked by Mr Shorter, touching hats to the
few passers-by. Shorter waving children out of the way. Wilkins looks
unhappily at the caretaker unlocking the chapel, who watches as they
pass.

ACKROYD. Look out, Gregory. You've been spotted.

They all laugh. Slow faces watching them as they go. No hurry. No rush.
No obvious interest. Heavy faces in close-up. Women in shawls, a child in
clogs. A milkman riding on the back of his cart.
    They are at the foot of the hill leading out of the town and they
dismount and begin to climb. Cut in shot of Edgar still trying to catch up.

14. Interior. Cross's house.

Cut to a middle class interior, a doctor's house, seen in a mirror behind the
face of a thin, pale young man in front of a cheval glass, dressed and ready.
He is a handsome, delicate-looking youth. His name is Cross. He walks to
the door and we see that he limps. He has a surgical boot on.

15. Interior. Cross's second bedroom.

Cut to interior of another bedroom. His mother's face, lying sideways on the pillow, eyes open. Listening to the uneven sound of his footsteps going down the stairs. Her husband asleep beside her.

16. Interior. Cross's hall.

A maid in the hall. Cut to Cross against the glass doors of the hall. The house is set above the town, with a drive, and steps up to the door.

17. Exterior. Cross's house. Drive and road.

He limps to his bike, but once on it he is freed from his deformity, cycling round and round the drive. His mother is watching him from the window as he rides out to the gate.

The road outside Cross's house is the road up which the cycling club is toiling. He waits for them.

Mr Shuttleworth would plainly like to take this excuse for a rest, but they go on.

SHORTER. Fall in behind, Mr Cross.

CROSS. Mr Shorter. Good morning, Mr Shuttleworth.

ACKROYD. Now then, Gerald.

CROSS. Arthur. Hurry yourself up, Edgar!

Edgar is coming up behind. The others are pushing their bikes, but Edgar rides his, standing up on the pedals in order to overtake them. Cross falls in behind, alongside Edgar.

18. Exterior. Top of hill.

The numbers are now complete, and as they reach the summit of the hill, still pushing their bikes, the sun comes out. They are on the edge of the moors, and the town (Halifax or Hebden Bridge) is below them. The older ones sit down to have a bit of a rest. Gibson, Edgar and Cross stay on their bikes.

ACKROYD. Here we are. The heights of Babylon.

SHORTER. Worst bit over.

BALDRING. Ay. I think I'll just have five minutes.

SHORTER. You're not jiggered already, Mr Shuttleworth?

MR SHUTTLEWORTH. Just taking in the view, Mr Shorter. Just taking in the view.

ACKROYD. There's your dark Satanic mills, Gerald.

WILKINS. Where's t'chapel. I can't see t'chapel.

GIBSON. It's down there, look. Can't you see your Mam waving her fist at thee?

WILKINS. Shut up.

ACKROYD. See, do you see Mason's? Down there. Do you see?

BOOTHROYD. Them's them new houses, Mr Shuttleworth. They've getten built up right to West Vale.

MR SHUTTLEWORTH. I can remember when all that were fields. It's where my grandma lived.

ACKROYD. There's going to be nought left o't'country if they're not careful. When I were little you could stand on t'steps o't'Corn Exchange and see t'moors. Nowadays there's nought but soot and smoke and streets and streets.

BOOTHROYD. Ay, but there's all this. It'll be a long time before they build up England.

19. Exterior. Different part.

Shots of them cycling along. They are coming flying down a hill.

ACKROYD. Hey up, lightning.

BOOTHROYD. Last one at t'bottom's a cissy, Mr Shorter.

Suddenly the tandem comes through the middle of the group.

MR TETLEY. (*Shouting.*) Can't stop . . . can't stop . . . no brakes.

The tandem crashes. The others look back at the scene of the crash. No damage has been done. Ernest mumbles a lot, while Mr Tetley fixes the handlebars of the bike.

[This crash wasn't in the script, but occurred while we were shooting.

Fortunately the actors remained in character and the camera kept turning.]

20. Exterior. Different part.

Shots of them cycling along easily now, down hills, through moors and fields, in their characteristic ways: Edgar with no hands, Shuttleworth and Shorter leading the way, but passed and re-passed by the more adventurous ones. Close shots of the actual mechanical workings of the bikes – pedals, etc. and a close shot of the strap arrangement that enables Cross to keep his boot in the pedal.

21. Exterior. Pub.

The party arrives outside a pub.

MR SHUTTLEWORTH. Here we are, lads. (*They get off their bikes and leave them in the hedge.*) I hope you'll allow me to do the honours. It's my birthday this year.

SHORTER. Mr Shuttleworth, you have a wry tongue. A wry tongue, Mr Shuttleworth. A right wry tongue.

MR SHUTTLEWORTH. Good morning. Give them all their pleasure, landlord, and let me know the damage.

[A speech improvised by the actor, David Waller, at this time working with the Royal Shakespeare Company.]

They sit drinking their beer at tables in the pub garden.

BALDRING. This'll lay the dust a bit.

EDGAR. Ay, this is right beer, this is. Make your hair curl. This'll put lead in your pencil, Gerald.

SHORTER. There's some folks have too much lead in their pencil, I reckon.

EDGAR. Who're you taking that for?

Cross is carrying out a bottle of lemonade.

GIBSON. It's Arthur. He's temperance.

BOOTHROYD. No, I like a drink, but I don't go mad with it.

ACKROYD. I've seen that many families ruined with it.

GIBSON. By, that looks strong stuff, Arthur. Here, let's have a sup.

He snatches the glass.

ACKROYD. Nay, give us it here. Sithee . . . damn you, you've spilt it. You lout.

GIBSON. Shurrup, you great lass.

BOOTHROYD. It's not the drink does harm. It's the social consequences, that I'm reckoning on. Drink retards progress. Did you ever think why we haven't had a revolution in this country? There's two reasons. One is drink, and the other *paradoxically* is Methodism . . .

The camera has meanwhile drifted away from Boothroyd, though his voice continues over the next sequence, showing:

22. Exterior. The orchard and kitchen garden behind the pub.

BOOTHROYD. (*V.O.*) . . . both of them in their different ways, distracting the mind of man from his immediate social conditions. Putting him into a false Nirvana. Intoxicated with beer, intoxicated with heaven. It's the same thing. Nirvana.

Baldring is sat happily on the earth closet in the garden with the door open, listening drowsily to the birds.

23. Exterior. Different part.

Cycling along again. They halt at a gate while Mr Shuttleworth consults the map.

MR SHUTTLEWORTH. I think we can take advantage of a short cut here, Mr Shorter. Hey, lads. Short cut here.

Mr Shuttleworth goes through first, Shorter holding the gate.

SHORTER. Thank you, Mr Shuttleworth.

They come up against a gate. Along it is strung a line of dead rooks and moles.

ACKROYD. Poor little buggers. (*Gibson touches one of the moles gingerly.*) Why do they have to hang 'em up?

GIBSON. It's like a warning to the others.

ACKROYD. How do you mean . . . a warning? What're they warning 'em about? They're born moles, aren't they? They can't do ought about it. Barmpots.

They cycle on. Close up of Shuttleworth's back tyre which is gradually deflating. Mr Shuttleworth tries to glance round at it as he rides, wobbling, almost coming off and stopping.

MR SHUTTLEWORTH. Hold it, lads. Quite flat, I'm afraid.

Shorter and Ackroyd dismount and look at the tyre, and gradually the ones ahead stop and ride back. Shorter takes charge, first of all upending the bike.

MR SHUTTLEWORTH. Mind my paintwork, Mr Shorter.

SHORTER. I'm doing my best, Mr Shuttleworth.

BOOTHROYD. Take it steady. take it steady. Don't fullock it.

Baldring is already sat down and half asleep.

BALDRING. Ay, take it steady.

BOOTHROYD. A bowl of water's the first requirement. All hands to the pumps. You make a better door than a window, lad.

Ackroyd goes and knocks at a cottage and comes back with a bowl of water.

MR SHUTTLEWORTH. I've never been mechanically-minded, for all I ride a bicycle.

SHORTER. No.

MR SHUTTLEWORTH. I wouldn't know where to start.

BOOTHROYD. You're an artist, Mr Shuttleworth.

MR SHUTTLEWORTH. Well, that way on, any road.

SHORTER. There's an art in *this*, like there is in all these things. Now everybody. Don't wander off. This halt isn't on the agenda, you know.

BALDRING. (*Asleep.*) I'll keep in the vicinity, Mr Shorter.

BOOTHROYD. What're you reading then, Gerald? (*Cross shows him.*) Allus got your nose in a book. Is it a tale? Oh ay, H. G. Wells. Is it a good one?

CROSS. Yes. Yes it is.

BOOTHROYD. *He's* a socialist, too. Does it come through?

CROSS. A bit, I suppose. Yes, a bit.

BOOTHROYD. That's good.

The tyre bubbles air in the bowl of water.

MR TETLEY. There she blows.

MR SHUTTLEWORTH. It is aggravating.

MR TETLEY. Gumption, that's what's required.

SHORTER. A puncture of this size is a serious business. It can jeopardise the whole wall of the tyre. Is that tacky yet, Mr Ackroyd?

Meanwhile Gibson is taunting Ernest with a lemonade bottle, pretending to give him a drink, then taking the bottle away.

MR TETLEY. Ernest! Come over here, Ernest!

The puncture is almost mended. In close up we see a small box from the puncture outfit opened and powder rubbed onto the newly applied patch, as in voice over Shorter says:

SHORTER. Apply it to the affected part and dust with the powder provided.

MR SHUTTLEWORTH. Champion, champion.

While the puncture is being mended, Edgar gives the glad eye to a woman watching the proceedings from her cottage doorway. He pops his bike against the hedge, and is about to go in when her husband, who has been bending down behind the hedge, straightens up and confronts Edgar.

EDGAR. Oh heck!

MAN. 'Morning.

EDGAR. How do you do.

When someone throws the water away after the puncture is mended, it goes quite close to Shorter.

SHORTER. Mind out. This suit's new on.

BALDRING. By, I'm hot. I wish I'd never put a vest on.

He peels an apple, very carefully and fastidiously.

GIBSON. What you do that for? T'skins the best part.

BALDRING. For them as likes it. For them as likes it.

Gibson takes the skin, and waits for the core. Baldring looks at Gibson, then throws it away.

GIBSON. (*Going after it.*) Soft bugger.

BALDRING. I think I'll just have five minutes.

CROSS. It doesn't seem like Sunday, somehow.

BOOTHROYD. It would if you were in t'mill all week like most folks.

WILKINS. They'll miss me, you know. It's my morning for taking t'plate round.

24. Exterior. Another part.

The puncture mended they are cycling along again, Boothroyd singing 'Did you not hear my lady, Go down the garden singing'.

[These shots, redolent of high Edwardian summers, had to be abandoned because of the bitter weather, the chestnut trees scarcely in leaf, let alone in flower.]

They cycle past a line of village boys, all in their Sunday best, walking along a white and dusty road in indian file. The front one looks round. They ride along in clouds of white dust, in bright sunshine, then under chestnut trees.
They ride through puddles. A watersplash. Some going over the bridge, and others the adventurous way through the stream. One man riding a cart-horse. A farm cart, with the mother and father up front and the daughter facing over the back of the cart.
Edgar rides for a while with his hand on the back of the cart while she giggles, until her mother looks round, the father whips up the horse and Edgar nearly goes flying.
Riding very slowly along, Mr Shuttleworth farts. Edgar giggles and Ackroyd winks. A dog runs after Mr Shuttleworth, barking and snapping at his ankles.

SHORTER. Take no notice, Mr Shuttleworth. He's more frightened of you than you are of him.

WILKINS. Be careful. We don't want hydrophobia.

GIBSON. Gerron, you little bugger.

SHORTER. Don't race it, don't race it. You make it worse. And watch your language.

25. Exterior. Different road section.

They are cycling along.

ACKROYD. Breathe in, breathe this air.

They pass a manure heap and are thrown into confusion.

EDGAR. By heck! Smell that!

ACKROYD. Breathe in! It's a grand country smell, is that. It fair does you good.

CROSS. (*Imitating him.*) Make your hair curl will that, Edgar. (*And winks.*)

They lift their bikes over a style.

SHORTER. Mind your oily great bike on my socks, Edgar. You've no thought. They've no thought, Mr Shuttleworth. Allow me.

He helps Mr Shuttleworth with his bike.

26. Exterior. Field.

The party wheel their bikes across a field.

SHORTER. Mind where you're putting your feet. This field's in a disgusting state.

WILKINS. That's one good thing about Halifax . . . no cows.

EDGAR. Oh I don't know. I've come across one or two cows in Halifax.

SHORTER. Damnation.

ACKROYD. Never mind. It's good clean muck.

SHORTER. My missus doesn't distinguish between sorts of muck, Mr Ackroyd. Muck is muck to her. And it's anathema.

Baldring and Boothroyd cycling along a road. Boothroyd is singing.

BOOTHROYD.   'O, saw you not my lady, out in the garden there;
Shaming the rose and lily, for she is twice as fair.'

[Everything conspired against making this a lyrical film. In the text I had given this and another song ('O maiden, my maiden') to Boothroyd, intending them to mark moments of sadness and warmth.

Boothroyd was played by Brian Glover. No slouch at acting, Brian does not sing in tune. The moment still has a limited pathos: it's a man who can't sing, trying to.]

Various shots of individual members of the group cycling along. They cross a final field and come to a halt overlooking some monastic ruins.

ACKROYD. Here we are. Journey's end.

MR SHUTTLEWORTH. Well, isn't that a picture?

BALDRING. I know one thing. My bum's numb.

They go down to the ruins, and the afternoon is spent there.

27. Exterior. The ruins.

The party is sitting by the stream in the abbey ruins eating their sandwiches. Some have lunch in handkerchiefs, others in odd bits of newspaper which they read. Mr Shuttleworth takes no part in the conversation but has the largest and most elaborate lunch of all, which he eats with deliberation and contentment, oblivious of the envious eyes cast on it.

GIBSON. I reckon we ought to share.

SHORTER. Share! But you've only got two scrutty little sandwiches. I've got some spice cake.

ACKROYD. Did you know sandwich isn't an original word? In olden days they didn't have sandwiches. They were brought in by the Earl of Sandwich (*mouth full*) hence the name.

Gibson tries to pinch some of Wilkins' lunch.

WILKINS. Take your hands off. You can have a bit of my cake, but I'm hanged if I'm sharing.

BOOTHROYD. In my day that was known as paternalism.

SHORTER. Well in my day it was known as generosity.

GIBSON. (*Eating.*) It's as hard as the devil.

WILKINS. They'll just be coming out now. They'll think I'm poorly. I never miss. Happen they'll go round home and find out.

EDGAR. Nay, that's not what you've got to worry about, Gregory. It's him up there writing it all down. 'Sunday May 17, 1911. Skipped chapel. T'singing from Mount Zion sounds a bit thin to-day, Peter. Have we got somebody off?'

CROSS. 'It's Wilkins, O Lord. He's . . . he's gone cycling.'

EDGAR. 'Wilkins? Gone cycling! Cycling? And him a Deacon. Write it down, lad, write it down.'

Mr Shuttleworth wanders round the abbey, earnestly examining the ruins. At one point during his wanderings he comes upon Gibson, who is carving his initials on a pillar.

MR SHUTTLEWORTH. That's not going to get us any further, is it Eric?

GIBSON. Sorry, Mr Shuttleworth. (*Who has already passed on. Gibson looks after him.*)

MR SHUTTLEWORTH. If we all went round carving our names, there'd soon be no ruins left. Desist, lad, desist.

Ackroyd and Boothroyd are also doing a tour.

ACKROYD. They were Cistercian monks here. From Cîteaux in France. (*He has a guide book.*)

GIBSON. What made 'em want to come here for, soft things?

BOOTHROYD. It's an unnatural life, separating yourself off like that.

ACKROYD. 'They always selected sites of great remoteness away from the temptations of civilisation.'

Gibson laughs coarsely.

BOOTHROYD. You don't always want to be with men. You don't always want to be with your own sort. You want variety, a mixture.

ACKROYD. Ay but there would be all sorts, carpenters, builders, gardeners . . . it wouldn't be as if they were all parsons.

BOOTHROYD. There wouldn't be any kids, would there? And allus getting down on their knees. It's no sort of life . . . You want to get out and get something done, not be stuck here waiting for it to happen, waiting for God to put things right.

ACKROYD. No. No. (*Conversation fading.*) . . . it would be a little community.

In some of these conversations we do not see the talkers, but simply a meadow, covered in long grass. Occasionally someone sits up above the level of the grass or a hand comes up to swat a fly with a cap.

[A remnant of the original script and its presumption of high, cloudless days. In retrospect I think this sequence was no great loss: there is a limit to the interest of grass as a shot.]

Baldring, as usual, has found himself a comfortable spot.

BALDRING. I think I'll just have five minutes.

28. Stepping stone. Stream.

Mr Shuttleworth, Edgar, Shorter and one or two others are sat by the stepping stones. Edgar is skimming stones across the river.

CROSS. That's a good one.

Two girls start to come across the stepping stones. One pretty, one plain. Edgar aims a stone which splashes them, upsets the balance of the pretty one who teeters on the edge of a stone hitching up her skirts and shouting with delight. This is watched in strained silence by the men on the bank.

MR SHUTTLEWORTH. She's a well-set up lass is that.

SHORTER. I think you've caught the mood of the company, Mr Shuttleworth.

The girls reach the shore.

PLAIN GIRL. Grown men. You ought to be ashamed of yourselves.

Edgar tosses another stone, that sends the pretty girl into more laughter and brings shouts of protest from the others.

SHORTER. Nay, Edgar, mind out. That's gone on Mr Shuttleworth's trousers.

ACKROYD. It's grand to get away from folks. Just fancy being fastened in.

BOOTHROYD. You see, I see Man going on from strength to strength. And it's a pretty straight road now, I reckon. We're finished with wars now. Folks won't stand for it. It's not us that makes wars. Worker's not going to take up arms against worker.

ACKROYD. You'll not alter folks, Henry, I don't care what you say.

BOOTHROYD. This'll seem like a dark age one day. A dark age.

EDGAR. If it's that easy, why hasn't it happened before?

Two youths in white shirts and riding breeches skirt the edge of the trees on large horses, looking incuriously at the trippers as they water the horses in the stream. Ackroyd catching butterflies with a net.

[Cut, alas. The butterflies were in charge of a butterfly handler (sic). The scene was set up and on a shout of 'Action' the butterfly handler loosed his troop of Thespian cabbage whites. Whereupon the poor creatures took one look at the bitter weather and promptly fell dead of hypothermia.]

These scenes should overlap in time, so that when one scene is being played another is going on in the background.

SHORTER. They've no nobility about them, women. It's all mundane. One day to the next. No large view. No theory. All practice.

Nobody is listening to him. Ackroyd is feeding a squirrel, enticing it nearer and nearer with food. Gibson creeps up behind him and throws a coat over it.

[The butterfly handler doubled as a squirrel handler. The squirrel, though hardier than its butterfly colleagues, was in its way equally intractable. Animal handlers invariably claim an exact knowledge of the habits and intentions of their charges. This is seldom the case.]

GIBSON. That's copped him.

ACKROYD. Damn you.

He tries to kick Gibson.

BOOTHROYD. Nay, fair does, Arthur. They're nobbut rats.

GIBSON. Soft bugger.

At the ruins Ernest sits with his feet in the water, roaring.

BOOTHROYD. Are you singing, then, Ernest?

ERNEST. (*Roars.*)

MR TETLEY. That's right. (*They smile.*)

The next speech should be dreamlike, casting a spell which will be broken by the gun shots. As Boothroyd speaks in voice-over we see close-ups of Boothroyd, Cross, Shuttleworth, Shorter, Wilkins, Ackroyd, Edgar and Ernest.

[Another sequence which, due to the weather, had to be shot in close-up on the actors rather than in wide shot on the actors in a summer landscape.]

BOOTHROYD. This century, it's like letting the kids out into the fields. We're encamped on the edge of the twentieth century. Like an army after toiling upwards through slavery, wars, oppression, century after century. And now we're over the hill, into a great green place. You come up over the top of the hill and see it stretched out before you, the twentieth century.

The calm is suddenly broken by the sound of sudden reverberating shots.

29. Nave of abbey.

The gaunt, ruined walls. More shots. A gamekeeper is shooting rooks, watched by Gibson. He shoots more, and they fall to the ground. Gibson makes to fetch the birds.

GAMEKEEPER. Let the dog do it, man. That's what it's for.

Ackroyd and Wilkins come running in. And stop sheepishly when they see what's happening. The shots should be sudden, mysterious. No alarm. But puzzlement and mystery.
    As the shots sound, Cross is wandering through woods and undergrowth, having awkwardly crossed the stepping stones, once slipping with his bad leg into the water. He wanders through the woods and on the far side comes out onto a lawn in front of a country house.

30. Exterior. Lawn. Country house.

Two ladies are sat under a tree and their husbands play croquet. As Cross watches, a procession of butler and two maids come out very formally with tea.

MOTHER. (*Calling.*) Florence! Flo-e-rence! Te-a-a!

She stands up and looks towards the edge of the wood where Cross is standing. He steps back and turns away as the two young men on horseback appear. They wave to the croquet party. Cross goes back through the wood.

31. Stream. Woodland edge.

A girl is coming through the trees. She is about fifteen. She stings herself on a nettle.

FLORENCE. Damn. (*Seeing him.*) I stung my hand.

CROSS. Get a dock leaf.

He picks a dock leaf and puts it on her wrist. Distant calls of 'Florence.' 'Tea. Tea.' 'Florence.'

FLORENCE. Thank you. You'll catch it if they find you here, you know.

The gamekeeper who has been shooting in the ruins comes through the undergrowth.

GAMEKEEPER. Now then, young fellow me lad. You've no business here.

Girl still dusting down her frock.

FLORENCE. It's all right, Gateacre.

GAMEKEEPER. (*Still suspicious.*) Her ladyship's calling, miss.

FLORENCE. I don't know why you have to shoot on a Sunday, Gateacre.

GAMEKEEPER. Pests, Miss. Pests. (*Turning away and going off disgruntled:*) They don't know it's Sunday. (*Turning and almost shouting it back at her:*) Vermin ain't no Sundays.

The girl is going back through the wood with Cross. She sees he limps.

FLORENCE. Have you hurt yourself?

CROSS. No. (*Lifts his boot.*)

FLORENCE. Oh, sorry. Sorry. *I* stutter. (*He shrugs and they both smile.*) Come for tea. (*He hesitates and she pulls his coat.*) Come on.

They come out into the sunlight on the edge of the lawn.

32. Exterior. Lawn.

MOTHER. There she is. Oh. (*And looks askance at Cross.*) Harrison, you'd better bring another cup. (*The maid runs off across the lawn. Cross and the girl walk away to the other side of the lawn, as the two gentlemen playing croquet raise their hats, and go to the tea table. Faint conversation drifts after them.*) I don't know. I don't say anything. Nothing surprises me any more.

Intermingled with Cross talking to the girl.

AUNT. Sad face. Sad face.

MOTHER. That boot won't help the grass one bit.

GIRL. Have you come far?

CROSS. Halifax.

FLORENCE. Forsyth. Could we have some cake. Do you mind having a bad leg? Or is that rude? People don't mention it. I am pert.

CROSS. I do mind. It isn't rude. People don't mention it. You are pert. (*They laugh.*) It's all right on a bike. Then you're like everybody else.

FLORENCE. Or a horse. I know someone who rides beautifully and she's a terrible . . . cripple. (*Cross looks over at the tea-party.*) My mother and my aunt. And these are my brothers.

The two young men run onto the lawn. They wave and stand talking at the tea table or sprawl on the grass. Snatches of conversation drift over.

MOTHER. Someone Florence found in the undergrowth. Isn't it exciting?

Though it is quite plain that exciting is not what it is at all.

FIRST BROTHER. Give you a game.

SECOND BROTHER. Florence, give you a game. We'll take you on.

FLORENCE. Do you play croquet? Come on. It's terribly easy. We can be partners. Be a sport.

Cross shakes his head.

CROSS. I couldn't. No, I couldn't honestly.

FIRST BROTHER. We're really none of us much good.

CROSS. No. Thank you. No.

They play and he watches.

FLORENCE. I'm having the good mallet.

SECOND BROTHER. Right. Then it's me to start.

He hits ball through the hoop first time. Florence messes up her shot.

FLORENCE. Oh useless. (*Boy turns back to croquet her ball.*) No, Arthur, please. It's not fair.

FIRST BROTHER. Sorry, Florence.

FLORENCE. I've hardly started. (*Her brother fetches it a great whack and sends it shooting across the lawn.*) Damn. (*She runs after it. It has ended up quite near where Cross's abandoned tea cup stands on the edge of the lawn.*) Look you should have . . .

> *But Cross has disappeared. Forsyth comes over to take the tea cup away, as Florence stares at the rustling trees.*

FIRST BROTHER. You are a frightful tart, Florence.

33. Exterior. Another part of the wood.

By the bank of the stream, Edgar and the pretty girl lie in the grass. He has his hand inside her blouse. She watches him unsmiling and seemingly unresponsive. He tries to get his hand up her leg. It is all quite awkward, with the noise of clothes unbuttoning and the rustle of her dress very much in the foreground. The plain girl is sulking on the far bank of the stream.

PLAIN GIRL. Come on, Connie . . . Your Ma won't half play pop with you, Connie Sinker.

FLIRT. She won't know. (*Pause.*) Louisa . . . Louisa.

PLAIN GIRL. What?

FLIRT. She won't know.

PLAIN GIRL. I shall tell her.

EDGAR. She won't.

PLAIN GIRL. I shall.

EDGAR. Take no notice.

PLAIN GIRL. Connie. (*Connie is too busy with Edgar.*) Connie. Connie.

34. Exterior. Abbey ruins.

Baldring sits silent among the ruins. Cross watches. Ackroyd is catching butterflies. He puts them in a killing bottle.

[Cut. See above. No bottle was necessary: the air was killer enough.]

ACKROYD. It's a kind of gas, you see. They don't feel anything. It just puts them to sleep.

> *A shot of them moving about in sunken parts of the ruins, the old drains and passages. So that their heads and shoulders are above ground, the rest*

*hidden, as if they were in trenches. And above this the rumble of thunder.
It ought to be another moment like the guns first sounding, a sudden pause
and a slight alarm.*

[Cut, again because of the weather. This scene makes the same point
as is made by the (altered) ending of the film at the War Memorial,
but it makes it better because less explicitly.]

BOOTHROYD. Are we going to have a game, then?

GIBSON. Aye, Come on.

CROSS. Bags foggy. Foggy innings. Come on, be sharp.

SHORTER. This is consecrated ground, you know.

ACKROYD. It never is. It's where they had their dinners. (*To Baldring.*)
Come on Percy.

BALDRING. I'd rather just spectate.

ACKROYD. Nay, come on.

BALDRING. I'll just field for a bit, then.

TETLEY. Can Ernest play?

BOOTHROYD. Can he play?

TETLEY. Ay, I think he's all right. Do you want to play cricket, Ernest?

Ernest roars.

BOOTHROYD. Aye, all right.

TETLEY. 'Appen just let him field, he'll be all right.

BOOTHROYD. Come on then. (*They play and Mr Shorter takes first go.*)
Look out, let Wilfred Rhodes have a go.

WILKINS. We'll get into trouble, playing in here. (*Shorter whacks the ball
into the water.*) In t'river's out.

SHORTER. It never is.

*Baldring goes to retrieve the ball from the water and in doing so glances
up at the archway over the stream.*

BALDRING. That's interesting. Do you see what they've done there?
Them arches, they've buttressed it. We'd never do that now. We'd brace
it. You don't buttress now. Mind you they're grand buttresses, are
them. T'feller at laid them stones knew what he was doing.

WILKINS. He'd be a monk.

BALDRING. I don't care if he were Charley Peace. He could lay right bricks.

Mr Shuttleworth calls out.

MR SHUTTLEWORTH. It says there's an echo. Hoo-ooh!

He positions himself, consulting the guidebook, and calls out again, but not a bit self-consciously. Boothroyd looks up from the game and winks at one of the others. Mr Shuttleworth calls out again. This time there is an echo and he nods satisfied, and comes on past where Boothroyd and Co. are playing cricket.

BOOTHROYD. Everything all right, Mr Shuttleworth?

MR SHUTTLEWORTH. Yes. Oh yes, yes.

Shorter looks and Wilkins throws the ball.

GIBSON. Owzat!

WILKINS. Out, you're out, Mr Shorter.

SHORTER. I never were.

WILKINS. You were.

SHORTER. Which is t'wicket?

WILKINS. That's t'wicket.

Points to a bit of the wall.

SHORTER. I were thinking that were t'wicket.

Points to another bit.

BOOTHROYD. Well then. You're out then.

SHORTER. No, I'm not.

GIBSON. You are.

SHORTER. Well I'm not playing then.

ACKROYD. Nay, come on. Disputed decision, here, Mr Shuttleworth. Would you care to arbitrate?

Gibson bowls and hits Shorter.

GIBSON. You're out now anyway. BBW.

SHORTER. What's that.

GIBSON. Bum before wicket.

SHORTER. I'm not having that sort of language.

He throws down the bat.

GIBSON. I don't know. It's nobbut a game. Are we playing or aren't we?

GIBSON. Here, catch, Ernest.

He hurls the ball at Ernest, who roars.

MR TETLEY. Nay, give over.

The game breaks up and the players drift away.

35. Exterior. Abbey gates.

They are ready to set off back. Wilkins picks flowers.

SHORTER. Late setting off, late going back. I don't know. Where is he?

CROSS. Edgar!

BALDRING. Edgar! Come on, sithee. We're late.

Gibson comes round a corner on his bike to find Mr Shuttleworth having a pee behind a buttress.

GIBSON. Sorry, Mr Shuttleworth.

MR SHUTTLEWORTH. Just obeying a call of nature.

CROSS. Edgar!

BOOTHROYD. Come on then, lads. Saddle up. Back to the rhubarb fields.

SHORTER. Aye, time we were off.

36. Exterior. Another part of the wood.

VOICES OFF. Edgar! Edgar!

Edgar pushes the girl away and gets up.

EDGAR. I mun go. (*He runs off into the trees, stopping to call back to the girl.*) I can't stop. We're a club.

GIRL . (*Disgustedly.*) Club!

37. Exterior. A road.

The others have set off. A shot of them silhouetted against the sky climbing a hill. Edgar catches up with them.

EDGAR. Lads.

BOOTHROYD. Been lakin' cricket. You missed a right good game, Edgar.

He winks at Shorter.

GIBSON. He's been lakin' a better game nor that, haven't you Edgar?

38. Exterior. Abbey ruins.

The girl rides through the empty ruins, then through the wood towards the road taken by the cyclists.

39. Exterior. Road and hill.

SHORTER. I shall sleep to-night. All this country air.

Mr Shuttleworth nods. He looks worried.

40. Exterior. Road by the woods.

Florence waits by the road, hoping to see Cross.

41. Exterior. A hill.

They are still coming up the hill, but not within sight of where Florence is waiting, when Mr Shuttleworth suddenly steers into Shorter.

SHORTER. Nay, look out, you'll have me over.

MR SHUTTLEWORTH. I think I'm going to have to sit down.

SHORTER. Nay, come on, Mr Shuttleworth. We've only just set off. (*Mr Shuttleworth has passed out. They lay him down by the side of the road and loosen his collar.*) Are you all right?

ACKROYD. He looks bad. (*He calls to the others who are still going up the hill.*) Nay, hold on.

SHORTER. You've had a funny turn.

MR SHUTTLEWORTH. Ay, I have. I have that.

ACKROYD. You've done too much. Are you all right?

MR SHUTTLEWORTH. I'm all right now. I've happen done too much.

SHORTER. You're not so young as you were.

BOOTHROYD. It were perhaps summat you had. Pork's a funny thing, I always think. And you were having pork.

MR SHUTTLEWORTH. Aye. I was. Happen so.

BOOTHROYD. I always steer clear of pork.

Edgar and Gibson are standing apart.

EDGAR. He's too old to be bikin' about.

GIBSON. That's put a right damper on things, that has.

ACKROYD. How do you feel now?

MR SHUTTLEWORTH. I'm right enough. I don't feel ought clever, but I'm right enough.

42. Exterior. Country house and lawn.

The lawn empty. Croquet mallets left. Lights going on. Maid collecting croquet sticks. Mother calling 'Flo-rence'.

43. Exterior. Road near woods.

Florence, still waiting. She hears her mother calling and slowly turns back into the wood.

44. Exterior. Hill.

They begin climbing the hill again, slowly.

SHORTER. And take it easy, Mr Shuttleworth. We don't want to lose our founder member.

They come up to the crest of the hill, where Florence had been waiting, but by now she has gone. It is getting dark. They ride along slowly

*silhouetted against the sky. Boothroyd sings 'O Maiden, My Maiden'.
The last shot is of them going over the edge of the hill back into the abyss
again.*

[The original script ended here, on a sequence of shots of the cyclists
wending their way home against the evening sun – country roads, long
shadows, lovely light – a perfect end to an almost perfect day, with the
abyss not so much Halifax as the war to come. The weather put paid
to such a sequence; the end we filmed (in the rain) is a poor
substitute:]

45. Exterior. War Memorial.

*The War Memorial from which the expedition set off at the start of the film.
It is now some years later. The Great War is over and the names of new
dead have been inscribed on the column. Those gathered round the Memorial
sing the hymn 'O Valiant Hearts . . .' Among them we see Mr
Shuttleworth, Wilkins, Shorter and Cross. As the hymn ends they look at
the wreaths at the foot of the monument. Shorter points with his umbrella at
one particular wreath. It is from the cycling club and carries its emblem.
They turn away and we hold on the Memorial for the closing credits.*

Intensive Care

FATHER   Frank Crompton
MIDGLEY   Alan Bennett
JOYCE MIDGLEY   Helen Fraser
AUNTY KITTY   Thora Hird
UNCLE ERNEST   Colin Douglas
HARTLEY   Derek Fowlds
JEAN   Madge Hindle
MARK   Jeremy Mosby
ELIZABETH   Karen Tunstall
VALERY   Julie Walters
ALICE DUCKWORTH   Elizabeth Spriggs
COLIN MIDGLEY   David Major
MRS MIDGLEY'S MOTHER   Jeanne Doree
MISS TUNSTALL   Joan Sanderson
TEACHER   Ted Beyer
MRS AZAKWALE   Lucita Lijertwood
MR HORSFALL   Jim Broadbent
HEADMASTER   Aubrey Morris
DENIS'S MOTHER   Alison Lloyd
DENIS'S FATHER (YOUNG)
Anthony Addams
DENIS AS A BOY   Kirk Wild
HEATHER   Karen Petrie
1ST NURSE   Pamela Quinn
2ND NURSE   Trish Roberts
INDIAN DOCTOR   Shope Shodeinde
FAT MAN   Frank Birch
YOUNG MAN ON TELEPHONE   Alan Hulse
ORDERLY/PORTER   Johnny Leeze
WOMAN ON STICKS   Frances Cox
DAY MATRON   Brenda Hall
WOMAN ON TELEPHONE   Olive Pendleton
VERY YOUNG DOCTOR   Peter Chelsom
HOSPITAL CLERK   Alan Starkey

Produced by Innes Lloyd
Directed by Gavin Millar
Designed by Humphrey Jaeger
Music by Jim Parker

1. Interior. Hospital corridor. Day.

A long, featureless corridor in a modern hospital. Empty. Double doors at the end. The camera tracks slowly along the corridor towards the double doors. Suddenly, the doors swing open and a trolley with an elderly man on it is pushed madly along the corridor by a resuscitation team, the camera retreating very rapidly before it until more double doors close off the scene.

2. Interior. Midgley's home. Kitchen. Day.

Midgley, a man of thirty-nine sits at a kitchen table looking into the camera. He has his overcoat on. A carving knife is in front of him on the table.

MIDGLEY. I just never expected it.

VOICE OVER (MISS TUNSTALL). On the many occasions Midgley had killed his father, death always came easily. He died promptly, painlessly and without a struggle. Looking back, Midgley could see that even in these imagined deaths he had failed his father. It was not like him to die like that. Nor did he.

MIDGLEY. The timing is good. It's only my father who would stage his farewell in the middle of a Meet The Parents week.

> *Mrs Midgley seizes the carving knife and slices the crust viciously from Midgley's sandwiches. She looks disgusted.*

3. Interior. Midgley's School. Day.

Midgley and another teacher come through double doors, thread their way through a crowd of parents and children and go into the school hall.

MIDGLEY. I notice how young the parents are getting. Fathers in particular. They even have permed hair, the odd earring . . . features I still find it hard to forgive in the children.

> *Miss Tunstall, the school secretary, hands them several folders.*

OTHER TEACHER. I saw one with a swastika necklace.

MIDGLEY. A boy?

OTHER TEACHER. A parent.

MIDGLEY. There's a mother somewhere with green hair.

MISS TUNSTALL. Not just green. *Bright* green. And then you wonder the girls get pregnant.

Miss Tunstall goes to the door of the hall and addresses the waiting crowd.

MISS TUNSTALL. Thank you.

Parents and children flood into the hall seeking out teachers. Cut to Midgley being interviewed by Mrs Azakwale, a large black lady.

MRS AZAKWALE. Coretta's bin havin' these massive monthlies, Mr Midgley. Believe me en twenty years I en never seen menstruatin' like it.

MIDGLEY. It's her poor performance in Use of English that worries me.

MRS AZAKWALE. She bin wadin' about in blood to her ankles, Mr Midgley. I 'en never out of the launderette.

Behind Mrs Azakwale, waiting his turn is Mr Horsfall, a large, dour man. He catches Midgley's eye and shakes his head in despair.

MIDGLEY. I worry about Coretta's attention span, Mrs Azakwale. (*Coretta is paying no attention at this moment, either.*) It's very short.

MRS AZAKWALE. I'm saying: she bin concentratin' on getting through puberty. Once that's out of the way I reckon it's all plain sailin'. (*Moving away.*) Now then, Coretta, pigeon, where's this Computer Sciences gentleman?

Camera follows Mrs Azakwale and Coretta as they go off, leaving Midgley facing Mr Horsfall and his son. The camera goes back to Midgley with Horsfall in full flow. His innocent-looking sports jacket notwithstanding, the boots, black trousers and blue shirt proclaim Mr Horsfall a policeman in mufti.

HORSFALL. He's had every chance. Every chance in the world. Chance after chance after chance. I've lost count of the number of chances he's had.

MIDGLEY. Martin is a little young for his age.

HORSFALL. Martin? Is that what you call him?

MIDGLEY. That's his name.

HORSFALL. His name is Horsfall. Martin is what we call him, his mother and me. For your purposes I should have thought Horsfall was sufficient. Are you married?

MIDGLEY. Yes.

HORSFALL. And you teach him English? He can scarcely string two words together. Why, Martin? Why? I can. Your father. I have to. People making their statements, who is it who finds them the right word? Me. At four o'clock in the morning after a day spent combing copses and dragging ponds, making house-to-house enquiries I can do it. The father. But not the son. Why? Say something, Martin. (*Martin says nothing.*) I mean: a school like this. Soccer facilities: tip top. Swimming bath: tip top. Gymnasium: tip top. You want to be grateful. We never had chances like that did we, Midgley.

Midgley, uncomfortable at finding himself handcuffed to Horsfall in the same personal pronoun, says nothing. There is a pause. Miss Tunstall comes up, anxious to attract Midgley's attention, but sensing this is an awkward silence and therefore part of what is being said, she waits a moment then makes little waving signs behind Mr Horsfall's head; who, a policeman and ever alert to mockery, turns round.

MISS TUNSTALL. (*Addressing Horsfall, not Midgley.*) The hospital's just rung. Mr Midgley's father's been taken ill. (*Only then does she look at Midgley.*) Your father's been taken ill.

4. Interior. School office. Day.

Midgley is on the telephone. Miss Tunstall is sitting at the desk, waiting to start typing.

MIDGLEY. They're ringing the ward. It's a stroke, apparently. And he's had a fall.

MISS TUNSTALL. You want to pray it's not his hip. That's generally the weak spot. The pelvis heals in no time, surprisingly. (*She doesn't sound surprised.*) Mother broke her pelvis. I thought it was the beginning of the end.

MIDGLEY. Hello?

MISS TUNSTALL. She took a nasty tumble in Safeways last week. They do when they get older. It's what you have to expect. I'm reconciled to it now. Their bones get brittle.

She cracks her fingers and begins to type.

MIDGLEY. No, I don't want Maintenance. I want Ward 7.

Miss Tunstall stops typing.

MISS TUNSTALL. It's these ancillary workers. Holding the country to ransom. Other people's suffering is their bread and butter.

She starts typing again softly.

MIDGLEY. Midgley. Midgley. (*She stops typing.*) I'm his son. (*He waits.*) I see. Thank you. (*He puts the phone down.*) He's critical. They say its touch and go.

MISS TUNSTALL. How old is he?

MIDGLEY. Seventy-two.

MISS TUNSTALL. My mother's eighty-two. Life is unfair.

Midgley is still standing by the telephone when the headmaster breezes in.

HEADMASTER. On the phone again, Midgley? I'm the one who has to go cap in hand to the Finance Committee.

MISS TUNSTALL. Mr Midgley's father's ill. It's touch and go.

She starts typing like the wind.

5. Interior. Headmaster's study. Day.

HEADMASTER. Of course you can go. Of course you must go. One's father. There can be no question. It's awkward of course. But then it always is. Was he getting on in years?

MIDGLEY. Seventy-four.

HEADMASTER. Seventy-four. Once upon a time I thought that was old. (*He looks at the timetable, a vast complicated affair.*) Let me see. It's English, Integrated Humanities and Creative Arts. Nothing else, is there?

MIDGLEY. Environmental Studies.

The Headmaster groans.

HEADMASTER. That's the bluebottle in the vaseline. Pilbeam's away on a course. That's the trouble with the environment. It involves going on courses. I shall be glad when it's a proper subject and confined to the text-books. Ah well. I have no parents. They were despatched years ago. A flying bomb.

The Headmaster makes this sound like a victory for common sense.

MIDGLEY. He must have been lying there two days.

HEADMASTER. A familiar scenario. Isolated within the community. Alone in the crowd. You must not feel guilty.

MIDGLEY. I generally go over at weekends.

HEADMASTER. It will give Tomlinson an opportunity to do some of his weird and wonderful permutations with the timetable. Though I fear this one will tax even Tomlinson's talents. . . .

He has opened the door to let Midgley out. They go back into Miss Tunstall's office.

6. Interior. School office. day.

HEADMASTER. . . . One must hope it is not as grave as it appears. One must hope he turns the corner. Corners seem to have gone out nowadays. In the old days the sick were always turning them. Illness now much more of a straight road. Why is that?

MIDGLEY. Antibiotics?

HEADMASTER. Ye-es. One has the impression modern medicine encourages patients to loiter. Mistakenly, one feels. God speed. (*He looks at the notice Miss Tunstall has been typing.*) Ah yes. Hooliganism in the swimming baths. (*He reads the notice.*) I'm not sure if we've couched this in strong enough terms. Daphne.

MISS TUNSTALL. It's as you dictated it.

HEADMASTER. I have no doubt. But I feel more strongly about it now. Nothing else is there, Midgley? (*Midgley shakes his head, smiles weakly at Miss Tunstall and goes out.*) A boy slips. Is pushed. We are talking about concussion. A broken neck. A fatality, Daphne. I intend to nail the culprits. I want them to know they will be crucified.

MISS TUNSTALL. Shall I put that?

The Headmaster looks at her sharply.

HEADMASTER. First this business of Midgley père. Ask Tomlinson to step over, will you? Tell him to bring his coloured pencils. And a rubber.

7. Interior. Midgley's home. Kitchen. Day.

The same scene as the second shot. Midgley sat with his coat on at the kitchen table, carving knife in front of him, while his wife prepares his sandwiches.

MIDGLEY. I have treated him so badly. All along. (*Mrs Midgley says nothing, but grimly spreads the bread.*) I wanted to go over this last weekend. It's my fault.

MRS MIDGLEY. Tomato or my jam?

MIDGLEY. Tomato. I just never expected it.

MRS MIDGLEY. I did. Last time I went over he came to the door to wave me off. He's never done that before. I think people know.

Pause.

MIDGLEY. He does come to the door. He invariably comes to the door.

Mrs Midgley shakes her head sensitively.

MRS MIDGLEY. He was trying to tell me something. I know a farewell when I see one. (*She puts the sandwiches, flask, in front of him and waits.*) Is there anything else you want?

8. Interior. Midgley's house. Sitting room. Day.

Another part of the house. Mrs Midgley is seen first, so that we at first think Midgley has gone. She is dusting. Her mother is sat in a chair, asleep. She is an old lady. No reference is made to her.

MIDGLEY'S VOICE. I'm not going to let him down. I want to be there when he goes. He loved me. (*Mrs Midgley picks up an item and dusts beneath it, viciously.*) Don't you think so?

He is stood in the doorway watching her.

MRS MIDGLEY. I do. Though why, I can't imagine. It's not as if you take after him. (*She dusts something else, grimly.*) One little bit.

Mrs Midgley's mother wakes up.

MOTHER. Is it Saturday today?

9. Interior. Midgley's house. The stairs. Day.

Midgley is sat on the stairs. Mrs Midgley is out of shot, still ruthlessly cleaning.

MRS MIDGLEY'S VOICE. He had strength. Our Colin is going to be strong. He loved Colin.

MIDGLEY. Does he know?

MRS MIDGLEY. Yes. It hasn't hit him yet. When it does he's going to be heartbroken. They both are. Poor old Frank.

Pause.

MIDGLEY. I've never understood why you call him Frank. He's my Father.

MRS MIDGLEY. He has a name. Frank is his name.

MIDGLEY. You're the only one who uses it. Everybody else calls him Dad. Or Grandad.

MRS MIDGLEY. I call him Frank because that's the name of a person. To me he is a person. That's why we get on.

Mrs Midgley's mother appears at the door of the sitting room.

MOTHER. Joyce.

MRS MIDGLEY. Yes, Mother?

MOTHER. When is that chiropodist coming?

MRS MIDGLEY. Yesterday, Mother. He came yesterday.

10. Interior. Midgley's house. Colin's bedroom. Day.

Loud music. The door opens. Midgley comes in and stands waiting. Colin, his teenage son switches the music off.

COLIN. Dad, I've told you before. Don't just walk in. Knock.

MIDGLEY. I did knock.

COLIN. This is my room. I could be doing anything.

MIDGLEY. I've got to go over to Bradford. To the hospital. Grandad's poorly.

COLIN. I know. Mum said. I thought you'd have gone by now. I'm really sorry.

Midgley closes the door and music starts again as he goes downstairs.

11. Interior. Midgley's kitchen. Day.

Joyce's mother sits on a kitchen chair throughout this.

MIDGLEY. Why don't you come?

MRS MIDGLEY. With mother? How can I?

MIDGLEY. Ta ra, then. (*He kisses her and goes to the back door and opens it, then stops.*) Anyway, it isn't.

MRS MIDGLEY. It isn't what?

MIDGLEY. It isn't why you get on: treating him like a person. You get on because you both despise me.

MRS MIDGLEY. Your father is dying. A good, good man is dying. And you hang about here resenting the fact that he and I were friends. I seem to have married someone very low down in the evolutionary chain. You might want one or two tissues.

Mrs Midgley takes some tissues and stuffs them in his pocket.

MIDGLEY. When you and he were together I didn't exist.

MRS MIDGLEY. Your father is *dying*. Will you exist now?

MIDGLEY. I'll make it right. I'll be there when he goes. I'll hold his hand. I shan't let him down. If I let him down now I'll never be able to make it right. He'd stay with me the rest of my life. I did love him, Joyce.

MRS MIDGLEY. I would like him to stay with you for the rest of your life. I hope he does stay with you for the rest of your life. As an example. As somebody to live up to. I think of his kindness. His unselfishness. His unflagging courtesy. The only incredible thing is that someone so truly saintly should have produced such a pill of a son. But I suppose that's your mother.

MIDGLEY. Shut up about my mother. My mother is dead.

MRS MIDGLEY. So is he, virtually. Dawdling. *Go.*

MIDGLEY. Then things will change, you'll see. I'll change. I'll be a different person. I can . . . go. Live. Start!

He kisses her quickly and goes out.

12. Exterior. Midgley's house. Day.

Midgley is about to get into his van when Mrs Midgley comes after him with his flask and sandwiches.

MRS MIDGLEY. *Start?* You're thirty-nine!

13. Montage. Midgley driving from Hull to Bradford. Day.

An old man waiting to cross at a zebra. As he goes across he holds up his hand to stop oncoming traffic. Halfway across he changes into Midgley's father. Thereafter Midgley see his father at every turn:
    Midgley's father sitting on a seat.
    Midgley's father waiting at a bus stop.
    Then Midgley's mother and father, the father carrying the shopping bag.

14. Interior. Hospital. Long corridor. Day.

The same long corridor we saw at the start of the film. Midgley is walking down it with Aunty Kitty, a woman in her seventies, his father's sister.

AUNTY KITTY. I thought you'd have been here a bit since. I was here at 3 o'clock. You'll notice a big change. He's not like my brother. He's not the Frank I knew. I don't dislike this colour scheme. I always liked oatmeal. The doctor's black.

15. Interior. Intensive care. Waiting room. Day.

MIDGLEY. Did he know you?

AUNTY KITTY. The nurse says he doesn't know anybody. The Duchess of Kent opened this unit, apparently. The kidney department's world-famous. (*A nurse comes in and Midgley gets up.*) This is my nephew, Mr Midgley's son. You father's got a room to himself, love.

NURSE. They all do, at this stage.

16. Interior. Intensive care. Father's room. Day.

Single ward. Midgley's father is lying motionless with his eyes open. Monitors etc. on his chest. A window cleaner is washing the windows, but with professional discretion avoids his gaze.

MIDGLEY. Dad. Dad. It's me, Denis. I've come. I've come, Dad. It's all right. (*He pulls his chair up to the bed and holds his father's hand.*) I'm sorry Dad.

A nurse looks in at the door.

NURSE. Are you next of kin?

MIDGLEY. Son.

NURSE. Not too long.

Midgley waits, holding his father's hand. Aunty Kitty comes in.

AUNTY KITTY. I wonder where he is? What does that look on his face mean?

MIDGLEY. It means that he is dying, and it's my fault.

A nurse comes and stands at the door and they go out to the waiting room again.

17. Interior. Waiting room. Day.

AUNTY KITTY. It's just a case of waiting now. There's a lot of waiting done in hospitals. Ninety per cent of it's waiting. (*Stroking the upholstery.*) Would you call this chestnut or russet? (*Pause.*) I always thought I'd be the one to go first. They've never got to the bottom of my complaint. They lowered a microscope down my throat. Nothing there. I even went on this machine the Duke of Gloucester inaugurated. That drew a blank as well. Mr Conway Lewis said they were baffled. (*There should be comings and goings through this.*) I asked the nurse, I said: 'Is he just unconscious or is he in a coma?' She didn't know. They don't get the training now.

MIDGLEY. Aunty. (*Aunty Kitty stops.*) What was my Dad like?

AUNTY KITTY. He never had a wrong word for anybody, your Dad. He'd do anybody a good turn. Shovel their snow. Fetch their coal in. He was a saint. (*Pause.*) You take after your mother more.

18. Interior. Waiting room. A little later. Day.

MIDGLEY. I feel I lack his sterling qualities. Grit. Patience. That willingness to shoulder other people's burdens. Virtues bred out of adversity.

AUNTY KITTY. I think you change when you go to university.

MIDGLEY. Deprivation, for instance. I was never deprived, Aunty Kitty. That way he deprived me, do you see?

AUNTY KITTY. I should have gone to secondary school. I left school at thirteen, same as your Dad. You wouldn't think they'd have curtains in a hospital, would you? You'd think it wouldn't be hygienic.

MIDGLEY. I know I had it easier than my Dad. But I was grateful. I didn't take it for granted. It's not particularly enjoyable, education.

AUNTY KITTY. You used to look bonny in your blazer.

MIDGLEY. He gave me what he'd wanted. Why should that be enjoyable?

AUNTY KITTY. You ought to be ringing round. Telling Ernest, Hartley and Christine. Mark's just got his bronze medal.

MIDGLEY. I'll wait and see the doctor first.

AUNTY KITTY. You'd have thought they'd have had all these complaints licked, what with these silicone chips. Somebody's got their priorities wrong. Then he's always been a right keen smoker, your Dad. Now he's paying the price. (*Pause.*) Robert Donat had bronchitis.

Midgley puts his head in his hands. Aunty Kitty, indicating a woman in a corner.

AUNTY KITTY. Her hubby's on the critical list. Their eldest girl works for Johnson and Johnson. They'd just got back from Barbados. (*The doctor comes into the waiting room. He is an Indian doctor. Midgley is dozing.*) Denis. It's doctor.

DOCTOR. (*Looking at his clipboard.*) Mr Midgley? Your father has had a stroke. How severe, it is hard to tell. However, when he was brought in he was also suffering from hypothermia. Our old enemy. He must have fallen and been lying there for two days at least.

MIDGLEY. I generally go over at weekends.

DOCTOR. Pneumonia has now set in. His heart is not strong. I do not think he will last the night.

He puts the clipboard under his arm, and we see there is nothing on it.

19. Interior. Hospital telephone area. Day.

Telephone in hospital: helmet type. A young man on one telephone, a fat man waiting.

FAT MAN. Only three phones and two of them duff. You wouldn't credit it. (*He is standing. Midgley is sitting.*) Say you were on standby for a transplant. It'd be all the same.

He jingles his coins. The young man puts his head outside the helmet.

YOUNG MAN. I've got one or two calls to make.

FAT MAN. Oh hell.

PASSING NURSE. There's a phone outside physio. Try there.

FAT MAN. I'll try there.

Midgley waits, watching the young man. The young man watches Midgley but does not see him, while the following conversations ensue.

YOUNG MAN. Hello, Dorothy? Dorothy, you're a grandma! A grandma. Yes. Well, guess. (*Pause.*) No. Girl. Seven and a half pounds. At 5.35.

Both doing well. I'm ringing everybody. Bye . . . *grandma.* (*Midgley half rises, but the young man makes another call.*) Hello, Neil. Hi. You're an uncle. Yes. Just now. 5.35. Well, guess. (*Pause.*) No, girl. *No.* It's what we really wanted. I'm over the moon. So tell Christine, she's an aunty and yes, a little cousin for Josephine. How's it feel to be an uncle? Bye. (*Midgley gets up and stands but the young man, while looking at him, ignores him.*) Betty? Congratulations. You're an Aunty. I won't ask you to guess. It's a girl. Susan's over the moon. And I am. I'm just telephoning with the glad tidings. Bye, *Aunty!*

MIDGLEY. Could I just make one call.

YOUNG MAN. Won't it wait? I was here first. I'm a father.

MIDGLEY. I'm a son. My father's dying.

YOUNG MAN. There's no need to take that tone. (*He steps out of the helmet.*) You should have spoken up. There's a phone outside physio.

He waits while Midgley telephones.

MIDGLEY. Uncle Ernest? Denis. Dad's been taken poorly. He's had a stroke. And a fall. And now he's got pneumonia. (*The young man looks away, abashed.*) Can you ring round, tell anybody who might want to come? The doctor says he won't last the night. I'm in a box. There are people waiting.

He puts the telephone down.

YOUNG MAN. You never know. They can work miracles nowadays.

20. Interior. Outside the hospital lift. Early evening.

UNCLE ERNEST. Did you ring our Hartley? (*Midgley nods.*) Tied up? Secretary, was it?

MIDGLEY. He's coming as soon as he can get away.

UNCLE ERNEST. Was he in a meeting? I'd like to know what they are, these meetings he's in that he can't speak to his father. Who are they in these meetings? Don't they have fathers? I thought fathers were universal. Instead of which, I have to make an appointment. 'I'll just look at his book.' Sons, fathers, you shouldn't need appointments, you should get straight through. You weren't like that with your Dad. Frank thought the world of you.

21. Interior. A large hospital lift. Evening.

UNCLE ERNEST. This is what I'd call an industrial lift. (*He taps the side of it with his boot.*) It's not an ordinary passenger lift, this. It's as big as our sitting room. It'd be a stroke. He's only seventy-two. I'm seventy-four.

The lift stops and a porter gets in with a trolley with a woman on it.

PORTER. Is it working? (*The little head closes its eyes.*) We've just had a nice jab. Had a nice jab and we're going for a ta ta.

UNCLE ERNEST. She'll be on five thousand a year, Hartley's secretary. That's a starting salary these days.

PORTER. Gangway.

He wheels his trolley out.

22. Interior. Hospital. Long corridor. Evening.

UNCLE ERNEST. I came on the diesel. It's only one stop. I use my railcard. I go all over. I went to York last week. Saw the Railway Museum. There's stock in there I drove. Museum in my own lifetime. Tell you one thing: I wouldn't like to have to polish this floor. You still school-teaching?

MIDGLEY. Yes.

UNCLE ERNEST. Pleased your Dad, did that. No. I've been all over since your Aunt Edith died. Take a flask. Sandwiches. I plan to visit Barnard Castle next week. Weather permitting.

23. Interior. Outside Intensive Care. Evening.

Uncle Ernest pauses.

UNCLE ERNEST. Is your Aunty Kitty here?

MIDGLEY. Yes.

UNCLE ERNEST. I thought she would be. Where no vultures fly.

24. Interior. Waiting Room. Evening.

Aunty Kitty sees them come in and, as if her grief were too great for words, solemnly embraces her brother, shaking her head and dabbing her nose.

AUNTY KITTY. I always thought I'd be the first to go.

UNCLE ERNEST. You still might. He's not dead yet.

AUNTY KITTY. Go in, Ernest. Go in.

25. Interior. Intensive Care. Father's room. Evening.

Father alone with his brother. Ernest stands. Then sits awkwardly.

UNCLE ERNEST. This is summat fresh for you, Frank. (*Pause.*) You were always such a bouncer. (*Pause, He gets up and looks at the scanner, then sits down again.*) I went over to York last week. It's the first time I've been since we used to bike over when we were lads. It hasn't changed much. They haven't spoilt it like they have Leeds. (*The nurse looks in, says nothing, and goes away.*) Though there's one of these precincty things. (*Pause.*) I went on my Railcard. It's still wicked. (*Pause.*) I'll say ta ra then, butt. Ta ra.

  He jogs his brother's foot in farewell, just as the nurse comes in and sees.

NURSE. (*Reprovingly.*) He's very ill. And this is delicate equipment.

26. Interior. Hospital lift. Evening.

Hartley, Uncle Ernest's son, Jean his wife and their two children, Mark and Elizabeth.

HARTLEY. Now think on, the pair of you, don't be asking for this, that and the other in front of your Grandad.

JEAN. Are you listening, Mark? Your father's talking to you. We don't want him saying you're spoiled.

HARTLEY. Though you are spoiled.

JEAN. Whose fault is that? (*The lift doors open and Mark nearly knocks down a nurse.*) Mind that nurse, Mark. Sorry.

27. Interior. Hospital long corridor. Evening.

Uncle Ernest is coming down the corridor with Midgley.

HARTLEY. Look out. Here's you grandad. Now then, Dad. Denis.

JEAN. Grandad. (*She kisses him.*) Give your Grandad a kiss, Elizabeth. (*The little girl does so.*) Mark.

MARK. I don't kiss now.

JEAN. You kiss your grandad.

The boy does so shamefacedly.

HARTLEY. How is he?

UNCLE ERNEST. Dying. Sinking fast.

HARTLEY. Oh dear, oh dear, oh dear.

MIDGLEY. They don't think he'll last the night.

JEAN. How've you been keeping?

MIDGLEY. Champion.

HARTLEY. I had the receiver in my hand to give you a ring, yesterday, Dad, only a client came in.

UNCLE ERNEST. That one of them new watches?

MARK. Yes.

He shows him it.

JEAN. He had it to save up for. You had it to save up for, didn't you Mark?

ELIZABETH. He didn't.

UNCLE ERNEST. I didn't have a watch till I was twenty-one. 'Course they're twenty-one at eighteen now, aren't they?

Pause.

HARTLEY. We'd better be getting along to the ward if it's that critical.

JEAN. Shall we see you soon, Grandad?

UNCLE ERNEST. I was thinking of going to Barnard Castle next week.

JEAN. Whatever for?

UNCLE ERNEST. I've never been.

HARTLEY. Say goodbye then.

JEAN. Kiss your Grandad.

The children kiss him again.

MIDGLEY. I'll just see you to the lift.

Hartley and Jean and their children go along the corridor.

JEAN. I'll give you such a clatter when I get you home, young lady. He did save up.

ELIZABETH. Only a week.

HARTLEY. Now, when we get there we shan't have to go in all at once. It'll just be two at a time.

JEAN. What's he doing going to Barnard Castle? He can't be short of money, taking himself off to Barnard Castle.

28. Interior. Intensive Care. Father's room. Evening.

Dad in bed, as before. Hartley and Martin come in.

HARTLEY. Hello, Uncle. It's Hartley. There's Mark too. We're all here. (*They stand awkwardly waiting. Hartley's attention is increasingly caught by the television monitor. The boy goes on looking distastefully at the bed.*) You see this screen, Mark? It's monitoring his heart beats.

MARK (*Witheringly.*) I know, Dad.

HARTLEY. I was only telling you. You want to learn, don't you?

MARK. Dad. We made one of those at school. Is he going to die?

HARTLEY. Well, I don't know. Why?

MARK. Jill says that if we get the chance of seeing someone dead we ought to take it. Jill says death is a part of life.

HARTLEY. Who's Jill?

MARK She takes us for Modern Studies.

29. Interior. Waiting Room. Evening.

ELIZABETH. Are you crying, Mam?

JEAN. Yes.

The little girl looks at her mother.

ELIZABETH. There aren't many tears.

JEAN. You can cry without tears.

ELIZABETH. I can't. How do you do it, Mam?

JEAN. I'll give you such a smack in a minute, your Uncle Denis's father is dying.

Elizabeth starts to cry.

JEAN. There, love. It's all right. He doesn't feel it.

ELIZABETH. I'm not crying because of him. I'm crying because of you.

30. Interior. Waiting Room. Evening.

Midgley, Hartley and an Indian father and son, who are sat in a corner. The father is weeping and hugging the child very tightly. The child peers under his father's arm at them.

HARTLEY. I wouldn't have another Cortina. I used to swear by Cortinas. (*Midgley looks at the Indian family.*) You still got the VW? (*Midgley nods.*) I might go in for a Peugeot next. A 604. Buy British.

Jean and Elizabeth come in, having been to see Father.

JEAN. (*Mouths at Hartley.*) How long are we stopping?

HARTLEY. I think we ought to wait just a bit, don't you, darling?

JEAN. Oh yes. Just in case.

HARTLEY. He was a nice old chap.

Aunty Kitty comes in.

AUNTY KITTY. I just had one coffee and a Wagonwheel, and it was forty-five pence. And it's all supposed to be voluntary.

MARK. There isn't a disco, is there?

JEAN. Disco? Disco? This is a hospital.

Aunty Kitty looks shocked.

MARK Leisure facilities. Facilities for visitors. Killing time.

JEAN. Listen. Your Uncle Denis's father is dying and you talk about discos.

MIDGLEY. It's all right.

HARTLEY. Here. (*Handing him a pound.*) Go get yourself a coffee.

Aunty Kitty closes her eyes in despair.

31. Interior. Long corridor. Evening.

A woman on sticks painfully hobbling to a radiator. She looks out of the window, alone. She speaks to no one in particular.

WOMAN. I do love chrysanths.

HARTLEY. You want to make it plain at this stage you don't want him resuscitating.

Midgley, Hartley and his family are walking down the corridor.

JEAN. That is if he doesn't want him resuscitating.

HARTLEY. I wouldn't.

JEAN. Denis might. You don't know.

Midgley looks as if he doesn't know either.

HARTLEY. You often don't get the choice. They'll resuscitate anybody, given half a chance. You read about it. Shove them on these life support machines. It's all to do with cost effectiveness. They invest in this expensive equipment, and then of course they have to use it.

The woman looking out of the window watches them go.

32. Interior. Outside hospital lift. Evening.

JEAN. Miracles do happen, of course. I was reading about these out-of-body experiences. Have you read about them, Denis? Out-of-body experiences. Where sick people float in the air above their own bodies. I think it won't be long before science will be coming round to an afterlife. Bye bye, love.

Shot of the whole of Hartley's family as the lift door closes.

33. Interior. Hospital. Long corridor. Evening.

Midgley goes down the corridor. The woman is still at the window.

WOMAN. They've put me down for one of these electric chair things. Once I get one of them I shall be whizzing about all over.

34. Interior. Waiting Room. Evening.

The Indian father and son are both asleep. Aunty Kitty and Midgley are the only other occupants of the waiting room.

AUNTY KITTY. Money's no good. Look at President Kennedy. They've been a tragic family. (*Pause.*) The Wainwrights got back from Corfu. They said they enjoyed it but they wouldn't go again. (*Pause.*) If I go now I can just get the twenty to.

MIDGLEY. I'll come down and phone Joyce.

Aunty Kitty looks at the sleeping Indians.

AUNTY KITTY. The little lad's bonny. They've got feelings the same as us. They're fond of their families. (*They are out into the corridor.*) More so probably, because they're less advanced than we are.

35. Interior. Hospital. Telephone area. Evening.

Midgley on the telephone.

MIDGLEY. I've got to be here.

36. Interior. Midgley's home. Sitting room. Evening.

Mrs Midgley's mother asleep. His son watching televison. Mrs Midgley on the telephone.

MRS MIDGLEY. You've done all that's necessary. Nobody would blame you.

37. Interior. Hospital. Telephone area. Evening.

MIDGLEY. I've got to be here. I must be here when he goes. Can't you understand that?

38. Interior. Midgley's home. Sitting room. Evening.

MRS MIDGLEY. I understand you. It's not love. It's not affection. It's yourself.

She puts the telephone down.

COLIN. Dad?

MRS MIDGLEY. He's hanging on.

Pause.

COLIN. Who?

MRS MIDGLEY. Your *grandad*. Wake up, Mum. Time for bed.

39. Interior. Intensive Care. Father's room. Night.

Midgley is sitting by the bed. We see the day nurse with her cloak on, outside, and the night nurse taking over. The night nurse, Valery, comes in and does jobs round the bed.

MIDGLEY. Am I in the way?

VALERY. No. Stop there.

He watches her. She is less pert than the others, more sloppy. She smiles at him and goes out.

40. Interior. Intensive Care. Father's room. Night. Later.

Night nurse looks in.

VALERY. Cup of tea?

41. Interior. Intensive Care. Night nurse's desk. Night.

Midgley is having his tea. She is working on various forms.

VALERY. Slack tonight. Still, it just takes one drunken driver. (*Midgley is dropping asleep.*) I thought you were going to be a bit of company. You're tired out. Lie down.

She gives him a pillow and they go out to the Waiting Room.

42. Interior. Waiting Room. Night.

VALERY. I'll give you a shout if anything happens.

The Indians are also asleep.

43. Interior. Intensive Care. Father's room. Night.

Four in the morning. His father's screen regularly blipping. His father's face.

44. Interior. Waiting Room. Day. Next morning.

Midgley is being shaken by the day nurse, as unsympathetic as the night nurse had been the reverse.

DAY NURSE. You can't lie down. You're not supposed to lie down.

Midgley sits up. The Indians have gone and in their place two anonymous people are staring at him expressionlessly.

MIDGLEY. The nurse said she'd wake me up.

DAY NURSE. What nurse?

MIDGLEY. If anything happened to my father.

DAY NURSE. Which is your father?

MIDGLEY. Midgley.

DAY NURSE. Is that a hospital pillow?

MIDGLEY. Mr Midgley.

DAY NURSE. No. No change. But don't lie down. It's not fair on other people.

45. Interior. Intensive Care. Father's room. Day.

Midgley and his father. Midgley looking rough and unshaven. His father pink and clean and fresh.

46. Exterior. Hospital. Day.

Midgley walks round the hospital and goes to his van in the car park. He looks at himself in the car mirror, then gets out and walks round the outside of the hospital. It is a modern building, built in identical units, so that one ward looks much the same as another. A woman is stood at a window suckling a baby. He looks at her, then a nurse appears behind her and draws the blinds. Midgley walks on. He finds himself outside Intensive Care. He looks up at his father's room. There is a nurse stood with her back to the window. She moves back to allow someone else in. Midgley can see someone in a white coat, another nurse. The room seems full of people.

He begins to scramble down the bank to try and get into this section of the building. He tries a door: locked. He scrambles along the bank, round the outside of the building, tries another door. A man on a telephone sees him: puts the telephone down and picks up another.

Midgley scrambles on, eventually finding himself in some bushes. He runs through the bushes, across a muddy flowerbed and finds himself at the main entrance.

47. Interior. Intensive Care. Father's room. Day.

Midgley rushes past the desk into his father's room.

MIDGLEY. Is he dead?

The nurses look round.

MATRON. Dead? Certainly not. I am the matron. Look at your shoes.

As the nurses bustle Midgley out he looks back and we get a glimpse of his father's face and he could be smiling.

MIDGLEY. But I want to see a doctor.

MATRON. Why? Have you a complaint?

MIDGLEY. The doctor yesterday said my father wouldn't last the night. He has, so I was wondering if there was any change.

MATRON. No change. I should go home. You've done your duty.

48. Interior. Waiting Room. Day.

Aunty Kitty has got her knitting, a flask, biscuits. She is quite settled in. The Indians are back waiting, too.

AUNTY KITTY. I've just been to spend a penny. When you consider it's a hospital, the toilets are nothing to write home about. (*She is immersed in Country Life.*) I wouldn't thank you for a house in Portugal. Loggia. Swimming pool. I just want somewhere I can get round nicely with the Hoover. Where've you been with your shoes? (*Midgley looks at his muddy shoes.*) You'd better ring your Uncle Ernest. He'll want the latest gen.

49. Interior. Hospital. Gent's toilet. Day.

Midgley gets some toilet paper and cleans the mud off his boots. He has put his shoes on again and is standing with the muddy toilet paper in his hand when an orderly comes in, looks at him and the paper with incredulity and disgust, and goes into a cubicle shaking his head.

ORDERLY. The bastard public. The nasty, dirty, bastard public.

Midgley looks at the paper and puts it in the bin.

50. Interior. Hospital. Telephone area. Day.

Midgley waiting. No sense of urgency. A woman is on the telephone.

WOMAN. Cyril. It's Vi. Mam's had her op. Had it this morning, first thing. She's not come round yet but apparently she's fine. Yes, fine. I spoke to the Sister, and she says it wasn't what they thought it was, so there's no need to worry. I don't know what it was, she did tell me the name, but the important thing is that it wasn't what they thought it was. No. Completely clear. The Sister would know, wouldn't she? Oh yes, I think it's good news, and she said the surgeon is the best. People pay thousands to have him, she said. Anyway I'll see you later. I'm so relieved. Aren't you? Yes. Bye.

Midgley goes to the telephone.

51. Interior. Intensive Care. Father's room. Day.

Uncle Ernest looking at him.

UNCLE ERNEST. Jillo, Frank. We can't go on like this, you know. I can't run to the fares.

52. Interior. Waiting room. Day.

Uncle Ernest and Hartley are leaving. Midgley with them.

AUNTY KITTY. It's Frank all over. Going down fighting. He loved life. He won't go without a struggle . . . It's their eldest daughter . . . (*She indicates an elderly couple waiting.*) Just choosing some new curtains in Schofields. Collapsed. Suspected brain haemorrhage. Their other son's a vet.

53. Interior. Hospital. Long corridor. Day.

UNCLE ERNEST. It's a wonder to me how your Aunty Kitty's managed to escape strangulation so long. Was he coloured, this doctor?

MIDGLEY. Who?

UNCLE ERNEST. That said he was on his last legs.

MIDGLEY. Yes.

UNCLE ERNEST. That explains it.

HARTLEY. Dad.

UNCLE ERNEST. What do you mean 'Dad'?

HARTLEY. I mean I'm vice chairman of the Community Relations Council, that's what I mean. I mean we've got one in the office and he's a tip top accountant. We all have to live with one another in this world.

UNCLE ERNEST. You're young.

54. Interior. Outside the lift. Day.

UNCLE ERNEST. I'll not come again. Again and again. It gets morbid. I'd go back home if I were you.

Midgley says nothing.

HARTLEY. He's got to play it by ear.

UNCLE ERNEST. There's no need to go through all this performance with me, you know. Come once, and have done. Mind you, I'll be lucky if you come at all.

The lift doors open.

HARTLEY. Shall I drop you?

UNCLE ERNEST. I don't want you to go out of your way.

HARTLEY. No, but shall I drop you?

Midgley watches the doors close on them still arguing. It is like a play within a play of his relations with his own father.

55. Interior. Hospital. Long corridor. Day.

Midgley walks back.

WOMAN ON STICKS. I'm getting one of these mobile trolley things. Once I get that I'll be up and down this corridor.

56. Interior. Intensive Care. Father's room. Night.

The night nurse comes in with a bowl and a sponge.

VALERY. (*Night Nurse.*) He doesn't want to leave us, does he? (*As she washes his father's thighs Midgley gets up suddenly and stares out of the window.*) I can see his attraction even though he's old. I can imagine women going for him.

Midgley isn't liking any of this.

MIDGLEY. Women didn't go for him. Only my mother.

VALERY. I don't believe that. (*Midgley turns just as she is sponging between his father's legs. He turns away hastily.*) What was he?

MIDGLEY. How do you mean?

VALERY. His job?

MIDGLEY. Plumber.

VALERY. What are you?

MIDGLEY. Teacher.

VALERY. He's got lovely hands. Real lady's hands. You see that happen in hospitals. People's hands change.

Midgley turns and she is holding his father's hand.

57. Interior. Intensive Care. Night Nurse's desk. Night. Later.

A VERY YOUNG DOCTOR. There hasn't been any particular change. His condition certainly hasn't deteriorated. On the other hand it hasn't improved.

MIDGELY. The other doctor said he wouldn't last the night.

YOUNG DOCTOR. I don't know there's any special point in waiting. You've done you duty.

MIDGLEY. I don't think he is dying.

YOUNG DOCTOR. Living, dying. (*Shrugs slightly.*) There's nothing special about the moment of death. The screen will alter, that's all. You do *want* your father to live, Mr Midgley?

MIDGLEY. Yes, only I was told he wasn't going to last long.

YOUNG DOCTOR. Our task is to make them last as long as possible. We've no obligation to get them off on time. This isn't British Rail.

MIDGLEY. Look, how old are you?

The doctor turns away, pulls a small face at Valery, and goes.

58. Interior. Intensive Care. Night Nurse's desk. Night. Later.

She is being sympathetic.

MIDGLEY. I don't like fifteen-year-old doctors, that's all. I'm old enough to be his father.

VALERY. Why not go and sleep in your van? If anything happens I'll send somebody down.

MIDGLEY. Does nobody else wait? Does nobody else feel like me? (*Pause.*) What do you do during the day, when you're on nights?

VALERY. Sleep. I generally surface around three.

MIDGLEY. Maybe we could have a coffee? If he's unchanged.

VALERY. O.K.

MIDGLEY. I'll just have another squint, then I'll go. (*He goes into his father's room. Camera stays with her. Midgley returns, quickly.*) Come look. He's moved.

59. Interior. Intensive Care. Father's room. Night.

Valery goes briskly and professionally ahead of him into the room and looks at the old man.

VALERY. No.

MIDGLEY. Yes. (*She switches on the overhead light.*) He's kind of smiling.

VALERY. No.

MIDGLEY. If you look long enough you'll see a smile.

VALERY. If you look long enough you'll see anything you want. You're tired. Goodnight.

Midgley would probably kiss her, were his father not present.

60. Interior. Midgley's home. Night.

Mrs Midgley on the telephone. Her mother sits with her bag by the sitting room door.

MRS MIDGLEY. Sit down a second, mother. I'll be with you in a minute. Mum's waiting to go up. She's crying out for a bath. I'm just stealing myself. What do you do all day?

61. Interior. Hospital. Telephone area. Night.

Midgley on the telephone.

MIDGLEY. *I* need a bath.

62. Interior. Midgley's home. Night.

Mrs Midgley watching her mother, whose handbag has slipped to the floor; she is trying to retrieve it.

MRS MIDGLEY. Go over to your Dad's. It's not all that far. If it's not going to be any minute, you might as well. I'm going to have to go. (*Her mother nearly falls off the chair, but she stops her in time.*)

MOTHER. What am I doing sitting on this chair? I never sit on this chair. I don't think I've ever sat on this chair before.

63. Interior. Hospital. Long corridor. Night.

Midgley in the long corridor. The Matron comes down the corridor on her electric trolley, a vision like the first appearance of Omar Sharif out of the heat haze in Lawrence of Arabia. Midgley watches.

64. Exterior. Car park. Morning.

Nurse Lightfoot (Valery) is banging on the window.

VALERY (*Mouthing*). Just coming off. (*Midgley winds the window down.*) Isn't it a grand morning. I'm just coming off. I'm going to have a big fatty breakfast then to to bed. I'll see you at tea-time. You look terrible.

Midgley sees his face in the driving mirror. He does. She walks off and he starts up the van and drives after her.

MIDGLEY. I forget to ask you. How's my Dad?

VALERY. No change. (*She waves and runs down towards the nurses' flats.*) No change.

65. Exterior. Street in Leeds. Day.

A terrace house. Midgley's van outside.

66. Interior. Father's house. Day.

Midgley in his father's house: neat, silent. Photographs of father and mother. A wedding. Photographs of grandchildren.

67. Interior. Father's scullery. Day.

Midgley pours water from kettle into a bowl. He looks at his father's razor. Cleans it. Changes the blade. Finds his father's old shaving brush, worn down to a stub. Uses ordinary soap. Wipes his face on the towel on the back of the door. Takes his shirt off. Washes. Smells his shirt. Goes upstairs.

68. Interior. Parents' bedroom. Day.

Neat: dressing table set with glass dressing table set, mirror and brush etc. Looks in drawer. Finds a new shirt, still in Christmas paper. Puts it on. Too big. Looks at socks. Underpants.

69. Interior. Father's sitting room. Day.

Midgley, dressed, downstairs standing in front of the fireplace. He looks as if he's ready for a funeral. His father's pipe is on the mantelpiece. He looks at it. Puts it back. It falls to the hearth. He stoops to pick it up, then suddenly thinks of his father doing the same, falling and lying there.

70. Exterior. Father's house. Day.

Midgley then panics, thinking of his father dead and rushes out of the house and drives away very quickly.

71. Interior. Corridor in hospital. Day.

Midgley running down it.

72. Interior. Corridor. Intensive Care. Day.

A trolley being wheeled out, body sheeted. Midgley stops and it passes. It is followed by the Indian father and son.

AUNTY KITTY. I offered them my condolences but I don't think they understood.

73. Interior. Intensive Care. Father's room. Day.

MIDGLEY. I'm wearing your shirt, Dad. It's the one we gave you for Christmas. I hope that's all right. It doesn't really suit me but I think that's why Joyce bought it. She said it didn't suit me so it would suit you. (*The day nurse comes in. She raises her eyebrows, indicating she thinks he is mad, talking. Midgley coughs.*) They tell you to talk. I read it in *Reader's Digest*. It was in the waiting room.

NURSE. They say the same thing about plants. I think it's got past that stage.

74. Interior. Nurses' home. Valery's room. Day.

They have just had tea.

VALERY. People are funny about nurses. Men. You say you're a nurse, and their whole attitude changes. Do you know what I mean?

MIDGLEY. No.

VALERY. I've noticed it at parties. They ask you what you do, you say you're a nurse, and next minute they're behaving like animals. Perfectly ordinary people. They turn into wild beasts. I've given up saying I'm a nurse for that reason.

MIDGLEY. What do you say you are, medieval historian?

VALERY. No. I say I'm a librarian. But that's why I liked you. You're obviously not like that. (*Midgley is silent.*) Of course you've got other things on your mind.

MIDGLEY. What?

VALERY. He is lovely. Your Dad. I do understand the way you feel about him. Old people have their own particular attraction I think. He does anyway. (*Midgley is restive.*) Was your cake gritty?

MIDGLEY. No.

VALERY. Mine was. Mine was a bit gritty.

MIDGLEY. It was probably meant to be gritty.

VALERY. No. It was more gritty than that.

   Silence.

MIDGLEY. What would you say if I asked you to go to bed?

VALERY. I suppose it's with you being a nurse: they think you've seen everything. When? Now?

MIDGLEY. Yes.

VALERY. I can't now.

MIDGLEY. Why not? You're not on till seven.

VALERY. No. It's Wednesday. I'm on early turn.

MIDGLEY. Tomorrow, then.

VALERY. Tomorrow would be better. Though of course it all depends.

MIDGLEY. What on?

VALERY. Your father. He may not be here tomorrow.

MIDGLEY. No. I'd better go back then.

VALERY. Fingers crossed.

75. Interior. Intensive Care. Father's room. Day.

Dad unconscious still, Midgley whispering in his ear.

MIDGLEY. Hold on, Dad. Hold on.

76. Interior. Hospital. Telephone area. Day.

MIDGLEY. Colin. It's Dad. Is your Mam there?

77. Interior. Midgley's home. Day.

COLIN. She's upstairs with Gran. Mum. Dad wants you.

MRS. MIDGLEY. (*Shouting.*) I can't. I'm bathing your Grandma. I can't leave her.

COLIN. She says she can't leave her.

78. Interior. Hospital. Telephone area. Day.

MIDGLEY. You go up and watch her. I want to speak to your Mam.

79. Interior. Midgley's home. Day.

COLIN. Dad, she's in the bath. She's no clothes on. Dad, I won't.

Mrs Midgley puts her head round the bathroom door.

MRS MIDGLEY. Tell him if I can get a granny sitter I'm going to come over.

COLIN. She says she's going to come over.

80. Interior. Hospital. Telephone area. Day.

MIDGLEY. (*Alarmed.*) No. Don't do that. Tell her not to do that. There's no need. Are you there? Go on, tell her.

81. Interior. Midgley's home. Day.

COLIN. I'll tell her.

82. Interior. Hospital. Telephone area. Day.

MIDGLEY. You won't. You'll forget. Go up and tell her now.

Midgley waits.

83. Interior. Midgley's home. Day.

COLIN. Mum. Dad says there's no need.

MRS MIDGLEY. No need to what?

COLIN. Go over.

84. Interior. Hospital. Telephone area. Day.

MIDGLEY. Did you tell her? Good. Haven't you forgotten something?
'How's Grandad, Dad? Is he any better?' 'Nice of you to ask, Colin.
He's about the same, thank you.'

85. Interior. Midgley's home. Day.

*Colin putting the telephone down wearily, as Mrs Midgley comes in with a
wet towel and a bundle of underclothes.*

MRS MIDGLEY. How was your Grandad?

COLIN. About the same.

MRS MIDGLEY. And your Dad?

COLIN. No change.

86. Exterior. Hospital car park. The van. Day.

Bright sunshine. Midgley asleep. Someone gets into the van.

MIDGLEY. Who's that?

HIS FATHER. Only me.

MIDGLEY. Hello Dad.

FATHER. I thought we'd go for a drive.

They drive off.

MIDGLEY. When did you learn to drive?

FATHER. Just before I died.

MIDGLEY. I never knew that.

FATHER. There's lots of things you don't know.

87. Exterior. Montage. Day.

They are driving along. The scene should change dramatically and inexplicably. Country. Town. Back streets.

FATHER. Isn't that your Mam when she was younger? (*He stops the van and a pretty woman gets in.*) Mam.

MOTHER. Hello Dad. Hello Denis. What a spanking van.

FATHER. Move over, Denis. (*Midgley is suddenly a small boy.*) Let your Mam sit next to me.

They sit in a line and Midgley sees his dad's hand on his mother's knee.

88. Exterior. A field. Day.

Midgley as a boy, is sitting with his mother in a field.

MOTHER. This field is spotless. It's a lovely field. We can sit here all day. Just the two of us.

Midgley, as a boy, has turned round and on the edge of the field, unseen by his mother, is a huge slag heap. He is horrified.

Aren't you glad we brought a flask?

A man is running down the slag heap. The boy is frightened. The man runs through the grass. He is covered in grime. It is his father. His mother is in white.

BOY. Mam. Mam.

She looks round.

MOTHER. It's only your Dad, love.

She smiles and he sits down beside her, his black hand on her white frock.

89. Interior. Leeds market. Day.

Then Midgley and his mother and father, now old, are walking through Leeds market, the place empty, the stalls shuttered and closed.

90. Exterior. Motorway. Day.

The van is driving along a motorway. The turnoffs are marked with the names of places like Leeds, Barnsley, Sheffield. Then they change to Heart Disease, Cancer.

91. Interior. Hospital reception. Station. Day.

His father is sitting down and he is in the reception area of the hospital, but it is also some kind of station. His mother sits beside him. They kiss, and look round, but Midgley is not there.

Above their heads there is a station noticeboard, but instead of arrivals and departures it is marked 'Births and Deaths' and keeps clicking over with different names. She kisses his father goodbye and goes through the gates, just as Midgley comes up. He shakes the gates shouting 'Mam, Mam.' But she has gone. He turns round and looks at his father who is shaking his head. He is disappointed with him.

Midgley shakes the gates again, calling 'Mam, Mam' as it changes to Valery knocking on the window of the van to wake him.

92. Exterior. Hospital. Car park. Day.

He sits up. Valery is tapping on the window. She waves and goes off towards her quarters. Midgley sits thinking.

93. Exterior. Hospital. Car park. Day.

It is later on that day, and the car park is more full. A smart car draws up, driven by a woman. She gets out. She is elegantly dressed, and is in her late fifties or early sixties. She walks towards the hospital.

94. Interior. Father's room. Intensive care. Day.

Midgley comes into his father's room. The woman is sitting there, holding his father's hand. She is unruffled.

ALICE. Is it Denis?

MIDGLEY. Yes.

ALICE. I'm Alice Duckworth. Did he tell you about me?

MIDGLEY. No.

ALICE. No. He wouldn't, the old bugger. He told me about you. Never stopped telling me about you. It's a sad sight. Though that slut of a nurse says he's a bit better this morning. His condition's stabilised, whatever that means. Shouldn't think she knows. You look a bit scruffy. I've come from Southport. (*She gets up and puts the carnations in the bin.*) Carnations are depressing flowers. (*She replaces them with flowers she has brought herself.*) I'm a widow. A rich widow. Shall we have a meander round? No sense in stopping here. His lordship's not got much to contribute.

Alice and Midgley go out through the waiting room.

95. Interior. Waiting room. Day.

Aunty Kitty begins to get up, but Mrs Duckworth walks straight past her. Aunty Kitty follows them out.

96. Interior. Long corridor. Day.

Into the corridor. Mrs Duckworth is walking briskly off, followed by Midgley.

ALICE. That your Aunty Kitty? (*Midgley nods.*) I thought so.

97. Interior. Reception area. Day.

They are having coffee. Alice taking out a flask from her bag.

ALICE. Do you want a drop of this in it?

MIDGLEY. No thanks.

ALICE. I'd better, I've driven from Southport. I wanted to marry your Dad, did you know that? He said no. Why? Because I'd got too much money. My husband left me very nicely placed; he was a leading light in the soft furnishing trade. Your Dad would have felt beholden, you see. That was your Dad all over. Couldn't bear to be under an obligation. Still, you know what he was like.

MIDGLEY. He was good. Everybody says how good he was.

ALICE. He always had to be the one, did Frank. The one who did the good turns, the one who paid out, the one who sacrified. You couldn't do anything for him. I had all this money, he wouldn't even let me take him to Scarborough. We used to go sit in Roundhay Park. Roundhay Park! We could have been in Teneriffe. (*She blows her nose.*) Still, I'd have put up with that.

MIDGLEY. That's why I've been waiting. That's why I wanted to be here. I didn't want to let him down. And he wants me to let him down, I know.

98. Interior. Hospital. Long corridor. Day.

ALICE. What was your Mam like?

MIDGLEY. She was lovely.

ALICE. She must have had him taped. She looks a grand woman. He's showed me photographs. (*She makes herself up.*) Anyroads. I'll go and have another look at him. Then I've got to get over to a Round Table in Harrogate. Killed two birds with one stone for me, has this trip.

MIDGLEY. You don't know. If he comes round he might reconsider your offer.

She looks at Midgley and smiles, then gives him a kiss.

ALICE. And don't you be like your Dad, think on. You go your own way.

99. Interior. Waiting room. Intensive Care. Day.

AUNTY KITTY. Your Mother'd not been dead a year. I was shocked.

MIDGLEY. I'm not shocked.

AUNTY KITTY. You're a man. It wasn't like your Dad. She's got a cheek showing her face.

MIDGLEY. I'm rather pleased.

AUNTY KITTY. And her hair's dyed. A real common woman. Anyway they're sending him downstairs tomorrow. He must be on the mend. I'll not stop much longer. I hope when he does come round he's not a vegetable. Where are you going?

MIDGLEY. I said I'd see someone.

Aunty Kitty is left in the waiting room. A woman comes in from the ward.

AUNTY KITTY. How's your hubby? Still in a coma? (*She shakes her head in mute sympathy.*) There must be a purpose somewhere.

She pops a toffee in her mouth.

100. Interior. Valery's room. Day.

Midgley is brushing his teeth, out of the room.

VALERY. Maureen knows to ring if anything happens. Not that it will. His chest is better. His heart is better. He's simply unconscious now. I'm looking forward to him coming round. I long to know what his voice is like.

101. Interior. Valery's bathroom. Day.

Midgley in the bathroom. Midgley turns the tap off.

MIDGLEY. What?

VALERY. I long to know what his voice is like?

MIDGLEY. Oh. Yes.

He turns the tap on again.

102. Interior. Valery's room. Day.

VALERY. I think I know. I'd just like to have it confirmed. (*Midgley comes in.*) You don't like talking about your Father, do you? (*She is undressing.*) Nice shirt.

MIDGLEY. Yes. One of Dad's.

VALERY. Nice.

He goes to the bathroom and we see her take the telephone off the hook. Midgley gets into bed. She is already in bed.

MIDGLEY. Hello. (*Pause.*) It's a bit daft is this.

VALERY. Why? It happens all the time.

MIDGLEY. It's what people call living, is this. We're living. (*They kiss.*) I ought to have done more of this.

VALERY. What?

MIDGLEY. Living. This is going to be the rule from now on. I've got a lot of catching up to do. This, it's the thin end of the wedge.

VALERY. I've never heard it called that before.

MIDGLEY. Dirty bugger.

VALERY. You started it. 'What would you say if I said could we go to bed.' I mean.

MIDGLEY. That's technique, that is. It avoids direct confrontation.

VALERY. I think I could do with some confrontation.

MIDGLEY. You've done this before. Hey, stop. I hope this isn't one of those private beds. It's not BUPA is it, this? Otherwise I may have to leave. I'm opposed to that on principle.

VALERY. People do talk rubbish in bed.

MIDGLEY. Only place left. Only place where you can act daft. Not that we do. Mrs Midgley and me. If Joyce ever does anything fresh I know it's because she's been listening to some rubbish on *Woman's Hour*.

VALERY. You never asked me if I was married.

MIDGLEY. You're a nurse. You're above marriage. (*Pause.*) Are you married?

VALERY. He's on an oil rig.

MIDGLEY. I bloody hope so.

Midgley takes off his glasses and the scene fades out.

The same. Later.

MIDGLEY. I feel better after that, Nurse. (*Valery lights a cigarette.*) Can I have one of those?

VALERY. You don't smoke.

MIDGLEY. I don't do this, either. (*He lights a cigarette.*) I'm in bed in the afternoon, smoking a cigarette with another woman, post coitally. (*Pause.*) I was certain they were going to ring.

VALERY. No.

She smiles, shows him the receiver is off, and puts it back on. He frowns, then smiles.

MIDGLEY. That was a risk. Still, we are now going to be taking risks. The new, risky life of D. Midgley. Do you think I ought to be getting back?

VALERY. We've still got half an hour.

MIDGLEY. Hey, you're insatiable, you.

VALERY. I know.

They put out their cigarettes and are just settling down again when the telephone rings.

VALERY. Yes? Yes. (*She is looking at Midgley as she is speaking.*) You'd better go.

MIDGLEY. What's matter?

VALERY. Go.

MIDGLEY. Had she been trying before?

VALERY. You'd better go.

MIDGLEY. (*Frantic.*) Had she been trying?

VALERY. *Go.*

MIDGLEY. Where's my glasses?

103. Interior. Hospital. The corridor. Day.

Doors burst open and Midgley runs down.

104. Interior. Intensive Care. Father's room. Day.

Aunty Kitty, Mrs Midgley, Midgley.

AUNTY KITTY. It's the biggest wonder I hadn't popped into see Mrs Tunnicliffe. She's over in Ward Seven having a plastic hip – she's been waiting two years – but, I don't know what it was, something made me come back upstairs and I was sat looking at some reading matter when in walks Joyce, and we'd hardly had time to say hello when the nurse comes running out to say he had his eyes open. So we were both there, weren't we, Joyce?

MRS MIDGLEY. He just said, 'Is our Denis here?'

AUNTY KIRRY. And I said, 'He's coming, Frank. It's me, Kitty'. And he just smiled a little smile and it was all over. It was a beautiful way to go. I'm glad I was here to see it. I was his only sister. (*Pause.*) The dots do something different when you're dying. I wasn't watching it, naturally, but out of the corner of my eye I noticed it was doing something different during his last moments.

MRS MIDGLEY. He's smiling.

The body lies on the bed, sheet up to the neck. Midgley goes to the window.

MIDGLEY. Of course he's smiling. He's won. He's scored. In the last minute of extra time.

Mrs Midgley looks disgusted. Porters appear to transfer the body onto a trolley. Mrs Midgley goes out.

AUNTY KITTY. It's a pity you weren't here, Denis. You've been here all the time he was dying. What were you doing?

MIDGLEY. Living.

105. Exterior. Father's room. Intensive Care. Day.

They are coming out. Valery is there. Midgley looks, but says nothing.

AUNTY KITTY. He just said 'Is our Denis here?' then smiled that little smile, and it was all over.

106. Interior. Hospital office. Day

A counter. Hospital administrator, going through a form. Dad's folded clothes on the counter.

HOSPITAL ADMINISTRATOR. One gunmetal watch. Wallet with senior citizen's bus pass. Seventy four and a half pence in change. One doorkey.

He pushes the form over for Midgley to sign.

MIDGLEY. Have you something I can put them in?

HOSPITAL ADMINISTRATOR. They never bring bags. It's not our job, you know, bags.

In the wallet there is a photograph of Midgley and his mother, when younger, stood together laughing. He looks at this while the man roots about for a bag.

107. Interior. Midgley's home. Kitchen. Night.

Midgley sat at the kitchen table. Mrs Midgley sat at the table. Both still in overcoats.

MRS MIDGLEY. You didn't let him down. You went for a walk. That's not letting him down.

MIDGLEY. I wasn't there.

Colin comes in with a girlfriend.

COLIN. Hello, Dad. Long time no see. (*Midgley doesn't respond.*) Did Grandad die?

MRS MIDGLEY. This afternoon.

COLIN. Oh. Jane's just going to have some coffee.

MRS MIDGLEY. Take her in the other room. (*They go out. She calls:*) Put the fire on.

She pours out the coffee.

108. Interior. Midgley's home. Hall. Night.

Midgley goes out of the kitchen and is about to go upstairs when he sees the sitting room door ajar. He pushes it open. Colin is kissing the girl. He watches for a second.

MIDGLEY. We've just lost your Grandad. You might show some feeling.

Mrs Midgley appears behind him with the coffee as Midgley goes.

MRS MIDGLEY. Take no notice. He's upset. There's nothing to be ashamed of. It's only your Father.

She smiles sweetly.

109. Interior. Midgley's school. Miss Tunstall's office. Day.

Miss Tunstall is typing.

MISS TUNSTALL. Well, at least he didn't suffer.

MIDGLEY. Oh no.

She stops typing and reaches for her cigarettes.

MISS TUNSTALL. When my mother finally pulls her socks up and dies I'm going to go on a world cruise.

MIDGLEY. (*Reaching for a cigarette.*) May I?

MISS TUNSTALL. I didn't know you smoked.

MIDGLEY. I thought I might start.

MISS TUNSTALL. Bit late in the day.

MIDGLEY. What's this?

He reaches over and takes the notice she is copying.

MISS TUNSTALL. It's one of his 'privilege not a right' notices.

MIDGLEY. (*Reading.*) 'Pupils are reminded that coming to school in their own cars is a privilege, not a right. There have been several unsavoury incidents recently . . .' I like 'unsavoury'. ' . . . of pupils resorting to their cars in the lunch hour to indulge in sexual intercourse.'

Miss Tunstall hurriedly retrieves the notice to check this is just Midgley's joke.

MISS TUNSTALL. 'Immoral behaviour.'

MIDGLEY. 'Immoral behaviour.' Where are you going to go on this world cruise?

Miss Tunstall shrugs and starts typing again.

MISS TUNSTALL. Bridlington, I expect.

110. Interior. Midgley's School. Long Corridor. Late afternoon.

Midgley walks down the long corridor. He is in his overcoat and carrying his briefcase. A small boy is looking out of the window. Midgley walks on down the corridor.

111. Interior. Hospital. Long corridor. Night.

The double doors and long corridor at the hospital, the credits over.

An Englishman Abroad

GUY BURGESS   Alan Bates
CORAL   Coral Browne
CLAUDIUS   Charles Gray
ROSENCRANTZ   Harold Innocent
GUILDENSTERN   Vernon Dobtcheff
GENERAL   Czeslaw Grocholski
THE BOY   Matthew Sim
HAMLET   Mark Wing-Davey
HOTEL RECEPTIONIST   Faina Zinova
TOBY   Douglas Reith
GILES   Peter Chelsom
TESSA   Judy Gridley
SCARF MAN   Bibs Ekkel
TOLYA   Alexei Jawdokimov
MRS BURGESS   Molly Veness
TAILOR   Denys Hawthorne
SHOE SHOP ASSISTANT   Roger Hammond
GEORGE   Charles Lamb
PYJAMA SHOP MANAGER   Trevor Baxter

Produced by Innes Lloyd
Directed by John Schlesinger
Designed by Stuart Walker
Music by George Fenton

A few years ago a stage play of mine, *The Old Country* was running in
the West End. The central character, Hilary, played then by Alec
Guinness, is an embittered, ironic figure living in the depths of the
country. Visitors arrive, and in a small *coup de théâtre* halfway through
the first act the audience suddenly realise that the country is Russia.
Hilary is a traitor, a former Foreign Office official now in exile. At the
end of the play he is induced to return home and face the music.

The play had some success, with Hilary being understandably, though
to my mind mistakenly, identified as Philby. Indeed soon after the play
opened the *Daily Telegraph* correspondent in Moscow found himself
sitting next to Philby at the opera and mentioned the play. The spy said
he'd been told about it, but that it didn't sound at all like him. This
wasn't surprising since, if I'd had anybody in mind when writing the
play it was not Philby but W. H. Auden; the play seeming to me to be
about exile, a subject that does interest me, rather than espionage, which
interests me not a bit. Still, Philby or Auden, the play ran and who was
I to complain? It should perhaps be said that this was a couple of years
before the unmasking of Professor Blunt and the great spy boom.

During the run of *The Old Country*, as happens, friends and well-
wishers would come round after the performance to greet Alec
Guinness, often with personal reminiscences of Philby and of his
predecessors, Burgess and Maclean. Hints would be dropped as to the
identity of spies still ensconced in the upper reaches of the Foreign
Office or the Diplomatic, and when I next dropped into the theatre I
would be given a précis of these titbits, though necessarily at second
hand. I remember feeling rather out of it; I may not be interested in
espionage but I am a glutton for gossip.

Happily, I did get to hear one story at first hand. Coral Browne came
to the play and afterwards Alec Guinness took us both out to supper at
the Mirabelle. I mention the restaurant only because the mixture of
Moscow drabness and London *luxe* was a part of the telling of the tale,
as it is a part of the tale told. It was over a meal very like the one that
concludes *An Englishman Abroad* that Coral told me of her visit to
Russia with the Stratford Company in 1958, and the particular incidents
that make up this play.

The picture of the elegant actress and the seedy exile sitting in a dingy
Moscow flat through a long afternoon listening again and again to Jack
Buchanan singing 'Who stole my heart away?' seemed to me funny and
sad, but it was a few years before I got round to writing it up. It was
only when I sent the first draft to Coral Browne that I found she had
kept not merely Burgess's letters, thanking her for running him errands,
but also her original notes of his measurements and even his cheque

(uncashed and for £6) to treat her and one of her fellow-actors to lunch at the Caprice.

I have made use of Burgess's letters in the play but another extract deserves quoting in full. His first letter, dated Easter Sunday, 1959, begins: 'This is a very suitable day to be writing to you, since I also was born on it . . . sprung from the womb on April 16 1911 . . . to the later horror of the Establishment of the country concerned.' Coral had apparently urged him to visit Paul Robeson when the singer visited Moscow: 'In spite of your suggestion and invitation to visit Paul Robeson, I found myself too shy to call on him. You may find this surprising, but I always am with great men and artists such as him. Not so much shy as frightened. The *agonies* I remember on *first* meeting with people I really admire, e.g. E. M. Forster (and Picasso and Winston Churchill, but not W. S. Maugham).' There is some irony in these remarks, particularly with regard to Paul Robeson, when one recalls a quip of Burgess's in happier days. When he was sent to Washington as Second Secretary at the British Embassy his former boss, Hector McNeil, warned Burgess to remember three things: not to be too openly left-wing, not to get involved in race relations and above all not to get mixed up in any homosexual incidents. 'I understand, Hector,' said Burgess. 'What you mean is that I mustn't make a pass at Paul Robeson.'

I have put some of my own sentiments into Burgess's mouth. 'I can say I love London. I can say I love England. I can't say I love my country, because I don't know what that means,' is a fair statement of my own, and I imagine many people's, position. The Falklands War helped me to understand how a fastidious stepping-aside from patriotism could be an element in the make up of characters as different as Burgess and Blunt. Certainly in the spy fever that followed the unmasking of Professor Blunt I felt more sympathy with the hunted than the hunters. In the play it is suggested that Burgess was a spy because he wanted a place where he was alone, and that having a secret supplies this. I believe this to be psychologically true, but there is a sense too that an ironic attitude towards one's country and a scepticism about one's heritage is a part of that heritage. And so, by extension, is the decision to betray it. It is irony activated.

In his essay 'The Well of Narcissus' Auden imagines Narcissus not as young and beautiful but as fat and middle-aged. Drunk, he gazes at himself in the glass, and says, 'I shouldn't look at me like that if I were you. I suppose you think you know who I am. Well, let me tell *you*, my dear, that one of these days you're going to get a very big surprise *indeed*!' That seems a fair description of Burgess's character and one not unfamiliar to the people among whom he was to end up. 'He exemplified that favourite type in the classical Russian novel, the buffoon; the man always playing the fool, not only for his own amusement love of exhibitionism, but also with the object of keeping everyone in the dark as to his own inner views and intentions.' Not Burgess, but the poet Yevtushenko as described by Anthony Powell.

In the play Burgess says, 'I lack what the English call character, by which they mean the power to refrain.' The remark was actually made by the Oxford aesthete, Brian Howard. The contradictions in the Cambridge Burgess turned him to treachery, the Oxford Howard to art. Howard's drunken, outrageous behaviour flouted convention much as Burgess's did, but with a conventional excuse: he was a failed writer. Burgess had no ambitions in that department and, diplomacy being a less crowded field than literature, his failure turned out more of a success. As a second-rate poet or novelist, not a Second Secretary at the Washington Embassy, Burgess would have seemed, if not commonplace, at any rate not unfamiliar. He would also have been much easier to forget.

So far as the general issues in the play are concerned, I find it hard to drum up any patriotic indignation over Burgess (or any of the so-called Cambridge spies for that matter). No one has ever shown that Burgess did much harm, except to make fools of people in high places. Because he made jokes, scenes and most of all passes (though not at Paul Robeson), the general consensus is that he was rather silly. It's paradoxical that Philby is thought of as a more respectable figure, because more serious (no jokes); though that seriousness consisted in handing over agents to torture and death.

Auden's name keeps coming up. Burgess wasn't a close friend, but the night before he left the country in May 1951, and before it became plain that he would have to go the whole hog and accompany Maclean, Burgess thought of lying low with Auden on Ischia. There would have been a nice appropriateness in this, secret agents and sudden flight being potent elements in Auden's poetic myth ('Leave for Cape Wrath to-night'). However, the projected visit didn't come off. On the crucial evening Auden, then staying with Stephen Spender failed (or forgot) to return Burgess's call. And this omission was also appropriate. Auden's poetry in the 30s often sounded like a blueprint for political action, but set against subsequent events some of his verse rang hollow. Or so Auden began to think while in America during the war. Burgess 'running naked through Europe' and turning up on Ischia would have been like a parody of early Auden, a reminder of a poetic past, some of which Auden was anxious to forget, or at any rate re-edit. Burgess on

Ischia would have been an artistic as much as a social embarrassment. Though that too would make a nice play.

I have taken a few liberties with the facts as Coral Browne told them to me. The scene in the British Embassy, for instance, did not occur; but since the Old Vic Company were warned by the British ambassador to 'shy away from that traitor Burgess, who's always trying to get back to England' it seemed no great liberty.

I hardly need to add how much in the preparation of the play I have been indebted to Coral Browne and also to John Schlesinger.

Unlike the other scripts printed here, that of *An Englishman Abroad* is as it was originally submitted to the BBC. It lacks scene numbers and headings, and the directions are general, not particular to any shot or scene. I have left it in this first state partly because, at the time of going to press, the play had not yet been filmed, but also to show the form in which all the other scripts were originally submitted.

A second printing of this book after *An Englishman Abroad* has been broadcast allows me to add a few more notes. When I wrote the script I had no idea where it would be filmed, and while I included some exterior shots I kept them to a minimum, thinking that, without going abroad, Moscow-like settings would be hard to find. In the event the film's designer, Stuart Walker, came up with some very convincing locations in Glasgow and Dundee, enabling John Schlesinger to open up the film and include many more exteriors. We see the outside of the theatre (Caird Hall, Dundee), the front of the British Embassy (back of Glasgow Town Hall), and the final shot of the film, vaguely described by me as 'Moscow streets', has Burgess strolling in his new togs across the Suspension Bridge in Glasgow, luckily in a snowstorm.

Searching for locations educates the eye. The Suspension Bridge on Clydeside doesn't look particularly Russian in itself. What makes it seem authentic is a long Georgian building on the far bank of the river, which is in the very back of the shot. This building happens to have been painted in two shades of pink in a way that maybe looks more like Leningrad than Moscow, but which certainly suggests Eastern Europe. The exterior of Burgess's flat was filmed at Moss heights in Glasgow, an early post-war block of flats, and the interior built in the small concert room at the Caird Hall. The magnificent marble staircase of the British Embassy is in Glasgow Town Hall, but when Coral Browne leaves the two young diplomats and goes down the staircase she travels five hundred miles between frames, as the room in the Embassy is actually at Polesden Lacey in Surrey.

Odd lines were put in. 'It's strange' says Coral as she and Burgess walk past a military-looking establishment with soldiers parading, 'Sybil Thorndyke *loved* it'. That building is Dundee High School. A more poignant exchange occurs as they are leaving Burgess's flat and he casually enquires whether she had known Jack Buchanan, whose record he has been playing her. 'Yes,' says Coral. 'We nearly got married.' Burgess gives her a second look, not sure that she isn't pulling his leg. She isn't. It had come out casually in conversation with Coral just before we started filming. Slipped in right at the end of the sequence it focuses what has gone before, both of them listening to a record that to Burgess means something very general and to Coral someone very particular. Its the kind of coincidence which, had it been invented, would have seemed sentimental.

It was pointed out, appropriately in the *Daily Express*, that it was not in Coral's dressing room that Burgess was sick, but in that of Michael Redgrave next door. This is true and was part of the story as Coral originally told it to me, Redgrave having called her in to help clean up an Englishman who was being sick in his room, but without introducing him. In an article about the Moscow visit in *The Observer* in 1959 Regrave mentions Burgess coming round, but does not mention him being ill. The kernel of our film is the meeting in the flat and, wanting to centre the story on Coral and leave Hamlet out of it as far as possible, I transferred the incident entirely to her dressing room. When Sir Michael's autobiography, *In My Mind's Eye*, came out in 1983 after the film had been made he recalls the incident as it actually happened, which might suggest that Coral had plagiarised the story. She hadn't. I had rearranged it for dramatic reasons.

There was only one point in the interpretation of the script where John Schlesinger and I differed and that was at the conclusion of the scene in the pyjama shop. Snobbish though I'd made the salesman, I felt he did have a point and that the balance of the scene ought in the end to go his way. When he revealed that the shop was Hungarian I wanted the tone of the scene to change and for it suddenly to cease to be about snobbery and reveal real issues. The film is set after all in 1958, only two years after the Hungarian uprising. John felt that an audience would not grasp this. We argued and left it open until the last moment when I deferred and gave the scene a jokier ending. On reflection I still think I was right and that those Mayfair scenes should end on a sourer note. But it was an amicable disagreement and our only one on what to make was a very enjoyable film.

Opening sequence.

A Soviet poster or banner fills the screen. It is a medallion of a bust of Stalin against a red background. Over this is played a record of Jack Buchanan singing 'Who stole my heart away?'. Mix through to busts of Stalin, Marx and Lenin adorning the front of a public building. Then to those of literary figures . . . Shakespeare, Tolstoy, Dante, etc. on the same building: it is a theatre.

Mix through to a further bust, as monumental as the rest, that of an impassive usherette stationed outside the main doors of the theatre auditorium. A play is in progress. We cut to the auditorium. It is Hamlet, *Act Two, scene 2.*

The stage of a large theatre.

CLAUDIUS.   . . . Something have you heard
    Of Hamlet's transformation; so I call it,
    Sith nor th'exterior nor the inward man
    Resembles that it was. What it should be,
    More than his father's death, that thus hath put him
    So much from th' understanding of himself,
    I cannot dream of. I entreat you both,
    That being of so young days brought up with him,
    And sith so neighboured to his youth and haviour,
    That you vouchsafe your rest here in our Court
    Some little time, so by your companies
    To draw him on to pleasures, and to gather
    So much as from occasion you may glean,
    Whether aught to us unknown afflicts him thus
    That opened lies within our remedy.

Claudius and Gertrude are talking to Rosencrantz and Guildenstern. During the speech, which should be shot fairly full close-up, with make-up, wig lines etc. pretty obvious, we cut away to a small section of the audience, all intent on the play except for one middle-aged man in a battered navy pinstripe suit and wearing an Old Etonian tie. He may be drunk and is certainly sleepy. His head keeps lolling onto the shoulder of the plump, plain woman beside him. To her intense distaste.

GERTRUDE. Good gentlemen, he hath much talked of you,
    And sure I am, two men there is not living
    To whom he more adheres. If it will please you

To show us so much gentry and good will
As to expend your time with us awhile,
For the supply and profit of our hope,
Your visitation shall receive such thanks
As fits a King's remembrance.

*During this speech we have again cut back to the audience, cued by
Gertrude being distracted and distanced from her role by a small
disturbance in the stalls.*

*The Englishman in the pinstripe suit is Guy Burgess. He wakes up and
lurches to his feet, stumbling over his two neighbours towards the aisle. He
is slightly drunk.*

BURGESS. You will excuse me, madam. I must pay a call of nature. A
piss, madam. I must piss.

*The solid neighbours around Burgess are put out, but do not protest.
Other high-ranking generals and officals register his departure by
determinedly ignoring it. But the disturbance has reached the stage.*

Stage.

GERTRUDE. (*Played by Coral Browne: aside*). One bugger's just walking
out. Charming.

Auditorium.

Burgess stumbles up the aisle. He pauses at the door.

BURGESS. What a pleasure in this day and age to hear the language so
beautifully spoken. I'm not walking out. I just have to go for a piss. (*To
an impassive usherette.*)

*Burgess continues through the theatre corridor and foyer, occasionally
explaining his mission to other impassive ladies.*

BURGESS. Wet my whistle. (*He descends a grand staircase, announcing:*)
Going to the Excuse Me.

*At the foot of the staircase a boy of about sixteen in an awkward suit
appears at a doorway and watches him, as he finds the door of the
lavatory and goes in.*

Theatre lavatory.

A large and ornate room. Burgess has a pee, which take a long time. He starts singing:

BURGESS. O God, our help in ages past,
    Our hope for years to come,
    Our shelter from the stormy blast
    And our eternal home.

As he is singing, the door opens slowly. Burgess notices this in the mirror, but goes on singing. The feeling should be that, though drunk, there is a part of him that remains watchful and alert. However, it is only another massive female attendant. He finishes. Buttons up his fly with some difficulty (some of the buttons are missing), then goes across to the washbasins.

BURGESS. No soap. Never any soap. Why? But answer came there none. (*This obviously excuses him from washing, and he goes towards the door. He stops by the woman attendant.*) Do I want to be sick? (*He considers.*) No. Not yet. You know, you remind me very much of a stoker I once knew.

There is no response. He comes out into the foyer.

Foyer

As Burgess comes out there is the sound of distant applause, and the attendants all stand up expectantly. Burgess heads for the main doors, and we hold on the doors as, a moment later, the boy in the awkward suit follows.

Stage door.

I imagine this not like the stage doors of an English theatre. Double doors, perhaps, and more like the entrance to an old-fashioned block of flats. Another attendant is sitting there. She too is carved out of granite. Burgess is arguing with her.

BURGESS. Dear lady, I do assure you. One is an old chum of the leading actor. We were at Cambridge together. They've come such a long way. One must just put one's head round the door. (*She puts out her hand.*) My pass? (*He begins to search through the pockets of his untidy but well-cut suit.*) My pass. My pass. (*She watches impassively.*) I'm sure I'm not the first to remark on your pronounced resemblance to the late Ernest

Bevin. You could be *sisters.* (*He produces a battered pass and hands it to her. She looks at it, and then at him.*) I know. It's a shocking likeness, but quite amusing. One looks such a tremendous villain. But then, I suppose one is. Oh, do hurry, woman. One is not feeling at all well.

She presses something. The door opens and he rushes in. Cut to:

Other side of the door.

Burgess has just rushed through. The door is stopped by a hand just before it closes, and pushed open again by the youth in the awkward suit, who comes through. He needs no pass.

A Corridor.

Burgess lurches along it. He passes actors in costume. Tries to look at the names on the door, but he is obviously not feeling at all well. Eventually he just opens the nearest door and rushes in.

Coral Browne's Dressing Room.

Coral, who plays Gertrude, is sitting there smoking. Burgess bursts through the door.

BURGESS. The drink! The drink! It is the drink!

He throws up in the basin while we hold on Coral's aghast face. Cut to:

Corridor Outside.
The boy is walking down it, not sure where Burgess has gone. He listens at various doors.

Inside Dressing Room.

Burgess is kneeling at the basin, moaning.

CORAL. Aren't you feeling well?

Burgess slowly gets to his feet and turns round.

BURGESS. Thank you. I'm perfectly all right.

He then hurriedly turns round and is sick again.

CORAL I'll get the woman. (*She opens the door, and nearly falls over the boy, who is on his hands and knees at the keyhole. Startled, she closes the door rapidly.*) I am in a French farce. It's Feydeau. Run the tap, for God's sake. (*Burgess does so, then washes.*) I wouldn't care, but it's only the interval. If you want to come round and be sick you might at least save it for the end of the performance.

BURGESS. Pear's soap. Mmmm.

He then dries himself. On her towel.

CORAL. Who are you? Who is that boy outside?

Burgess, still drying himself, goes to the door, opens it and looks down imperturbably at the youth, who is still on his knees. Then he closes the door in his face again.

BURGESS. Don't know. Haven't seen that one before. Could I have one of these? (*He takes a cigarette.*) Love your frock.

CORAL. You're very rude. Are you from the Embassy?

BURGESS. Not exactly.

CORAL. There can't be many other Englishmen in Moscow. Who are you?

BURGESS. I was at Cambridge with Hamlet.

CORAL. Well, why don't we tell him you're here? He's only down the corridor.

Burgess bars the way.

BURGESS. All in good time. The question is, you see: are we as welcome as ever?

CORAL. I know your face.

BURGESS. Craven A. For your throat's sake. Mmmm.

CORAL. Are you enjoying the play?

BURGESS. Adoring it. I like the look of Laertes. He goes rather well into tights.

CORAL. Yes. That's what he thinks.

BURGESS. He looks as if he's put a couple of King Edwards down there. How do you like Moscow?

CORAL. Loathe it. I cannot understand what those three sisters were on about. It gives the play a very sinister slant.

A call boy knocks at the door (Russian or English? I don't know.)

BURGESS. A Scotch would help.

CORAL. Haven't you had enough? (*She gets him one nevertheless.*) If you're not at the Embassy what do you do?

BURGESS. Liaise.

CORAL. Press?

BURGESS. Sort of.

CORAL. You're not feeling sick again?

BURGESS. I think I am, rather.

CORAL. Oh God.

BURGESS. One of the few lessons I have learned in life is that when one is sick it is always in threes. (*A second call at the door:* Miss Browne.) Yes. Here it comes.

CORAL. Don't panic. (*She rapidly clears her clothes and articles to a safe distance from the basin, at which Burgess is now kneeling.*) I'll send somebody in. I must go. But do try and feel better, and go home.

She leaves him, his head laid against the edge of the basin. As she leaves, Burgess straightens up. He is obviously perfectly well. He looks round the room. Smells the soap deeply as he checks what's on the dressing table. He lights another cigarette and puts the whole packet in his pocket. Takes a drink of Scotch from the bottle and nicks that too. He sits down at the dressing table and looks at himself in the mirror. He puts on some of Coral's make-up.

Corridor.

Burgess comes out of Coral's room. He goes down the corridor looking at names on the doors. As he does so he nearly bumps into Claudius who is hurrying along, late for his call.

CLAUDIUS. Sorry, my fault, my fault.

BURGESS. (*In Russian.*) Not at all.

As Claudius goes on he suddenly stops and does a take, looks back down the corridor towards where Burgess is lumbering towards the stage door. Claudius is plainly in two minds whether to go after him. Maybe he even says 'Guy?', but he is late for his call and has to rush on towards the stage.

Wings.

Coral is talking to another actor.

CORAL. Haven't the faintest idea. Came in. Threw up in the basin. It was like being back in Australia. (*Claudius slips in ahead of her, out of breath.*) Cutting it fine, darling.

CLAUDIUS. (*Taking her hand ready to make a ceremonial entrance.*) Guess who I've just seen. Coming down the corridor. Guy Burgess.

CORAL. Who?

CLAUDIUS. Guy Burgess, dear. The spy. The missing diplomat.

They make their entrance.

CLAUDIUS. What Gertrude? How does Hamlet?

Coral has dried. Claudius looks at her. We hear the prompter's voice:

PROMPTER. Mad as the seas and wind when . . .

GERTRUDE. (*Recovering.*) Mad as the seas and wind when both contend
Which is the mightier: in this lawless fit
Behind the arras, hearing something stir,
He whips out a rapier, cries, 'A rat, a rat,'
And in his brainish apprehension kills
The unseen good old man.

Auditorium.

A shot of Burgess's seat in the stalls. Empty.

Empty Corridor. Backstage.

Distant applause. Applause ends. Hamlet comes along down the corridor and goes into his dressing room. Then Coral and Claudius, Coral carrying a bouquet. Laertes passes them and Claudius waits until he is out of earshot before he speaks.

CLAUDIUS. Mum must be the word. Truly.

CORAL. Why?

CLAUDIUS. We don't want anyone ringing the *Express*. He's got fatter.

CORAL. You knew him?

CLAUDIUS. Oh. I used to run across him years ago, the way one did, you know.

CORAL. Of course, you're rather that way, aren't you?

CLAUDIUS. What way?

CORAL. Left.

CLAUDIUS. I was. Everyone was in those days.

CORAL. I liked him. For all he was sick in my basin. Bags of charm. But you're right. I wouldn't set the *Express* on my worst enemy. Drink? (*She goes into her dressing-room as Claudius lingers in the doorway.*) It's gone. My drink. (*She looks round.*) My ciggies. My soap. Oh, darling. The rotter.

CLAUDIUS. Bags of charm.

Hotel Metropole, Moscow. Night.

Coral comes up the vast, empty stairs, along the broad corridor towards her room. She is with one of her fellow actors. A woman attendant, like those in the theatre, sits at the end of the corridor.

ACTOR. If it's like mine, it's vast. Let's see.

Coral opens the door of her room and they go in. It is ridiculously grand. Vast, pelmeted curtains. Grand doors. A huge bed.

CORAL. I feel as if I'm in *King's Rhapsody*. It's all too Ivor Novello for words. (*She goes to the window, puts one hand on the curtain, and sings:*) 'I can give you the starlight, I can give you the moon . . .'

This is interrupted by a thunderous knocking at the door. The actor opens it. It is the attendant. She is gabbling in Russian. She points at the actor and shakes her head.

ACTOR. What's the matter?

CORAL. I think what Flora is saying, dear, is that no men are allowed in the room.

ACTOR. Why not? It is a ludicrous country. Good night.

He leaves, and Coral closes the door and goes into the bathroom. There is a small sound. She comes back in a bathrobe. There is an envelope on the mat by the door. Coral picks it up, opens it and reads it. She opens the door. Looks down the corridor. There is just the blank-faced attendant.

CORAL. Who came? (*Silence.*) Who came? (*Nothing.*)

Coral and the woman stare at one another for a moment, and then Coral closes the door.

Hotel Lobby. Reception Desk. Next Morning.

The Receptionist is looking at Coral blankly.

CORAL. (*Crossly.*) Well somebody must be able to tell me how to get there.

She has the note in her hand. Claudius comes up.

CLAUDIUS. Problems?

CORAL. No. No. (*She puts the note in her pocket.*) I thought I might pop across and see Comrade Lenin and Comrade Stalin sleeping the sleep of the just.

CLAUDIUS. I'll come.

CORAL. No, darling. On such occasions one wants to be alone.

She sweeps elegantly away, leaving Claudius looking after her.

Theatre.

It is empty. A cleaner is swabbing the steps. Coral goes to her dressing room and takes down one of her costumes. She deliberately, though with some difficulty, makes a large rip in the skirt.

Theatre. Wardrobe.

The wardrobe master is there with Laertes, sewing up a split in Laertes' tights. While the wardrobe master chatters, we see Coral purloin a tape-measure.

WARDROBE MASTER. I said to him, 'I don't like foreigners. I never have liked foreigners. I'm not ashamed of it. It's simply a matter of taste. After all, some people don't like Bette Davis. (*He looks at the tear in Coral's dress.*) How did you do this, dear?

CORAL. Acting.

WARDROBE MASTER. Over-acting, if you ask me. Leave it with me, dear.

Theatre. Stage Door.

Coral is showing the note she has received to the stage doorkeeper.

CORAL. Where?

The doorkeeper shrugs and says nothing.

Street.

Coral asks a policeman. The same result.

The British Embassy. Day.

A vast, ornate room, sparsely furnished and with bits of furniture inappropriate to the setting. A filing cabinet here; a utility desk there. In a corner, away from the main action, a girl is typing. Coral is talking to two upper-class young men, one thin, named Giles, the other plump, named Toby. There has obviously been some conversation. Coral has the note in her hand.

TOBY. (*Looking at the room.*) The place was built for somebody's fancy woman around the turn of the century. Shows, too.

Pause.

CORAL. (*Looking out of the window.*) What do you *do* here? I should die.

GILES. No. No. Lots and lots to do. We play table tennis. Ping pong. We have a tournament. I'm rather interestingly placed at the moment. I'm playing the winner of Siddall versus Gittins.

TOBY. You'll be slaughtered. He'll be slaughtered. And of course if you like paintings, that takes care of the afternoons. The Impressionists are staggering.

CORAL. I should die.

GILES. No. Some of the Americans, for example, are delightful. All right, Tessa? (*To Coral.*) Tessa is cross with us today. (*Tessa glances at them across the vast room, without ceasing to type.*) It beats school, I can tell you.

TOBY. Giles is a Marlburian. You see, we couldn't let you go wandering down any old street. You're our responsibility.

CORAL. I just want to know where the place is. How do I get there? I thought that was what embassies were for.

TOBY. You have to remember the gentleman in question was a spy. I believe he still holds a British passport, so technically he is still a British subject, but we have no obligations towards him. In England he would be languishing in gaol.

GILES. He's rather languishing here, actually.

TOBY. (*Looking at the note.*) 'Bring a tape measure.' Bring a tape measure.

CORAL. Mr Burgess has asked me to lunch.

TOBY. With a tape measure?

GILES. Watching his waistline.

CORAL. You can't stop me going to lunch. It's a free country. Or rather, it isn't.

GILES. Have lunch here. Tuesday: Kedgeree. Delicious! (*Calling.*) Tuesday, Tessa! Kedgeree. Tessa doesn't think we take her seriously.

Toby plays with the Venetian blinds, so that the light changes on their faces.

TOBY. Was he a chum of yours?

CORAL. He popped by my dressing room last night and threw up in the basin. it was our first meeting.

GILES. How Brideshead!

TOBY. You've never had any contact with him before?

CORAL. No.

TOBY. You didn't meet him when he was at the Foreign Office?

CORAL. No.

TOBY. Or the BBC?

CORAL. No.

TOBY. What about Maclean?

CORAL. No.

GILES. Odd he should come into your dressing room.

CORAL. It's understandable he should want to hear an English voice, isn't it?

TOBY. Quite. Except ladies aren't exactly his line.

CORAL. Are they yours?

GILES. Of course, if all he wanted was to be sick, that would figure.

CORAL. He was coming round to see one of the actors.

TOBY. Which one?

CORAL. No idea.

GILES. You're probably right. He's lonely. Poor old thing. Sad. Everybody says how amusing he used to be. Maclean was the clever one, of course, and he seems quite happy here. Burgess didn't like Maclean, though, that's the joke. Altogether an unfortunate elopement. People are silly.

TOBY. You're not being paid by the *Daily Express*? They're very keen to get hold of him.

GILES. I should give up the idea. Have lunch with us. Go on.

CORAL. I have no intention of having lunch with you. He has asked me to call. (*She walks across the room, very cool and elegant, to where Tessa is typing.*) Do you know where this is?

Tessa is quite plain, not at all elegant and may have been crying.

GILES. Tessa doesn't know, do you Tessa?

TOBY. Tessa's just a skivvy. Tessa is just marking time until she gets her face on the front page of *Country Life*.

GILES. After the advertisements.

TOBY. For gate-legged tables.

Tessa looks away, shakes her head at Coral and goes on typing.

TOBY. (*In the middle of the empty room.*) Stalin is dead. Exchanges are taking place. For the first time in 10 years our friends the foe are just beginning to play ball.

GILES. We don't want them to take their bat home do we?

TOBY. Burgess and Maclean. They're yesterday's breakfast. The point is we don't want any fuss at this point. No scenes. This is grownup stuff.

CORAL. I am going to lunch. A quiet little meal. I am an actress. Actresses are fools. It's a well established fact. Why should there be any fuss?

Toby is poised to tear up the note.

TOBY. May I?

Coral snatches it.

CORAL. Certainly not. The impudence!

She puts it in her bag and makes to go.

GILES. Stay to lunch. There'll be jokes.

TOBY. Giles knows lots of jokes. Only we've heard them all. New people make such a change. Tessa wants you to stay, don't you Tessa?

TESSA. (*Unwinding the last sheet of her typing.*) I think you're both shits.

She runs out.

GILES. (*Calling.*) One was only teasing. Oh dear. That means we won't be on speakers for a week.

CORAL. Don't show me out.

She sweeps out, down an ornate corridor. Doors. Filing cabinets. Tessa is hiding in one of the doorways.

TESSA. Show me that address.

Coral does so, at which point Toby appears at the end of the corridor.

TOBY. (*Calling.*) Tessa. Naughty.

TESSA. (*To Coral.*) Sorry.

Coral leaves.

Moscow Streets.

Coral walks alone. She is stared at by people. She stops someone. Shows them her paper. They shake their heads and go on. She approaches someone else. The same.

She is going down another street. It is empty except for one man coming towards her. Coral shows him the paper. He looks round. Looks dubious. Fingers her scarf. Coral is reluctant to lose it, but offers it him. He looks round, takes it and stuffs it in his pocket. He walks on, motioning her to keep her distance. He rounds a corner. Pause. She appears, following him.

Cut to the man approaching a block of flats. The man goes past it. Coral goes past it. The man stops. Crosses the road suddenly, and is gone. Coral looks up at the block of flats. The same boy we have seen at the theatre is lounging on the steps. Coral goes in.

Interior of Flats.

Dirty and unfinished. Concrete joists still showing unpainted. Cement dust. Lots of pot plants outside doors and on window-sills. Builder's rubbish. Rubbish outside doors.

She picks her way fastidiously up the stairs, not sure which of the many doors to knock at. Faintly, she hears an English voice, and she begins to go up the stairs towards it.

BURGESS'S VOICE. On either side the river lie
Long fields of barley and of rye,
That clothe the wold and meet the sky;
And thro' the field the road runs by
        To many-tower'd Camelot;
And up and down the people go,
Gazing where the lilies blow
Round an island there below,
        The island of Shalott.

Coral goes up the stairs as Burgess's voice, reciting Tennyson, comes nearer. She passes other doors. From one a wary Muscovite housewife

*peers out, then closes it quickly. Coral has spotted a door which is half
open on a landing. She listens and then slowly pushes it open. Burgess,
who gives no sign of knowing she is there (though he does) is shaving in
front of the mirror. The one-room apartment is very untidy.*

BURGESS.   . . . From the bank and from the river
            He flash'd into the crystal mirror,
            'Tirra lirra', by the river
               Sang Sir Lancelot.

            She left the web, she left the loom,
            She made three paces thro' the room,
            She saw the water-lily bloom, . . .

Coral is in the room by this.

            She saw the helmet and the plume,
              She look'd down to Camelot.
            Out flew the web and floated wide;
            The mirror crack'd from side to side;
            'The curse is come upon me,' cried
              The Lady of Shalott.

CORAL. I suppose that's my soap.

BURGESS. It is, it is. And very nice too. Have a drink. (*He offers her a
bottle of vodka and takes a tooth glass from the washbasin.*) Sit down. (*He
sweeps some dirty clothes to the floor.*) I've just been tidying up.

*This is not obvious. Coral surreptitiously cleans the tooth glass on a
corner of her skirt. Burgess has gone back to the mirror to finish shaving.*

BURGESS. Quite honestly, I thought you'd chuck.

CORAL. I nearly did. You steal my soap, you steal my cigarettes, you even
stole my face powder.

BURGESS. I know. One should have asked. One is such a coward. (*He
wipes his face as she surveys the room.*) Hardly luxury's lap. (*One wall of
the room is bookshelves. There is a piano* [*or harmonium*]. *A plum-coloured
armchair. A gas stove in an alcove with a pan on it, steaming. A single bed
and another smaller bed in a far corner.*) A pigsty, in fact. I used to live in
Jermyn Street. Tragic, you might think, but not really: that was a pigsty
too. By their standards it's quite palatial. Even commodious. One is very
lucky.

CORAL. If that's our lunch, it's burning.

BURGESS. (*Unhurriedly.*) Yes. (*He peers into the pan and tastes it.*) Yes. One could salvage some of it, do you think? (*He hesitates.*) . . . No. (*He empties it into a bucket.*) All is not lost. I managed to scrounge two tomatoes and – quite a talking point – a grapefruit!

CORAL. (*Faintly.*) Treats!

He puts a tomato on a plate for her and eats his like an apple.

BURGESS. Garlic?

CORAL. No, thank you.

BURGESS. I love it. (*He eats several cloves.*) Now, tell me all the gossip. Do you see Harold Nicolson?

CORAL. I have *seen* him. I don't know him.

BURGESS. Nice man. Nice man. What about Cyril Connolly? He's everywhere.

CORAL. I haven't run across him either.

BURGESS. Oh. One somehow remembers everyone knowing everyone else. Everyone I knew knew everyone else. Auden, do you know him? Pope-Hennessy?

CORAL. (*Manfully.*) The theatre's in a terrible state. Three plays closed on Shaftesbury Avenue in one week.

BURGESS. Really? Some ballet on ice is coming here. The comrades are all agog. I'm rather old-fashioned about ice. I used to direct at Cambridge, you know. One thinks back and wonders did one miss one's way? You're not eating your tomato?

CORAL. I'm not hungry.

BURGESS. I am. Yum yum.

He takes it, studs it with several cloves of garlic, and wolfs it down.

CORAL. Do you see many people here?

BURGESS. Oh *yes*. Heaps of chums. You don't know what you're missing with this tomato.

CORAL. There's your other half, I suppose.

BURGESS. What? Oh yes. (*He points to the piano accordion on the other bed.*) He's a dab hand at the accordion. We play duets.

CORAL. *Maclean?*

BURGESS. Oh no. Not *Maclean*. (*He bursts out laughing.*) Maclean's not
my friend. Oh ducky. Oh no, not Maclean. He's so unfunny, no jokes,
no jokes at all. Positively the last person one would have chosen if one
had the choice. And here we are on this terrible tandem together . . .
Debenham and Freebody, Crosse and Blackwell, Auden and Isherwood,
Burgess and Maclean. Do you know Auden?

CORAL. You've asked me. No.

BURGESS. Don't look. The seeds get inside my plate. (*He goes over to the
basin and removes his false teeth and swills them under the tap.*) People ask
me if I have any regrets. The one regret I have is that before I came
away I didn't get fitted out with a good set of National Health gnashers.
Admirable as most things are in the Soviet Socialist Republic, the
making of dentures is still in its infancy. (*Pause.*) Actually, there's no
one in Moscow at all. It's like staying up at Cambridge for the Long
Vac. One makes do with whatever's around.

CORAL. Me.

BURGESS. No, no, no. And in any case I asked you here for a reason. Did
you bring a tape measure? (*Coral produces it from her bag. Burgess stands
up and puts on a jacket. He cuts a shabby figure, the knees of his trousers
darned and darned again.*) I want you to measure me for some suits.
From my tailor. I only have one suit. It's the one I came away in, and
I've fallen down a lot since then.

CORAL. Only I shan't know where to start. What measurements will he
want?

BURGESS. Measure it all. He'll work it out. He's a nice man.

*He gets her a pencil and paper. She draws the figure of a man on the
paper.*

CORAL. Won't the people here get you a suit?

BURGESS. What people?

CORAL. The authorities.

BURGESS. Oh yes, but have you seen them? Clothes have never been the
comrades' strong point. Besides, I don't want to look like everybody
else, do I? (*He bends his arm for her to measure.*) I seem to remember
doing that.

CORAL. Your arms can't have altered.

BURGESS. I never cared tuppence about clothes before . . . measure me round here . . . I was kitted out in the traditional clothes of my class. Black coat, striped trousers. Pinstripe suit, and tweed for week-ends. Shit order of course. Always in shit order. But charm. I always had charm.

CORAL. (*Measuring away.*) You still have charm. She said through clenched teenth.

BURGESS. Not here. Not for them. For charm one needs words. I have no words. And, short of my clothes, no class. I am 'The Englishman'. 'Would you like to go to bed with the Englishman?' I say. Not really. One got so spoiled during the war. The joys of the black-out. London awash with rude soldiery.

He says a Russian phrase 'Skolko zeem, skolko let', which is the Russian equivalent of 'Où sont les neiges d'antan'.

CORAL. Do you speak Russian?

BURGESS. I manage. I ought to learn, simply for the sex. Boys are quite thin on the ground here. I can't speak their language, and they can't speak mine, so when one does get one it soon palls. Sex needs language.

Coral is still busy, measuring, writing down.

CORAL. At least you've found a friend.

BURGESS. Tolya? I'm not sure whether I've found one or I've been allotted one. I know what I've done to be given him. But what has he done to be given me? Am I a reward or a punishment? He plays the accordion. I play the harmonium. It's fun. (*Coral doesn't look as if she thinks it fun.*) He's an electrician with the ballet. Of course, he may be a policeman. If he is a policeman he does it jolly well. Forster lived with a policeman, didn't he? You know him?

Coral shakes her head.

CORAL. I feel I'm somewhat of a disappointment in the friends department.

BURGESS. No matter.

CORAL. Nobody will believe me when I go home. 'What did you do in Moscow, darling?' 'Nothing much. I measured Guy Burgess's inside leg.

The camera should be on Burgess at this point. There is the same sense that one had earlier, that inside the drunken buffoon is somebody watchful.

BURGESS. I shouldn't think one's inside leg alters. It's one of the immutables. 'The knee is such a distance from the main body, whereas the groin, as your honour knows, is upon the very curtain of the place.'

CORAL. Come again.

BURGESS. Tristram Shandy. Of course you wouldn't do that.

CORAL. Do what?

BURGESS. Go round telling everybody. My people here wouldn't like that.

CORAL. (*Looking up at him from her knees.*) No?

BURGESS. No. A hat would be nice, I've written down the name of my hatters. And my bootmakers.

CORAL. It's a trousseau.

BURGESS. Yes. For a shotgun marriage.

CORAL. How do you know he won't say no? Your tailor.

BURGESS. It would be vulgar to say no. He won't say no.

CORAL. Well, I'll see what I can do.

She prepares to go. Burgess doesn't.

BURGESS. Don't go yet. I don't want you to go yet.

Coral plainly does want to go.

CORAL. Can't we go somewhere? You could show me the sights.

BURGESS. I can't go yet. I have to wait for the telephone call. When the telephone call comes I'm permitted to leave.

CORAL. Who from?

BURGESS. Oh . . . you know . . . my people. It's generally around four.

CORAL. That's another two hours.

BURGESS. Never mind. I can play you my record. (*He puts on a record. It is Jack Buchanan singing 'Who stole my heart away?' They listen to this in its entirety.*) Good, isn't it? Like to hear it again?

CORAL. Do you just have the one?

BURGESS. Just the one, yes.

CORAL. What's on the other side?

BURGESS. You don't want to listen to the other side. The other side's rubbish. I never listen to the other side.

He puts on 'Who' again. He is drinking. She isn't. Cut to:

The Block of Flats outside Burgess's Apartment.

The boy we have seen watching the entrance to the apartment is sitting on the balustrade, one storey down from Burgess's. A woman is sweeping the stairs. Faintly, the sound of Jack Buchanan from Burgess's falt.

Interior of Burgess's Flat.

Coral and Burgess are still listening to Jack Buchanan. Coral is plainly bored out of her skull.

CORAL. What do you miss most?

BURGESS. Apart from the Reform Club, the streets of London and occasionally the English countryside, the only thing I really miss is gossip. The comrades, though splendid in every other respect, don't gossip in quite the way we do, or about quite the same subjects.

CORAL. Pardon me for saying so, dear, but the comrades seem to me a sad disappointment in every department. There's no gossip, their clothes are terrible, and they can't make false teeth. What else is there?

BURGESS. (*Gently.*) The system. . . . Only, being English, you wouldn't be interested in that. (*Pause.*) What do people say about me in England?

CORAL. They don't much, any more. (*She gets up suddenly and starts frantically tidying up the room. Folding clothes, washing dishes. Sweeping. Burgess watches languidly.*) I thought of you as a bit like Oscar Wilde.

Burgess laughs.

BURGESS. No, no. Though he was a performer. And I was a performer. (*He is looking at himself in the glass.*) Both vain. But I never pretended. If I wore a mask, it was to be exactly what I seemed. And I made no bones about the other. My analysis of situations, the précis I had to submit at the Foreign Office, were always Marxist. Openly so. Impeccably so. (*She should be wiping the floor round his feet at this point, something very menial indeed.*) Nobody minded. 'It's only Guy.' 'Dear old Guy.' Quite safe. If you don't wish to conform in one thing, you should conform in all the others. And in all the important things I did conform. 'How can he be a spy? He goes to my tailor.' The average Englishman, you see, is not interested in ideas. Say what you like about political theory, and no one will listen. You could shove a slice of the Communist Manifesto in the Queen's Speech, and no one would turn a hair. Least of all, I suspect, HMQ. Am I boring you?

CORAL. It doesn't matter.

Fade in to Burgess at the piano, playing Elgar. Coral, having finished tidying up, sits. Then investigates the bookshelves. Takes a book out. Puts it back.

BURGESS. (*Shouting above the music.*) I'll think of 101 things to ask you when you've gone. How is Cyril Connolly?

CORAL. You've asked me that. I don't know.

BURGESS. (*Stopping playing.*) So little, England. Little music. Little art. Timid, tasteful, nice. But one loves it. Loves it. You see I can say I love London. I can say I love England. I can't say I love my country. I don't know what that means. Do you watch cricket?

CORAL. No. Anyway, it's changed.

BURGESS. Cricket?

CORAL. London.

BURGESS. Why? I don't want it to change. Why does anybody want to change it? They've no business changing it. The fools. You should stop them changing it. Band together.

CORAL. (*Getting up.*) Listen, darling. I'm only an actress. Not a bright lady, by your standards. I've never taken much interest in politics. If this is communism, I don't like it because it's dull. And the poor dears look tired. But then, Leeds is dull and that's not communism. And look at Australia. Only it occurs to me we have sat here all afternoon pretending that spying, which was what you did, darling, was just a minor social misdemeanour, no worse. And I'm sure in some people's minds much better than being caught in a public lavatory the way gentlemen in my profession constantly are, and that it's just something one shouldn't mention. Out of politeness. So that we won't be embarrassed. That's very English. We will pretend it hasn't happened, because we are both civilised people. Well, I'm not English. And I'm not civilised. I'm Australian. I can't muster much morality and outside Shakespeare the word treason to me means nothing. Only, you pissed in our soup and we drank it. So. Very good. Doesn't affect me, darling. And I will order your suit and your hat. And keep it under mine. Mum. Not a word. But for one reason: because I'm sorry for you. Now in your book . . . in your *real* book . . . that probably adds my name to the list of all the other fools you've conned. But you're not conning me, darling. Pipe isn't fooling pussy. I know.

The telephone rings.

BURGESS. Pity. I was enjoying that. (*He picks it up.*) You spoiled the lady's big speech. Da. Da. Spassibo.

He puts it down. He waits for Coral to go on.

CORAL. I just want to be told why.

BURGESS. Solitude.

CORAL. Solitude?

BURGESS. If you have a secret you're alone.

CORAL. But you told people. You told several people.

BURGESS. No point in having a secret if you make a secret of it. Actually, the other things you might get me is an Old Etonian tie. This one's on its last legs.

They have got up ready to go, when Tolya, a young Russian comes in.

BURGESS. Ah, here's Tolya. (*He kisses him.*) Tolya. This is Miss Browne. She is an actress. From England.

TOLYA. (*Pronouncing it very carefully.*) How do you do?

BURGESS. (*Protectively.*) Very good. If you give him an English cigarette he'll be your friend for life.

Coral does so.

TOLYA. Blagodaryou vas.

She lights it for him with her lighter. He is entranced with the lighter.

BURGESS. Oh dear. Sorry.

Tolya has taken the lighter, and now reluctantly offers it back.

CORAL. (*Resignedly.*) No, please.

BURGESS. He's a real Queen Mary. You . . . wouldn't be able to order him a suit, would you? He'd look so nice.

CORAL. (*Desperately.*) Anything. Anything.

Burgess and Tolya have a few words in Russian.

BURGESS. Tolya wants to play you a tune. Let him. He'd be so pleased. (*Burgess and Tolya embark on a duet, from HMS Pinafore, say. As they play Burgess calls out, indicating Tolya:*) What do you think? Reward or punishment?

Exterior of Flats.

Coral and Burgess are going down the steps of the flats.

CORAL. Where are we going?

BURGESS. Church. Do you like church? I adore it. (*They pass the watching boy on the stairs.*) This one, the singing is very good. The opera singers are in the choir, warming up for the evening performance.

CORAL. That's not another friend?

BURGESS. Good God, no. When I first came I used to be shadowed by rather grand policemen. That was when I was a celebrity. Nowadays they just send the trainees. Ironic, that. (*He waves to the boy, who pretends not to notice.*) Good afternoon. Not strong on irony, the comrades.

Russian Church.

Coral and Burgess are stood listening to the service. The singing is very good, but there are few people there. Coral looks at Burgess. Tears are streaming down his face. In the service a bell is rung at the altar for the sanctification. Cut to a shop in the West End, the bell ringing on the shop door.

A Tailor's in the West End.

Coral is looking at some clothes.

CORAL. I'd like to order some suits.

TAILOR. Certainly, madam.

CORAL. You've made suits for the gentleman before, but he now lives abroad.

TAILOR. I see.

Coral gets out the bit of paper with the figure drawn on it and her measurements.

CORAL. I took his measurements. I'm not sure they're . . .

Tailor takes the bit of paper.

TAILOR. Could one know the gentleman's name?

CORAL. Yes. Mr Burgess.

TAILOR. We have two Mr Burgesses. I take it this is Mr Burgess G.? How is Mr Burgess? Fatter, I see. One of our more colourful customers. Too little colour in our drab lives these days. Mr Guy favoured this pattern. It's a durable fabric. His suits were meant to take a good deal of punishment. I hope they have stood him in good stead?

CORAL. Yes. They have indeed.

TAILOR. I'm glad to hear it. Always getting into such scrapes, Mr Guy. Your name is . . .?

CORAL. Browne.

TAILOR. There is no need for discretion here, madam.

CORAL. Truly.

TAILOR. My apologies. And this is the address. I see. We put a little of ourselves into our suits. That is our loyalty.

CORAL. And mum's the word.

TAILOR. Mum is always the word here, madam. Moscow or Maidenhead, mum is always the word.

Interior of a Hatter's.

There is another customer in the shop, so Coral cannot speak plainly.

HATTER. What is the gentleman's name? (*She writes it down.*) If we have made a hat for the gentleman we should have his block. (*He looks at the paper.*) Would madam care to come downstairs?

Hatter's Basement.

A room lined with shelves of hat blocks. All the blocks labelled.

CORAL. Do you keep everybody's block?

HATTER. Only until death. Certain blocks we retain longer. The Duke of Wellington. Mr Gladstone. Mr Burgess's we had not expected to need again. . . . (*He comes to a block with its name turned to the wall.*) Here we are. One never knows. He'll want his initials on the band,'I take it. We always do that. G.B. (*He smiles.*) Great Britain.

The Caprice Restaurant.

Coral is just finishing lunch with Claudius.

CLAUDIUS. I wish you'd told me at the time. I'd have liked to have seen the old thing again.

CORAL. He wanted me to take you out to lunch. And he's paying. He sent me a cheque.

They toast him.

CLAUDIUS. To Guy. And no problem ordering any of the stuff?

CORAL. Nobody batted an eyelid. And why should they? It's all been sent off. Only now he's written wanting some pyjamas. I don't anticipate any difficulty there.

She shows Claudius the letter.

CLAUDIUS. (*Reading.*) 'What I really need, honestly, the only thing more, is pyjamas. Russian ones can't be slept in, are not in fact made for that purpose. What I would like is four pair of White or Off-White, and Navy Blue Silk. Quite plain and only those two colours. Then at last my outfit will be complete, and I shall look like a real . . . agent again.'

CORAL. What? (*She takes the letter.*) No, dear. 'Then I shall look like a real gent again.'

Smart West End Outfitters.

Coral is talking to an assistant. We do not hear the conversation. The assistant goes into the back of the shop, while Coral, obviously quite confident of the success of this final errand, surveys the shop. One other

upper-class customer there, who will observe what follows. The Manager
returns. He should be played very gently and without arrogance.

MANAGER. I'm afraid this gentleman no longer has an account with us,
madam. His account was closed.

CORAL. I know. But he wishes to open it again.

MANAGER. I'm afraid that's not possible.

CORAL. Why?

MANAGER. (*A little nonplussed.*) Well . . . we supply pyjamas to the Royal
Family.

CORAL. So?

MANAGER. The gentleman is a traitor, madam.

CORAL. So? Must traitors sleep in the buff?

MANAGER. I'm sorry. We have to draw the line somewhere.

CORAL. So why here? Say someone commits adultery in your precious
nightwear. I imagine it has occurred. What happens when he comes in
to order his next pair of jim jams? Is it sorry, no can do?

MANAGER. I'm very sorry.

CORAL. (*And in this speech her indignation should bring out her Australian
accent much more than hitherto.*) You keep saying you're sorry, *dear.*
Jesus Christ! You were quite happy to satisfy this client when he was
one of the most notorious buggers in London, and a drunkard into the
bargain. Only then he was in the Foreign Office. 'Red piping on the
sleeve, Mr Burgess, but of course.' 'A discreet monogram on the pocket,
Mr Burgess? Certainly.' 'And perhaps if you'd be gracious enough to
lower your trousers, Mr Burgess: we could plunge our tongue between
the cheeks of your arse.' But not any more. Oh no. And why? Because
the gentleman in question has shown himself to have some principles,
principles which aren't yours and, as a matter of interest, aren't mine
either. But that's it so far as you're concerned. No more jamas for him. I
tell you, it's pricks like you that make me understand why he went.
Thank Christ I'm not English.

MANAGER. As a matter of fact, madam, our firm isn't English in origin,
either.

CORAL. Oh? And what is it?

MANAGER. Hungarian.

This should stop Coral short, and the scene suddenly cease to be funny.

Burgess's Apartment, Moscow.

It is empty, but the floor is strewn with cardboard boxes, a chaos of torn tissue-paper and opened parcels.

Moscow Street.

Burgess is walking down it alone. He is in his new clothes and very elegant. In Voice Over, Burgess is singing at the piano, with piano accordion accompaniment, the song from HMS Pinafore *which, as the scene progresses, is taken up by full chorus and orchestra.*

BURGESS. For he himself has said it,
      And it's greatly to his credit,
      That he is an Englishman.
      For he might have been a Roosian,
      A French or Turk or Proosian,
      Or perhaps I-tal-ian.
      But in spite of all temptations.
      To belong to other nations,
      He remains an Englishman.
      He remains an Englishman.

Just into the edge of frame at the end of the song comes the figure of the boy who is still following him.

Credits over the actual notes of the measurements, fragments of letters and finally the cheque for lunch, all in Burgess's handwriting.

Acknowledgements

'I've Got Sixpence': words and music by
Box, Cox and Hall © 1941 Bradbury Wood Ltd
(Chappell Music Ltd)

'I Can Give You the Starlight' from
The Dancing Years: music by Ivor
Novello, words by Christopher Hassall
© 1939 Chappell & Co Ltd

Photographs
All photographs BBC copyright. Photographers as follows:
Don Smith: Cover photograph, pages 11, 33, 85, 112, 115,
170, 174 and 206.
Tony Russell: pages 49 and 50.
Warwick Bedford: page 31
John Jefford: pages 216, 229, 247 and 252.